GREEN VOICES

THE UNIVERSITY COLLEGE OF RIPON AND YORK ST. JOHN
YORK CAMPUS

Please return this book by the date stamped below
- if recalled, the loan is reduced to 10 days

Fines are payable for late return

GREEN VOICES

Understanding contemporary nature poetry

Terry Gifford

MANCHESTER UNIVERSITY PRESS
Manchester and New York

distributed exclusively in the USA and Canada by St. Martin's Press

Copyright © Terry Gifford 1995

Published by Manchester University Press
Oxford Road, Manchester M13 9NR, UK
and Room 400, 175 Fifth Avenue, New York, NY 10010, USA

Distributed exclusively in the USA and Canada
by St. Martin's Press, Inc., 175 Fifth Avenue,
New York, NY 10010, USA

British Library Cataloguing-in-Publication Data
A catalogue record is available from the British Library

Library of Congress Cataloging-in-Publication Data
Gifford, Terry.
    Green voices : understanding contemporary nature poetry / Terry
Gifford.
        p.   cm.
    Includes bibliographical references.
    ISBN 0–7190–4345–X (hbk.). —— ISBN 0–7190–4346–8 (pbk.)
    1. English poetry——20th century——History and criticism.
2. Pastoral poetry, English——History and criticism.   3. Nature in
literature.   I. Title.
PR508.N3G54   1995
821007.9140936——dc20   94–28631
                                                                  CIP

ISBN 0 7190 4345 X hardback
ISBN 0 7190 4346 8 paperback

Photoset in Linotron Joanna
by Northern Phototypesetting Co. Ltd, Bolton
Printed in Great Britain
by Biddles Ltd, Guildford & King's Lynn

If you have infected the sky, and the earth
Caught its disease off you – you are the virus
Ted Hughes, "If", Three Books

Speaking of nothing more than what we are –
How exquisitely the individual Mind
(And the progressive powers perhaps no less
Of the whole species) to the external world
Is fitted; and how exquisitely too –
Theme this but little heard of among men –
The external world is fitted to the mind.
Wordsworth, "Home at Grasmere"

Like two gods of mud
Sprawling in the dirt, but with infinite care

They bring each other to perfection.
Ted Hughes, "Bride and Groom Lie Hidden
for Three Days", Cave Birds

Contents

Acknowledgements

This book began as doctoral research supervised with sympathetic and astute guidance by Professor Kenneth Graham until his retirement from Sheffield University Department of English Literature. For supervision of the final stages of that research I am grateful for rigorous conversation and climbing with Professor David Craig, both in the University of Lancaster and and "the University of the Wilderness".

My sincere thanks are extended to Dr Izabel de Fatima de Oliveira Brandão, poet and scholar of the University Federal de Alagoas, Brazil, who, during her own research at Sheffield University, extended my thinking about nature and my ability to write about it.

I am also grateful for comments on all or parts of the text from Professor Edna Longley of Queen's University Belfast, Dr Keith Hanley of Lancaster University, Professor Rand Brandes of Lenoir-Rhyne College, USA, Dr David Jones of Wakefield District College, Dr Linden Peach of Bretton Hall College of Leeds University, the 'green group' of poets: John Sewell, Diana Syder and Colin Sutherill. I am delighted to thank the participants of the international summer school "The Challenge of Ted Hughes" at the University of Manchester, July 1990, who will recognise reflections on our debates in Chapter 6. I would especially like to thank the conference director Dr Keith Sagar for support during my earliest work on Hughes. I owe a debt to Dr Neil Roberts of Sheffield University for previous collaborations on the work of Ted Hughes.

Thanks also to the writers George Mackay Brown, Gillian Clarke, Debjani Chatterjee and Ted Hughes for their co-operation in answering my questions. Thanks for permission to quote at length from "Against Looting" are due to David Craig and Littlewood Arc. Thanks also to Iain Crichton Smith and Carcanet Press for permission to quote "Going Home" from *Collected Poems*. The Chief Librarian of The Orkney Library, R. K. Leslie, has been extremely helpful, as have the library staff at Bretton

Hall College of Leeds University who continue their unfailing good humour and professionalism.

Bretton Hall College of Leeds University has given me financial support and research time to work on this book. I would also like to thank my students for their enthusiasm in testing out ideas and readings of texts in programmes of research-based teaching.

Part of Chapter 5 was explored in 'Saccharine or Echo Soundings? Notions of Nature in Seamus Heaney's *Station Island*', in *The New Welsh Review*, No. 10, autumn 1990, pp. 12–17. Some of the ideas in Chapters 1 and 6 were first explored in 'Gods of Mud: Ted Hughes and the Post-Pastoral', in *The Challenge of Ted Hughes*, ed. Keith Sagar, London: Macmillan, 1994.

Finally, thanks to my parents for their bibliographical service from Cambridge, to Tom for leading through, Ruth for her poems and her patience, and to Gill Round for the most important support of all.

Terry Gifford
Bretton Hall College, Leeds University

1
The social construction of nature

NATURE poetry is having a bad time.

I was going to begin with this sentence. When, in 1985, I was drawing up the first outline for this study of notions of nature in contemporary poetry this statement seemed to be true in terms of the current debate. The Penguin Book of Contemporary British Poetry,[1] edited by two young arbiters of taste, the deputy literary editor of the Observer and the poetry editor at Chatto & Windus, had recently declared that "the spirit of post-modernism" had changed the preoccupations of poetry. The interest was not in content but in style: "Most of the devices developed by young poets are designed to emphasise the gap between themselves and their subjects."[2] But what was curious about this anthology was that here, on the first page, was Seamus Heaney's poem "Churning Day":

> After the hot brewery of gland, cud and udder
> cool porous earthenware fermented the buttermilk.

Surely this was more about the spirit of nature than post-modernism, more about the human activity of "fermenting" continuing the natural process of the cow's "hot brewery" than emphasising a gap between work in the kitchen and work in the cow. The work of churning day leaves people slightly changed, Heaney says at the end of the poem: "And in the house we moved with gravid ease." Surely here was a personal descriptive celebration of a human unity with natural processes in which the writer, with a phrase like "gravid ease", is emotionally inside it. Indeed, might this not serve as a recognisable definition of not just poetry about nature, but "nature poetry"? According to the editors, Blake Morrison and Andrew Motion, this

1

anthology represented "a radical departure from the empirical mode".[3] But using a phrase of Heaney's to characterise the other writers in their anthology, the editors attempted to contradict the apparent evidence of their opening poem: "These poets are – to borrow a phrase from Seamus Heaney's "Exposure" – "inner emigrés": not inhabitants of their own lives so much as intrigued observers, not victims but onlookers, not poets working in a confessional white heat but dramatists and story-tellers".[4]

In the bitter political context of Heaney's moving from Northern Ireland to live in the Republic, to which he is partly alluding in "inner emigré", this is in fact a phrase derived from "confessional white heat". But if this claim by the editors was a distortion of Heaney's poetry, it was a more accurate account of the renewed interest in narrative poetry and of the stylistic self-consciousness represented elsewhere in the anthology. So in 1982 Morrison and Motion could confidently assure us that "Ted Hughes is a remarkable writer but no longer the presiding spirit of British poetry."[5] Nature poetry was having a bad time. A decade later The New Poetry[6] is noted for the absence of nature poetry from the fifty-five poets anthologised. "We seem to have lost our nature poets", comments one reviewer.[7] The anthology's publisher, Neil Astley of Bloodaxe, boasts, "We don't publish much landscape poetry."[8] Nature poetry is having a bad time.

I was going to start with this statement, not only because it was true of polemics within the current literary debates, but because it would demand a definition. What is the difference between "nature poetry" and poetry about nature? Why is "nature poetry" a term of abuse?[9] Why have both survived in our urbanised, post-industrial society? These are questions to which this book will return. The urgency of the need for answers to these questions is best illustrated by my hesitation in suggesting that nature poetry is still having a hard time outside these canonising anthologies. The editors of The New Poetry may not have noticed, but quite quickly everything has turned green.

In the spring of 1988 Mrs Thatcher turned green[10] and in the summer of 1991 the Ministry of Defence turned green.[11] In the spring of 1992 the Queen turned green.[12] Suddenly the adjective has become a noun (my father always urged me to eat them, but now he too could be one of the Greens) and a verb ("Greening of Cities Challenges Urban Planners"[13]). The poetry business also discovered that it was green. The summer 1990 issue of Poetry Review declared itself to be "the green issue".[14] Writers not usually known for their nature poetry offered a green poem. At the same time *Poetry Wales* also produced a "Special Green Issue" which reviewed four new anthologies of green poetry.[15] In 1985 would these books have been anthologies of "nature poetry"? One reviewer, Hilary Llewellyn-Williams, was aware of this irony:

> Poets need no longer apologise for writing about Nature. The new Nature poetry is more than merely descriptive: it deals with the tensions between us and our environment, our intense and often destructive relationship with it, our struggle to come to terms with the fact that we're a part of the world out there and not simply observers and manipulators.[16]

That she was speaking for herself, as well as a new generation of poets from Wales and elsewhere, we shall see in Chapter 7.

The old writing about "nature" then, was "merely descriptive". This is the sense in which the term "nature poetry" has come to be used. As Raymond Williams points out, this poetry had its origins in the earliest Greek and Latin pastorals of Theocritus and Virgil, but it represented a shift in attitude towards nature that was

> now the nature of observation, of the scientist or tourist, rather than of the working countryman. Thus the descriptive element in original pastoral could be separated out, and a whole tradition of "nature poetry", strong and moving in these separate ways, could be founded to go on its major course, over several centuries into our own time.[17]

In our own time, "nature poetry" has become a pejorative term and it is therefore difficult to use the phrase without inverted commas in a purely descriptive way to refer to poetry that is concerned with nature, as I insist upon doing in this book. I reserve the term "green poetry" for those recent nature poems which engage directly with environmental issues. In a more general sense one might use the term "green voices" to include the diversity of nature poetry being written today. Indeed, it is important that nature poetry of all kinds can be addressed in current literary discussion, for it needs to be critically confronted in the poetry of writers as culturally diverse as Sorley MacLean, Ted Hughes, Gillian Clarke, Seamus Heaney, Grace Nichols and Debjani Chatterjee.

The reason for the negative implications of "nature poetry" in current discourse almost certainly lies with Georgian poetry. Commentators from Leavis in the 1930s[18] to Wiener in the 1980s[19] have recognised the sentimentality and escapism of the poetry edited by Edward Marsh in five anthologies of *Georgian Poetry* between 1912 and 1922. These five volumes contained poems by Rupert Brooke, A. E. Housman, W. H. Davies, John Masefield, Edmund Blunden, Walter de la Mare and others. In fact, R. H. Ross in his book *The Georgian Revolt* says that "as early as 1913 Richard Aldington had taken several of the pre-war Georgians to task for their naiveté in supposing that good poetry could be created out of the mere facts of botanical germination, florescence, and decay".[20] Of course, accusations of comfortable escapism in nature cannot be true of every poem in all five volumes. D. H. Lawrence's "Snap-Dragon", for example, is an ambitious and subtle poem in which external nature (the snap dragon) is a vehicle for exploring the inner nature of a lover. It ends by celebrating the joy that "Shall have risen red on my night as a harvest moon".[21] It ends with the statement that "Death, I know, is better than not-to-be." This is Lawrence using nature in a challenging manner to explore his developing vision of what it is for him to be fully alive.

Other poets have also been associated with the Georgians, most notably Edward Thomas, whose work did not appear in any of Marsh's *Georgian Poetry* anthologies. It is worth looking briefly at a poem by Edward Thomas because, as Edna Longley puts it, "he stands 'On a bridge alone' ("The Bridge") between Romantics and Moderns".[22] He also stands between England and Wales, between "nature poetry" and "green poetry", and between Edna Longley and Stan Smith who have an instructive disagreement about the poem which Thomas referred to as "Bob's Lane"[23] but which they refer to as "Women He Liked". The poem begins:

> Women he liked, did shovel-bearded Bob,
> Old Farmer Hayward of the Heath, but he
> Loved horses. He himself was like a cob,
> And leather-coloured. Also he loved a tree.

Along an unnamed lane he planted elms because he loved "the life in them". But the result turns out to be a useless pathway that comes to have a name:

> Many years since, Bob Hayward died, and now
> None passes there because the mist and rain
> Out of the elms have turned the lane to slough
> And gloom, the name alone survives, Bob's Lane.

If readers share Bob's view of nature, it is clear that the "slough/ And gloom" of the lane do not greatly matter. Great trees have a life there. But the community remembers Bob as having destroyed a pathway, and this is the irony with which Thomas choses to conclude the poem. The tensions within the poem therefore ask a question about the reader's attitude towards nature which the poem itself does not resolve. Are the trees to be valued more than the lane? The last words of the poem hold in ambiguous tension the life in trees that Bob loved, against the "slough/And gloom" of the lane. Stan Smith takes the community's view: "Love can destroy that which it wishes to serve, celebrate and enhance."[24] He goes on to counter Edna Long-ley's answer to the poem's question: "This poem is not the celebration of a countryman's 'indissoluble ... organic relationship with land-scape' which Edna Longley finds it (*Poems and Last Poems*, p. 357). It is a powerful little myth of degeneration and waste, of a countryside in decay."[25]

What is interesting about this difference of interpretation is that it is actually a difference in readings of the notion of nature that under-pins the poem. I have argued that it is an ambiguous one that deliber-ately challenges readers to clarify their own attitude towards nature.

This debate illustrates the need for a theoretical framework for the discussion of notions of nature in poetry. The need is urgent because nature is back on the agenda not only in the form of green poetry, but in the form of "literary ecocriticism". The latter term was launched upon the literary world in 1991 by Jonathan Bate in his book *Romantic Ecology: Wordsworth and the Environmental Tradition*.[26] In the same year a book published in the USA provided a discussion of "language and ecology" in the later poetry of Ted Hughes.[27] If nature poetry was bad, ecological poetry must be good, presumably by avoiding some-how being nature poetry at all. And where does this leave green poetry? Is "Bob's Lane" a nature poem or a green poem? What would it have meant if it had been included in the "Special Green Issue" of *Poetry Wales*?

In that issue Llewellyn-Williams characterises "the new Nature poetry" as engaged with tensions of relationships and responsibility, participation and power. One could argue that the best of the old writing about nature tackled just such tensions and much of this book will be examining precisely that issue. But the sense of a "new Nature poetry" is, of course, part of a wider social concern with the future of our planetary environment that has demanded a re-examination of our relationship with the natural world. Underlying this current concern is a debate about the nature of "nature". It is in this cultural context that the literary debate needs to be located.

An indication of the diversity of the notions of nature being offered by scientific commentators in recent years can be made by contrasting the theory of *The End of Nature* proposed by Bill McKibben[28] with James Lovelock's Gaia theory.[29] Briefly, McKibben argues that the meaning of nature has changed for us since we have so deeply penetrated all of its processes that it no longer exists as a force uninfluenced by human activity. "We have ended the thing that has, at least in modern times, defined nature for us – its separation from human society."[30] Because "we have substantially altered the earth's atmosphere", McKibben dramatically suggests that "a child born now will never know a natural summer, a natural autumn, winter, or spring".[31] We may, he says, be able to counteract our most damaging effects, but from now on the result will be an engineered environment. "Instead of a world where rain had an independent and mysterious existence, the rain [has] become a subset of human activity."[32] The implications of this for references to rain in poetry would be profound were not the actual event of feeling rain much the same as that before we entered this so-called "post-natural world".[33] We can still get soaked to the skin in it. Nevertheless, inside the heads that are getting soaked we know that the rain has been altered, as anticipated by two songs emerging from the Cuban missile crisis of 1963: "A Hard Rain's A-Gonna Fall" by Bob Dylan[34] and "What Have They Done To The Rain?"[35] Today, after Chernobyl, the signification of a phrase like "rain storms/Spiralling out of Russia"[36] has changed again. Dylan's "hard rain" has fallen in Europe.

"The green issue" of *Poetry Review* contained an essay by James Lovelock in which he summed up his Gaia theory:

> But what if . . . the earth is a vast living organism? In such a living system species are expendable. If a species, such as humans, adversely affects the environment, then in time it will be eliminated with no more pity than is shown by the micro-brain of an intercontinental ballistic missile on course to its target. If the earth is like this, then to survive we face the hard task of reintegrating creation. Of learning to be part of the earth and not separate from it.[37]

What is interesting here is that notions of nature, in this case the idea that the earth is a self-regulating organism indifferent to human survival, are now being proposed and debated in *Poetry Review*, the journal of The Poetry Society. One might argue that poets had been "learning to be part of the earth and not separate from it" for some time before Lovelock's Gaia theory. But what are contemporary poets to make of the very diversity of notions of nature presented in our culture beyond either Gaia or "the end of nature"? Indeed, it is not always clear precisely what significations underlie images of nature in their current cultural contexts. Four examples will have to represent this cultural confusion about what nature is.

The first two examples are taken from the *Guardian*. Readers opening the newspaper on 21 February 1991 will have learned that they could "create a brand new planet" for only £39.95 if they bought from Ocean Software a computer game called Sim Earth, "a planet simulator that takes on board the Gaia theories of Professor James Lovelock". A feature article enthuses about this "software toy" in the weekly computer (rather than environmental) section of the paper.

If this is rather overwhelming, the reader can always turn to the daily dose of "A Country Diary" which began in the *Manchester Guardian* in 1904.[38] The function of this column, which appears on the same page as the leading articles and letters, seems to be unchanged since Edwardian times. Its style is detailed, descriptive and celebratory. Experts on natural history and country matters speak to a largely urban audience. On behalf of urban readers the *Guardian* sends out its octogenarian Country Diarist, Harry Griffin, to get, in his own words, "soaked to the skin" on the Lakeland fells.[39] It is indeed good to know that spotted orchids are still to be found in Oxfordshire,[40] but one can sometimes get the impression that, underneath the leaders and letters, all's well with the world in the small box of "A Country Diary".

However, in the laboratories of Oxfordshire a third, very different conception of nature is at work. Genetic engineering has brought us to the stage where "genetically engineered plants and animals can be patented and sold as 'life products' ".[41] Greenpeace has expressed concern that "transnational companies will be able to monopolize and manipulate markets in favour of the genetically engineered life forms which they own".[42]

The manipulation of markets using images of nature takes place every day on our television screens, from which my fourth example is taken. Despite the fact that in Britain our diet contains too much sugar, a television advertisement encourages an increased intake on the grounds that sweetness is common in nature. Similarly butter and beer, both sources of health problems in our society, are advertised by their producers as having nothing but goodness because they have some natural ingredients. If McKibben is right in saying that "Nature has become a hobby for us",[43] often mediated through the spectacular images of a TV "nature programme", when such images are used in the commercial breaks we often have no direct experience of those exotic images of nature by which to evaluate the message attached to them. In this context, does the screening of a green poem such as Heathcote Williams's *Whale Nation* become merely another pretty commercial?[44]

In literary theory an echo of the wider cultural unease about the nature of nature is to be heard in French feminist theory and American ecofeminism. "Is Female to Male as Nature is to Culture?", asked the American anthropologist.[45] "Woman is body more than man is", argues the French theorist Hélène Cixous[46] in accepting that Culture/Nature = Man/Woman = Superior/Inferior in a patriarchal society. Her call for women to "write the body" is intended as an act of subversion and liberation which Toril Moi, for one, condemns as "biological essentialism".[47] Moi offers a distinction between "feminine and "female": " 'feminine' represents nurture, and 'female' nature".[48] This then begs the question posed by the American Ann Rosalind Jones: "Is women's sexuality so monolithic that the notion of a shared, typical femininity does justice to it? What about variations in class, in race, and in culture among women?"[49]

This anti-essentialist/pro-essentialist debate is replicated in American ecofeminism, which sees the exploitation of women as the same mind-set as that which exploits the earth. Ecofeminists ask "What is the point of partaking equally in a system that is killing us all?"[50] Rejecting the nature/culture dualism of early work like Mary Daly's *Gyn/ecology*,[51] many ecofeminists seek a holistic concept of nature through intuitive knowledge gained by spiritual practices.[52] Theodore Roszak believes that "precisely because they have found the daring to throw off conventional academic restrictions, ecofeminists have, through the arts and through ritual practices, discovered new ways to recreate the animist sensibility".[53] And what has happened, one might ask, to the Green Man?[54] That ecofeminism is post-feminist is indicated by the female editors of one ecofeminist reader placing as the penultimate chapter Yaakov Jerome Garb's essay on contemporary earth imagery, in which he writes: "Bring on the Sky Goddesses, the Earth Gods, and all the wild and fecund creatures of psychic life – restore to both men and women those richly creative images of self-hood and earth-hood so long banished from our culture."[55]

So if, from the media to literary theory, we are offered such diverse and contradictory notions of nature, how can poets and readers share a language of reference to nature? And why bother, since most of us now live or work apparently out of direct contact with nature? This brings us back to the question of how and why nature poetry has survived.

Firstly there is the question of whether, especially as urban dwellers, we share any unmediated experience of nature. Do we all experience the same rain before we write of it? And is rain inside our heads before it falls on the outside of our heads? Is there any longer a distinction to be made between the signified and the signifier? I am writing this at my home in Sheffield. If I turn my head a little away from the frame of the screen on which I am writing, I look through the frame of a window. This frame is filled by two things: tree and sky. Both are constantly changing, although at different rates. The Japanese cherry has just finished its two weeks of flowering. Now as I look out into the top of the tree I see branches and leaves. In the winter I shall look through the branches to the top of a terrace of houses dipping away to miles of industrial buildings and housing estates. Above the tree the blue sky is filling with clouds. It has started to rain. The newly-arrived swifts have disappeared. The rain gets heavier. I see it and hear it.

Do you? I have not described it, so what has the word "rain" signified to you here? Presumably you have imagined water falling past my window and not custard, or cats and dogs? Perhaps not. Your own direct experiences of rain will have been framed by your contexts, but you will know what it generally looks, sounds and feels like so that the word "rain" works in a broad sense. The signified thus has a primacy over the signifier. However, as soon as I communicate in words my own context or frames, I am mediating "rain" for a reader. To convey more of what it has meant to me would require the suggestibility of poetry, which in turn would require in the reader some degrees of experience of rain for the signifiers to make distinctions. The Amhara people of Ethiopia have one word for all rain.[56] A German correspondent recently sent me sixty-four German expressions for rain.[57] Rain can be a concept, such as fertility or pollution, but the feel of rain, snow or sun is a direct contact with external nature

9

that we lose touch with at our peril. If we lose direct experience of seasonal changes how are we to understand growth and decay in ourselves?

So this book is not ultimately about reading and writing poetry, but about our living relationship with the material reality we sometimes call "the environment" or "nature" or "our inner selves" or "our bodies". This is a material world in which we live but from which we have become strangely alienated. There is much evidence to show that those of us living in large industrial cities – and that is most of us – need to have unmediated contact with nature. A study of the therapeutic value of trees for hospital patients found that, compared with patients whose windows looked out on to brick walls, those whose windows gave them a view of trees required fewer painkillers and were discharged earlier.[58] The frame here is a healing one. We not only need this sort of contact, we need to communicate it, examine it and share its meaning through our symbolic sign-systems. Our semiology of nature keeps us sane by reminding us that we are animals.

In *The Living Landscape*, Fraser Harrison describes the importance for him of living with a sweet chestnut tree. In his attempt to explain the significance of this he defines the reason why nature poetry has survived:

> The cycle of life and death in nature offers the most accessible and emotive representation of our own biological fate. This metaphysical view of nature helps us reconcile ourselves to those aspects of our flesh and blood existence which are least compatible with our self-knowing intelligence. By identifying our feelings and life story with animal behaviour and the rhythms of renewal and decay in plants, we give meaning to the key moments of our existence, and keep up our courage in the face of our mortality and vulnerability to suffering. It is only "natural" that we should think of these biologically determined episodes – birth, growth, sexual bonding, nurturing, ageing, sickness and death, the mysteries that are at the heartland of any religion – in terms of symbolism drawn from the life processes of other organic creatures.[59]

Peter Redgrove takes this further, arguing that we have repressed our animal awareness of the invisible natural forces of, for example, electricity and magnetism. He traces a symbolic indication of this awareness, from ancient times to the present, around the figure of the Black Goddess. Quoting Mandelstam's "The earth moans with metaphors", Redgrove constructs a pattern of symbols which he interprets to confirm his part-scientific, part-Jungian evidence of "extra-sensuous perception". Redgrove's sense of nature can be summed up by his suggestion that "our approach to reality, our sense of reality, cannot assume that the text of nature, the book of life, is a cryptogram concealing just a single meaning. Rather, it is an expanding riddle of a multiplicity of resonating images."[60]

Redgrove's work represents an extreme case of the problems inherent in the simple proposition of Fraser Harrison that we need to understand nature in ourselves by symbolic reference to nature outside ourselves. The "riddles" Redgrove elucidates in his studies and recreates in his poetry present a unique set of problems for readers that will be examined in the final chapter.

In fact, recent social and economic changes have resulted in more people moving "back to nature" from the cities. But the move to the towns of the last quarter of the nineteenth century produced an urban culture which in some ways never really lost its roots in nature. I do not just mean that the city had to invent the allotment or the park, the urban garden or the window-box. I mean that socially every urban family in, say, 1950 had a direct line back to the country within only two, or at most three, generations. My own family made the move to the city comparatively recently. My grandparents worked a market-garden on the edge of the Fens. My father took those skills into the town as an urban professional gardener. I moved as a first-generation student into this large industrial city where my own children were born. In Britain cities are only two centuries old and they may be a failure, alienating us from earlier generations' knowledge of the cycles and forces of nature. Theodore Roszak suggests that it is only in the last few years of its long life that "Gaia has been stricken with City Pox."[61] But he argues that "City Pox may be approaching its terminal stage."

In post-industrial Britain the movement of population has been back to the rural areas, begun by middle-class people who still worked in the town. Howard Newby, the sociologist of rural England, says that as urban areas have declined in manufacturing employment, rural areas have been increasing, particularly in employment associated with new technology. "Consequently, for the first time since the Industrial Revolution, rural areas may participate in a technological breakthrough on an equal footing with urban centres. The relationship between hitherto 'rural' and 'urban' areas is likely to be fundamentally altered by these processes."[62] So our need for direct

11

contact with nature is being reflected in social and economic trends in post-industrial Britain. It is no accident that at the same time as notions of "rural" and "urban" are undergoing change, notions of "nature" are also in some confusion in our culture. It is time to turn to definitions.

In the USA most bookshops have a shelf of "Nature Writing" and each region is celebrated by its own nature writers. "Nature writing has become a genre of increased literary activity recently", reports the American poet Gary Snyder.[63] Ideas about "nature" in America are often explored through the concept of "wilderness" and there is a tradition of explicitly examining these notions which derive from the writings of Emerson,[64] Thoreau[65] and Muir[66] in the nineteenth century. Most recently two seminal works stand out: the historian, Roderick Nash, produced a thorough social history in *Wilderness and the American Mind*[67] and the philosopher, Max Oelschlaeger, in *The Idea of Wilderness*,[68] has written an analysis of conceptions of nature in the context of a history of philosophy. The latter includes a chapter on the early twentieth-century poet Robinson Jeffers and the influential contemporary poet Gary Snyder. Snyder's recently published selected poems are provocatively titled *No Nature*.[69] In his preface he says, "There is no single or set 'nature' either as 'the natural world' or 'the nature of things'." His idea of the human mind as a wilderness area is explored in his most recent collection of essays *The Practice of the Wild*.[70]

In Britain the pioneering work of Raymond Williams in *The Country and the City* and Keith Thomas in *Man and the Natural World*[71] has been followed by Peter Marshall's world survey *Nature's Web: An Exploration of Ecological Thinking*.[72] (In 1929 Edmund Blunden had produced an uncritical pastoral survey of *Nature in English Literature*[73] which extended the Georgian search for "contentment".) Thomas's book is a historical study of the change from the Tudor and Stuart attitude of "hard-won human dominance"[74] over nature to the late seventeenth-century view that there were "no disharmonies between man's needs and those of subordinate creation".[75] Marshall's book is a retrospective ecological history of philosophy and science. But Raymond Williams's book remains the seminal study of changing attitudes towards nature within British literature. In it he uses the literary evidence to elaborate a pattern of social uses of "nature" in the form of images of "the country" that are in tension with assumptions about "the city". "Nature" is therefore used to reflect and to serve the social purposes of writers and readers. The theoretical basis of his approach is indicated by his definition of "nature" in *Keywords*.[76]

There Williams outlines three uses of "nature":

(i)   the essential quality and character of something;
(ii) the inherent force that directs either the world or human beings or both;
(iii) the material world itself, taken as including or not including human beings.[77]

This provides the reason why Wordsworth writes about nature (ii) and I have been writing about nature (iii). There are, of course, overlapping usages and Williams gives a brilliant illustration of six examples from *King Lear*.[78] But at the heart of his six pages of definition is the statement that "any full history of the uses of 'nature' would be a large part of the history of human thought".[79]

Here Williams is sharing the theoretical position of Nash and of Oelschlaeger from the USA, together with that of Thomas from Britain, that "nature" is a way of thinking. Notions of nature are, of course, socially constructed and determine our perception of our direct experiences, which, in turn, determine our communications about them. I see and hear the rain through my window, but already its meaning for me will be framed by my socialised perception of it. It may signify the source of life, or the pollution of life. Similarly my poem about it may be perceived by readers as a nature poem, or an ecological protest. Williams himself never formulated the phrase "the social construction of nature" and it has not been formulated by the few writers who have, in fact, been deploying the concept of "nature" as a cultural construct.[80] Since it provides a key theoretical basis for the study of notions of nature in contemporary poetry it needs further elaboration.

In 1967 two writers on the sociology of knowledge published an influential book with a challenging title. Peter L. Berger and Thomas Luckmann's *The Social Construction of Reality*[81] elaborated a theory of language which can now be seen to be post-structuralist and to have much in common with the rediscovery of Mikhail Bakhtin's theory of "dialogics". For Berger and Luckmann "language is capable of becoming the objective repository of vast accumulations of meaning and experience"[82] by which subjective experience is given shared cultural meaning. But "since socialization is never complete",[83] these meanings are continuously being qualified at an individual and at a social level: "the relationship between man, the producer, and the social world, his product, is and remains a dialectical one".[84] Of course poetry is one form of this dialectic, although the poet may choose the degree to which she challenges or qualifies or endorses this unstable shared meaning. Indeed, the poet may be aware that there is a diversity of conflicting categories of shared meanings in different social groups and one of those categories can be the expected poet's view. Thus Edward Thomas can ask, "And as for seeing things as in themselves they really are ... what is a fine summer's day as in itself it really is? Is the meteorological office to decide? or the poet? or the farmer?"[85] One does not think of Edward Thomas as a deconstructionist, but here he is deconstructing some significations of "a fine summer's day".

One development from the 1960s sociology of knowledge has been the 1980s study of "cultural politics". In a recent series of books under that general title, two by Simon Pugh deal directly with notions of nature. The second of them, *Reading Landscape: Country – city – capital*,[86] edited by Pugh, is dedicated to Raymond Williams. But it is in *Garden – nature – language* that Pugh, who is not a writer on literature but on garden history, makes the next generation's re-statement of Williams's pioneering six-page definition of "nature":

> The "natural" is the cultural meaning read into nature, meaning determined by those with the power and the money to use nature instrumentally, as a disguise, as a subterfuge, as a pretence that things were always thus, unchangeable and inevitable, which they never were. . . . The garden is a better re-made nature, but in respecting the inherent goodness of nature, what is unpleasant in the real world becomes "unnatural". In both cases "nature" is a recipient of social values and becomes a social construct. What nature really is is not in question. The implications of this for a world fast on the way to destroying its environment is [sic] self-evident.[87]

The last part of this is less than convincing. A concern for an environment under threat needs to be underpinned by some sense of "what nature really is". The problem with the deconstructionists of the "cultural studies" school is that their purely intellectual awareness of "nature" seems to prevent them from communicating a direct experience of nature from any perspective whatever. There are no smells in Pugh's garden. There is only the problem of "the pleasure of the capital wealth that it represents".[88] Raymond Williams, for all his tendency towards abstractions like "structures of feeling",[89] does take his starting-point from "the heavy smell, on still evenings, of the silage ricks"[90] outside his window.

The American Wordsworth scholar Alan Liu would deny that these sensuous realities are nature at all: they are simply themselves. When he says, "There is no nature",[91] he is pointing out that the word is a human construct: "Nature is the name under which we use the nonhuman to validate the human, to interpose a mediation able to make humanity more easy with itself."[92] Whilst Liu is right to identify the word "nature" as "a mediation", he is wrong to deny the general physical presence that is one side of that mediation. There has to be a nature to be called "nature". Whilst he is correct in pointing out that our use of the term "nature" is an "abstraction",[93] he is wrong to suggest that it makes humanity "more easy with itself". This holds true for pastoral poets, but for many contemporary poets their exploration of their relationship with nature is a matter of unease. As Jonathan Bate says in discussing Liu's proposition, " 'Nature' is a term that needs to be contested, not rejected."[94] If we contest these notions as Bate suggests, we can at least choose which conception of nature we can provisionally live with and explore in our poetry about nature. Ultimately this should lead to a debate about which notions are most useful to our survival and that of the planet.

The problem with those post-structuralists who contest everything at once and are therefore only able to answer a question with another question, is the pretence that they are not using provisional assumptions in order to communicate. Choosing provisional notions of nature is crucial to considered action. And whether we like it or not we act upon the environment every day. A similar pretence is perpetrated by the fashionable post-modernist construct of the fragmentation of experience. When my students say "But there are no 'grand narratives' possible any more", I say "We are living them. We call them 'growth and decay', 'the seasons', 'a river'." I point to my balding head as a not-so-grand narrative, in flux, capable of many representations and demanding constant questioning, but following a natural narrative of decay. Daily, post-modernists have to use an active, if tentative, concept of ageing, or of justice, or of environmentalism, however these concepts have been socially constructed.

So what I have termed, following Berger and Luckmann, "the social construction of nature", represents the view that there can be no "innocent" reference to nature in a poem. Any reference will implicitly or explicitly express a notion of nature that relates to culturally developed assumptions about metaphysics, aesthetics, politics and status, that is, in many cases, ideologies. In other words, in literature nature is culture. In poetry, with its particularly self-conscious discourse, culture is nature.

In order to discover whether the poet is contesting the perceived hegemony, this theoretical approach requires a reader to be aware of the social group from which a writer comes, together with the place and time in which the text is written. The trees of "The Woods of Raasay"[95] clearly have a very different meaning for the Gaelic poet Sorley MacLean from the trees inhabited by Seamus Heaney's "Sweeney Redivivus" in *Station Island*,[96] as will be shown in later chapters. The notions of nature at work in these poems are as different as history and myth, and as similar. This is further complicated by the cultural investment of meaning in, not just images, but in places. For example, some places about which a modern poet might write have been culturally reconstructed as locations for nature consumerism. W. H. Auden was clearly aware of the social construction of nature when he wrote,

Am I
To see the Lake District, then,
Another bourgeois invention like the piano?[97]

By contrast, Oscar Wilde appears to have been aware of the reader's personal construction of nature when he said of Words-worth, "He went to the lakes, but he was never a lake poet. He found in the stones the sermons he had already hidden there."[98]

A personal notion of nature will always be in dialectical relation to socially constructed notions of nature. The poem is a site where writer and reader negotiate that dialectic of personal and social meanings. Literary criticism is the exchange of reports from that imaginative encounter. It is an articulation of what has been provisionally taken for granted and what has been provisionally taken as suspect in the text. To put it another way, "Consciousness, mind, imagination and language are fundamentally wild. 'Wild' as in wild ecosystems – richly interconnected, interdependent, and incredibly complex. Diverse, ancient, and full of information."[99] Here Gary Snyder is implying that in articulating and evaluating that "information", literary criticism is one way of nature itself thinking. Through the elaboration and questioning of notions of nature in contemporary poetry the human species is learning, still, how to live on the earth now.

Of course, new notions of nature will be articulated in the old language with new meanings. Wordsworth's use of "ministry", for example, will be discussed in Chapter 5. Contemporary poets will inevitably be engaged in a dialectic not only between personal and social constructions of nature, but between notions of nature in contemporary culture and those traditions of nature poetry established in the literature of the past. The most complete account we have of those traditions is Raymond Williams's *The Country and The City*.

Williams suggests that, even after the Industrial Revolution radically changed the country and the city in England,

> attitudes to the country, and to ideas of rural life, persisted with extraordinary power, so that even after the society was predominantly urban its literature, for a generation, was still predominantly rural; and even in the twentieth century, in an urban and industrial land, forms of the older ideas and experiences still remarkably persist.[100]

The following chapters will examine contemporary poetry for the persistence of "forms of the older ideas" about nature and clarify the cultural uses of nature in the modern contexts within which that poetry is being written. Many of the key poets whose work is discussed by Williams will be referred to in relating contemporary poets to their traditions. But two central concepts in Williams's work will be taken into this examination of recent poetry.

The first is Williams's discovery of the recurring Golden Age. Each generation of writers, he shows with convincing detail, needs to construct an image of an only-just-passed, idealised relationship with nature which represents a source of stable values. Peace, decency and order, located in an idealised notion of nature, can "serve to cover and evade the actual and bitter contradictions of the time",[101] as he says of the period of the Enclosures. Sometimes an image of a particular Golden Age, "a myth functioning as memory, could then be used, by the landless as an aspiration",[102] rather than as a nostalgic retreat. (But it is in the latter category that Williams places the poetry of Edward Thomas, the only twentieth-century nature poet to whom he refers.[103])

This ever-present image of a Golden Age is one part of Williams's analysis of the pastoral. He traces the way in which what he calls "the primary activities" of the early pastoral of Virgil and Hesiod have been transformed by English aristocratic purposes into what he calls the "neo-pastoral" of court entertainment:

> What happened in the aristocratic transformation was the reduction

of these primary activities to forms, whether the "vaile" of allegory or the fancy dress of court games. It is a significant change, but it has been so prepotent – though its impulses, one would think, had been so long dead – that the ordinary modern meaning of pastoral, in the critical discourse of otherwise twentieth-century writers, has been derived from these forms, rather than from the original substance or from its more significant successors. "Pastoral" means, we are told, the simple matter in which general truths are embodied or implied.[104]

Williams might have been referring to Peter V. Marinelli's book, *Pastoral*,[105] published only two years before *The Country and the City*. Marinelli writes: "The pastoral is not by the widest stretch of the imagination an escapist literature in the vulgar sense."[106] At least a more recent editor of a Macmillan Casebook on *The Pastoral Mode* has to begin, "Pastoral is a contested term."[107]

What Williams demonstrated was that the pastoral served a class view of the country, falsifying the economic relations between workers and owners (even if, on occasion, the worker wrote the pastoral himself). "It is not easy to forget that Sidney's *Arcadia*, which gives a continuing title to English neo-pastoral, was written in a park which was made by enclosing a whole village and evicting the tenants. The elegant game was then only an arm's length – a rough arm's length – from a visible reality of country life."[108] "Pastoral" was therefore inevitably, for Williams, a pejorative term and it is in this sense that the term is used in this book. In fact Williams was followed by a number of younger critics who used his analysis of pastoral literature in their own work.

One of these, Roger Sales, in *English Literature in History 1780-1830: Pastoral And Politics*[109] defines his use of "Pastoral" by "the famous five Rs": "refuge, reflection, rescue, requiem, and reconstruction".[110] By "refuge" he means "the desire for escape". By "reflection" he refers to a selective evocation of the past in which positive values are "rescued". "Requiem" represents the way in which "the pastoral idiom affects a reflective melancholia at the transitory nature of life, but tries to locate and isolate still points of permanence".[111] Sales's notion of pastoral as "reconstruction" refers to what John Lucas has called "the deeply conservative ambition"[112] of the pastoral. Sales writes: "Refuge, reflection, rescue and requiem all sustain the illusion that pastoral deals with universally acknowledged truths. It is, however, deceptive and prescriptive. It offers a political interpretation of both past and

18

present. It is a propagandist reconstruction of history."[113]

But the most important work to follow *The Country and the City* has been *The Penguin Book of English Pastoral Verse* edited by John Barrell and John Bull.[114] Organised in historical sections, each with an introduction from the editors, this anthology is clearly complementary to Williams's book in its approach: "For the pastoral vision is, at base, a false vision, positing a simplistic, unhistorical relationship between the ruling, landowning class and/or the poet's patrons and often the poet himself and/or the workers on the land; as such its function is to mystify and to obscure the harshness of actual social and economic organisation."[115]

Included in this anthology is a section called "Anti-Pastoral" which includes writers such as Goldsmith, Crabbe, Duck, and Clare (whose poetry Williams discussed under the heading "Counter-Pastoral"). It remains true, however, that the tension between notions of pastoral and anti-pastoral persists into the present. This tension underlies the current uncertainty about the term "nature poetry" and recurs as a series of questions always to be asked of any contemporary poet who refers to nature, the country, landscape, or green issues. It is my intention to ask those questions of a selection of geographically representative poets' work: What are the notions of nature expressed in this poetry? How do those notions relate to Williams's definition of "pastoral" and "counter-pastoral"? Indeed, to what extent has contemporary poetry at its best outflanked these polarised attitudes? Might one be able to identify a "post-pastoral" poetry? Gary Snyder recently expressed a concern that European deconstructionists "who wish to decentre occidental metaphysics have begun to try to devalue both language and nature, and declare them both to be further inventions of ruling-class mythology".[116] Raymond Williams has shown that it is necessary to admit that the eighteenth-century pastoral was just that: nature serving a class interest. This is not to devalue nature itself. Indeed it is to clear the ground for a search for a post-pastoral poetry.

From contemporary England the literary ground of the archipelago of Britain and Ireland is still viewed with a cautious colonialist circumspection. The "Irish specialists" discuss poetry from the island of Ireland, and what English critics would write on Gaelic poetry in translation? Barrell and Bull make a curious comment that, had they extended their anthology of pastoral poetry into the latter part of the twentieth century, they might have included poets like Edwin

19

Muir and R. S. Thomas "and their several varieties of pessimistic frontier pastoral".[117] By "frontier" is presumably meant "at the furthest point of habitation in Britain", where a separation of urban and rural experience is still maintained. In fact, the experience is more inter-active than that in Wales, for example, as R. S. Thomas complains. So can pastoral poetry come from, say, Norman Nicholson's industrial town of Millom in Cumbria or the city of Derry in the North of Ireland to which John Montague refers? Indeed, if one is to examine in what ways contemporary poetry has got beyond the tensions of pastoral and anti-pastoral it seems important to consider the poetry coming from all the so-called "frontiers" of the archipelago. Literary studies in England, from which I am writing, have tended to neglect important writers living in Scotland, Ireland and Wales. In enquiring into the full range of the constructions of nature alive in poetry now, it is important not to repeat that geographical and cultural distortion. How is nature used in Gaelic poetry, for example? How does the "green language"[118] of Heaney, coming out of a culture under stress, differ from that of Hughes, the English Poet Laureate confronting an environment under stress? What can we learn from the notions of nature at work in the different cultures of our contemporary poetry?

My use of the term "contemporary poetry", which usually means poetry by living writers, has been flexible in order to consider the widest possible range of nature poetry. Of the writers whose work is given detailed attention here, only two are not alive today: Norman Nicholson died as recently as 1987 and Patrick Kavanagh died in 1967. To have excluded Kavanagh's *The Great Hunger* would have been to show neglect, yet again, of this most powerful (and after Heaney's essays[119] one can say influential) continuation of the anti-pastoral tradition in modern poetry. So the parameters of this book have been set from the publication of *The Great Hunger* in 1942 to the publication in 1994 of a poem by a young feminist rock-climber, Kym Martindale, discussed in Chapter 7.

But before considering Kavanagh and the anti-pastoral tradition there is the matter of Barrell and Bull's final challenge. Barrell and Bull end their anthology with Hardy and Yeats. They believe that "now and in England, the Pastoral, occasional twitches notwithstanding, is a lifeless form".[120] Their argument is that in the twentieth century, "as the possibility of social mobility and of economic progress increases, so the pastoral tradition, which had originally rested on a separation

20

of social worlds, is first threatened and finally almost fades away".[121] Well, given the notion of the social construction of nature, are the traditional features of the construct known as the pastoral evident in the poems of Norman Nicholson from England, of George Mackay Brown from Scotland, of John Montague from Ireland, or of R. S. Thomas from Wales?

Notes

1 Blake Morrison and Andrew Motion eds., Harmondsworth: Penguin, 1982.
2 ibid., p. 12.
3 ibid.
4 ibid.
5 ibid., p. 13.
6 M. Hulse, D. Kennedy and D. Morley eds., Newcastle upon Tyne: Bloodaxe, 1993.
7 John Greening, Poetry Review, Vol. 83, No. 2, summer 1993, p. 21.
8 The Guardian, 11 Aug. 1993, G2, p. 4.
9 As in, for example, "A friend who is ecologically aware, and himself a poet, was nonetheless able to refer to [the poems of Francis Horovitz] as 'nature poetry' and to use that phrase in a dismissive tone." K. Kaplin, Tongues in Trees, Bideford: Green Books, 1989, p. 209.
10 Her biographer, Hugo Young, writes: "What remained quite striking, how-ever, was the world's capacity, as she saw it, to adapt to her thinking rather than hers to bend before the fashions of the world. There was a single, conspicuous exception. Having made a first speech on the subject in 1988, she began to give environmental issues more serious attention through 1989" (One of Us, London: Macmillan, 1989, revised Pan edition, 1990, p. 562).
11 Launching a 21-chapter manual on conservation, the defence minister, Kenneth Carlisle, was reported as saying that "The germ warfare defence establishment at Porton Down in Wiltshire contains 11 square miles of the least disturbed chalk downland in Britain and some of the best conserved water meadows: scientists there were very proud of their record" (the Guardian, 5 Jul. 1991).
12 Under a headline of "Green Queen says time running out for planet", the Guardian reported that in her Commonwealth Day message for 1992 the Queen said: "Unless we take action now to halt the rise in global tem-peratures, rising sea levels will threaten the very existence of several islands and low-lying Commonwealth countries" (9 Mar. 1992).
13 The Guardian, 18 Apr. 1987.
14 Vol. 80, No. 2.
15 Vol. 26, No. 1, reviewed S. Rae ed., The Orange Dove of Fiji: Poems for the World Wide Fund for Nature, London: Hutchinson, 1989; Kaplin, Tongues in Trees; A. King and S. Clifford eds., Trees Be Company, Bristol Classical Press, 1989; H. Windrath ed., No Earthly Reason?: Poetry on Green Issues, Manchester: Crocus, 1989. To these

might now be added S. Dunn and A. Scholefield eds, *Beneath the Wide, Wide Heaven*, London: Virago, 1991 and W. Scammell ed., *This Green Earth*, Maryport: Ellenbank Press, 1992.

16 *Poetry Wales*, Vol. 26, No. 1, p. 69.

17 *The Country and the City*, London: Chatto & Windus, 1973, Paladin edition, 1975, p. 31.

18 "Mr Blunden is at any rate significant enough to show up the crowd of Georgian pastoralists." He does not, Leavis says, "draw . . . upon the common stock of Georgian country sentiment." *New Bearings in English Poetry*, London: Chatto & Windus, 1932, Peregrine edition, 1963, pp. 61, 59.

19 "The hallmark of the Georgians was pastoralism, an absorption in the English countryside. But they were not really nature poets; rather, they found in the country something of great value . . . the search for certainty in a disruptive world." M. J. Wiener, *English Culture and the Decline of the Industrial Spirit 1850–1980*, Cambridge University Press, 1981, p. 63. Wiener is surely wrong to suggest that they conducted this search through anything other than what must be called "nature poetry".

20 London: Faber & Faber, 1967, p. 253. Ross is referring to Aldington's satirical poem "To a Poet" published in *Egoist*, Vol. 1, No. 9, 1 May 1914, p. 161.

21 This quotation is taken from the earlier manuscript version in V. de Sola Pinto and W. Roberts eds, *The Complete Poems of D. H. Lawrence*, London: Heinemann, 1972, p. 955. The word 'Shall' is missing in the version in the main body of *The Complete Poems*, p. 126 as it is in Edward Marsh ed., *Georgian Poetry 1911–1912*, London: The Poetry Bookshop, 1912, eighth edition (*sic*), 1913, p. 116. Without this word the text appears to make no sense.

22 *Poetry in the Wars*, Newcastle Upon Tyne: Bloodaxe, 1986, p. 47.

23 See R. G. Thomas ed., *The Collected Poems of Edward Thomas*, Oxford: Clarendon Press, 1978, p. 336. The text is on p. 339.

24 *Edward Thomas*, London: Faber & Faber, 1986, p. 78.

25 ibid.

26 London: Routledge, 1991, p. 11.

27 This is the title of Chapter Five of L. M. Scigaj, *Ted Hughes*, Boston: Twayne, 1991.

28 Harmondsworth: Penguin, 1990.

29 *Gaia: a New Look at Life on Earth*, Oxford University Press, 1987.

30 *The End of Nature*, p. 60.

31 ibid., p. 55.

32 ibid., p. 83.

33 ibid., p. 55.

34 Copyright 1963 by M. Witmark & Sons, recorded on *The Freewheelin' Bob Dylan*, Columbia CL 1986/CS 8786.

35 Reynolds, copyright 1964 by Essex Music, recorded on *Meet The Seekers*, World Record Club (WRC) 1967, SM/202/6.

36 See "The Stone Spiral" by the present author on pp. 176–7.

37 Vol. 80, No. 2, summer 1990, p. 4.

38 Wiener, *English Culture and the Decline of the Industrial Spirit 1850–1980*, p. 182, No. 36.

39 *The Guardian*, 1 Jul. 1991.

40 13 Jun. 1990.
41 *Greenpeace Campaign Report*, May 1991.
42 ibid.
43 *The End of Nature*, p. 64. "We do sometimes watch a nature programme, an account of octopuses or wildebeest. Mostly, however, we watch 'LA Law' " (p. 65).
44 London: Jonathan Cape, 1988. The text of *Whale Nation* is discussed on pp. 167–9.
45 Sherry B. Ortner in Michelle Zimbalist Rosaldo and Louise Lamphere eds, *Women, Culture and Society*, Stanford University Press, 1974, p. 86.
46 "Sorties" in Catherine Belsey and Jane Moore eds, *The Feminist Reader*, London: Macmillan, 1989, p. 113.
47 ibid., p. 125.
48 ibid.
49 Elaine Showalter ed., *The New Feminist Criticism*, London: Virago, 1986, p. 369.
50 Ynestra King, "Healing the Wounds: Feminism, Ecology, and the Nature/Culture Dualism" in Irene Diamond and Gloria Feman Orenstein eds, *Reweaving The World: The Emergence of Ecofeminism*, San Francisco: Sierra Club Books, 1990, p. 106.
51 Boston: Beacon Press, 1978.
52 See Charlene Spretnak's "Towards an Ecofeminist Spirituality" in Judith Plant ed., *Healing the Wounds: The Promise of Ecofeminism*, Philadelphia: New Society Publishers, 1989, pp. 127–32.
53 *The Voice of the Earth: An Exploration of Ecopsychology*, London: Bantam Books, 1993, p. 246.
54 See William Anderson, *Green Man: The Archetype of our Oneness with the Earth*, London: HarperCollins, 1990.
55 *Reweaving the World*, p. 277.
56 I am indebted to my colleague Dr Peter Harrop for this information.
57 I am indebted to Eberhard Schulz of the Düsseldorf branch of the Deutsch-Englische Gesellschaft.
58 Reported on BBC Radio 4's "Today" programme, 4 Dec. 1987.
59 *The Living Landscape*, London: Pluto Press, 1986, p. 32.
60 *The Black Goddess and the Sixth Sense*, London: Bloomsbury, 1987, p. 110.
61 *The Voice of the Earth*, p. 219.
62 *Country Life: a Social History of Rural England*, London: Weidenfeld & Nicolson, 1987, Cardinal edition, 1988, p. 236.
63 "Nature Writing", *Resurgence*, March/April 1994, No. 163, p. 28. Available from Salem Cottage, Trelill, Bodmin, Cornwall PL30 3HZ.
64 *Selected Works*, Oxford University Press, 1990.
65 *Walden and Civil Disobedience*, Harmondsworth: Penguin, 1983.
66 T. Gifford ed., *John Muir: The Eight Wilderness-Discovery Books*, London: Diadem, 1992.
67 New Haven: Yale University Press, 1967, third edition, 1982.
68 New Haven: Yale University Press, 1991. A useful recent bibliography of American books about wilderness, nature and environmentalism is to be found in Peter Coates's *In Nature's Defence: Americans and Conservation*, Keele University: British Association for American Studies, 1993.

69 New York: Pantheon Books, 1992.

70 San Francisco: North Point Press, 1990. A summary of the thinking behind the notion of "mind as wild habitat – poem as a creature of the wild mind" can be found in *Resurgence*, March/April 1994, No. 163, pp. 28–30. See note 63 above.

71 London: Allen Lane, 1983.

72 London: Simon & Schuster, 1992.

73 London: Hogarth Press, 1929.

74 *Man and the Natural World*, p. 28.

75 ibid., p. 20.

76 Glasgow: Fontana, 1976.

77 ibid., p. 184.

78 ibid., pp. 186–7.

79 ibid., p. 186.

80 Smith, *Edward Thomas*, p. 104; Simon Pugh, *Garden-nature-language*, Manchester University Press, 1988, p. 2; and Alan Liu, *Wordsworth: the Sense of History*, California: Stanford University Press, 1989, p. 38.

81 Harmondsworth: Penguin, 1987.

82 ibid., p. 52.

83 ibid., p. 166.

84 ibid., p. 78.

85 *Daily Chronicle*, 14 Jul. 1903, quoted in Smith, *Edward Thomas*, p. 105.

86 Manchester University Press, 1990.

87 *Garden-nature-language*, p. 2.

88 ibid., p. 114.

89 *The Country and the City*, p. 22.

90 ibid., p. 12.

91 *Wordsworth: the Sense of History*, p. 38.

92 ibid.

93 "To believe that nature 'is' in the way a tree 'is' is to abstract the notion of essence while concealing the abstraction." ibid.

94 *Romantic Ecology*, p. 56.

95 *From Wood to Ridge*, Manchester: Carcanet, 1989, p. 171.

96 London: Faber & Faber, 1984, pp. 100, 113, 115.

97 Part III, "Mountains" of the poem "Bucolics", *Collected Poems*, London: Faber & Faber, 1976, p. 429.

98 "The Decay of Lying" in *De Profundis and Other Writings*, Harmondsworth: Penguin, 1984, p. 67.

99 *Resurgence*, March/April 1994, No. 163, p. 29.

100 *The Country and the City*, p. 10.

101 ibid., p. 60.

102 ibid., p. 57.

103 ibid., p. 308.

104 ibid., p. 32.

105 London: Methuen, 1971.

106 ibid., p. 11.

107 Bryan Loughrey ed., London: Macmillan, 1984, p. 8.

108 *The Country and the City*, p. 33.

109 London: Hutchinson, 1983.

110 ibid., p. 17.
111 ibid., p. 16.
112 *England and Englishness*, London: Hogarth Press, 1990, p. 118.
113 ibid., p. 17.
114 London: Allen Lane, 1974, and Harmondsworth: Penguin, 1982.
115 ibid., p. 4.
116 *Resurgence*, March/April 1994, No. 163, p. 29.
117 ibid., p. 432.
118 "The green language of the new Nature" is the language of connection which was forged by Wordsworth and made survival possible for Clare, Williams argues in *The Country and the City*, p. 175.
119 In *Preoccupations*, London: Faber & Faber, 1980, and *The Government of the Tongue*, London: Faber & Faber, 1988.
120 ibid., p. 433.
121 ibid., p. 7.

2

Some versions of contemporary pastoral? The poetry of Norman Nicholson, George Mackay Brown, John Montague and R. S. Thomas

THE EDITORS of The Penguin Book of English Pastoral Verse conclude the commentary on their final section with a strange and sudden curtailment:

> It would of course have been possible to extend the anthology yet further, to the poetry of the Georgians; to Muir, and to R. S. Thomas, and their several varieties of pessimistic frontier Pastoral; and to other poets still writing today. Indeed, with the current concern with ecology, it is not difficult to anticipate a revival of interest in the Pastoral – Industrial Man looking away from his technological Wasteland to an older and better world.[1]

But their perfectly reasonable argument that "today, more than ever before, the pastoral vision simply will not do" seems to be based upon a denial that any experience of the country can be differentiated today from urban experience: "The separation of life in the town and in the country that the Pastoral demands is now almost devoid of any meaning. It is difficult to pretend that the English countryside is now anything more than an extension of the town."[2]

Certainly the pastoral myth would be inadequate to today's multiple crises in our mismanagement of the British countryside and, indeed, the globe itself. All the more reason, one might have thought, for the need to examine the presence of this false vision in contemporary poetry. But to excuse themselves from this, by arguing that those who work in the country no longer experience the processes of nature more directly than city-dwellers, seems a final failure of nerve by the editors of what should have been important and perhaps salutary evidence of a pastoral continuum for contemporary poets and reviewers such as Heaney. With the exception of John F. Lynen's *The Pastoral of Robert Frost*[3] one looks in vain for studies of the pastoral in the modern poetry of our urbanised age.

Of course shepherds will have been making poetry in the form of songs before the development of urban culture. Folk-song collectors from Bartók to Bert Lloyd have found a vigorous continuing tradition to this day in Eastern Europe, for example. But pastoral poetry in its idealised form was from the earliest the product of an urban culture, as George Puttenham argued in *Arte of English Poesie* in 1589. "No doubt the shepheards life was the first example of honest fellowship", he wrote. But "the pastorall Poesie which we commonly call by the name of *Eglogue*" could not be the earliest form of poetry for "nor thereby was there yet any good towne, or city, or Kings palace".[4]

The eclogue to which Puttenham refers was a form deployed in his own time by Spenser in imitation of Virgil's earliest-known works (90–17 BC), *The Eclogues*. Here refined shepherds inhabited the landscape of Arcadia. But in the still earlier *Idylls* of Theocritus (c.316–260 BC) the Greek poet entertained the court with "idyllic" descriptions, based upon rural songs, of his native Sicily. Peter Marinelli suggests that the idyll "derived from the Greek 'eidyllion' (image or picture) does not define a poetic type so much as . . . characterise a short poem, descriptive or narrative, which possesses a picturesque or idealistic quality."[5] So in the two earliest forms of pastoral, the Greek and the Roman, there is an uneasy distinction between a real place described idealistically, and the "Arcadia" of the imagination that came to be deployed as a purely literary device. Ironically, "Arcadia", the concept, was based upon Virgil's knowledge that Arcadia was a real region of the Peloponnesus which the historian Polybius reported to be famous for its singing contests. Thus Bruno Snell can say that "Arcadia was discovered in the year 42 or 41 BC" by Virgil.[6] Both the real and imaginary places, Barrell and Bull point out, represent "an urban interpretation of rural matters".[7]

In fact, satisfying this urban construction of nature within modern poetry are four writers from different cultural contexts whose work represents a continuation of different but overlapping aspects of the pastoral tradition. From England Norman Nicholson's poetry exemplifies not only Georgian notions of nature, but more recent Freudian readings of pastoral. Writing about Orkney, George Mackay Brown has recreated in his poetry a Scottish Arcadia of remarkable consistency. In the face of the Troubles in the North of Ireland, John

Montague tries to avoid yearning for a pastoral retreat in his best-known work, *The Rough Field*,[8] and in the Welsh countryside R. S. Thomas has come to find a religious pastoral that has emerged from the reluctant pastoral of his early work.

The poet Norman Nicholson lived all his life (1914–87) in the small town of Millom on the west coast of Cumbria, where his grandfather was a foreman at the ironworks. The title poem of his last collection, *Sea to the West*, contains several elements of pastoral, but it is essentially an idealised description of a supposedly real place which offers a vision of nature in direct contrast to the town, in precisely the manner claimed by Barrell and Bull to be "now almost devoid of any meaning".[9] The poem begins:

> When the sea's to the West
> The evenings are one dazzle –
> You can find no sign of water.
> Sun upflows the horizon;
> Waves of shine
> Heave, crest, fracture,
> Explode on the shore;
> The wide bay burns
> In the incandescent mantle of the air.[10]

William Scammell is surely right to "register the shock of 'upflows' and the unshowy brilliance of the concluding image"[11] of this first stanza, in which this sky is made domestically familiar in the image of a gas mantle burning "the air". Yet the anachronism of this homely image is also typical of the poet's ultimate need for a cosiness and comfort expressed with a whimsy which renders the "unshowy" as pretentiously naive. In *Sea to the West* that comfort is found outside the town, as indeed it is in the title-poem.

The images of light on water which dominate the first two stanzas are contrasted in the third stanza with negative images of light on water in the town. It is uncertain whether the "purpling" of dykes is due to sunset or pollution, but the latter appears to be the most likely since purple seems an unnatural colour for red light on water. Similarly, it is unclear whether "black-scum shadows" that "stagnated between backyard walls" are actually on real water. "Stagnated" is clearly an image associated with dykes introduced earlier, but it could well be working as a metaphor derived from this pattern of water images. There is even a negative change in words of similar sounds:

"dazzle" has been replaced by "drizzle", and "sykes of light" are followed by the "purpling dykes" linked to the town.

This is not only a poem which offers a description of uplifting experience available outside the town – it offers an idealisation of that experience in the classic manner of the pastoral. For Nicholson this description is unproblematic. To be "blinded by looking" is not only unharmful, but to be wished for at the moment of death in the final lines of the poem: "Let my eyes at the last be blinded/Not by the dark/But by dazzle." There is no sense here of the potentially threatening power hinted at by Ted Hughes's phrase "the whelm of the sun", in the poem "Egghead".[12] Indeed to be "blinded by dazzle" would apparently be a comfort at the moment of death, to be preferred to a confrontation with the darkness of the final moment. The landscape of the typical pastoral offers a comfortable reconciliation of tensions. In "Windsor Forest" Pope expresses this comfortable notion of nature with a characteristic combination of deftness and forthrightness:

Here hills and vales, the woodland and the plain,
Here earth and water seem to strive again,
Not Chaos-like together crush'd and bruis'd,
But, as the world, harmoniously confus'd:
Where order in variety we see,
And where, tho' all things differ, all agree.[13]

The trick is to appear to admit that "all things differ", even "strive" against each other perhaps, but that ultimately all's well in the natural world because all conflicts are in balance. This underlying "agreement" in nature provides a source of comfort and a sense of constancy that seems to be a particular need for some poets of the latter half of the twentieth century.

"Sea to the West" also contains two further elements that recent criticism has defined as pastoral. The first is what Peter Marinelli calls "the retreat into childhood".[14] It is important for the poem's final effect that the vision to be desired at the moment of death originates in a memory of childhood placed at the age of fifteen. So "(five times, perhaps, fifteen)" can, as a parenthesis, remind the reader of a return to that experience of youth. "Pastoral", writes Roger Sales, "is the great escape from adult experience to childhood innocence. Small really was rather beautiful then. It is thus perfectly possible to have urban, and indeed suburban, versions of pastoral."[15] William Empson expanded the notion of pastoral to include what he called a "pastoral process of putting the complex into the simple".[16] So for Empson *Alice in Wonderland* was a pastoral. But it seems equally inadequate to define any kind of escapist process as pastoral. Where there is no possibility of glimpsing any representative of nature in the use of the word, a writer could be accused of a pastoral vision if he or she envisaged, for example, a city without crime, as in the case of Marshall Berman writing of Jane Jacobs's book, *The Death and Life of Great American Cities*: "Her vision seems positively pastoral."[17] The return to childhood in Nicholson's poem is better seen as an aspect of nostalgia for the perception of nature located in the past.

At the end of "Sea to the West" the natural revelation experienced first in childhood is retrieved in the form of an apostrophe: "Let my eyes at the last be blinded." The poem in its last stanza takes the form of a wish or prayer. Laurence Lerner, in defining the "illusion" of pastoral, quotes Freud:

> An illusion, Freud concludes, is a belief in which "wish-fulfilment is a prominent factor in its motivation". The wish to find in country life a relief from the problems of a sophisticated society formed itself, in Renaissance times, into a set of poetic conventions. These are the conventions of pastoral. Pastoral is the poetry of illusion: the Golden Age is the historiography of wish-fulfilment.[18]

This, then, is the second further feature of pastoral in Nicholson's poem. The wish-fulfilment which concludes "Sea to the West" leaves a wistful tone that is reminiscent of Georgian verse. Indeed Norman Nicholson might be justly regarded as a latter-day Georgian poet of the English Lake District. He describes the natural world in an unproblematic, idealised way that represents it as a constant. Yet many of his poems appear to deal with processes of change. How, then, can one come away from his poetry feeling that he has presented a sense of permanence in the natural world?

The poem "Beck" from *Sea to the West* begins:

> Not the beck only,
> Not just the water –
> The stones flow also,
> Slow
> As continental drift,
> As the growth of coral,
> As the climb
> Of a stalagmite.[19]

Images which emphasise the invisible slowness of change have the effect of reinforcing permanence, especially in a volume which also deals with faster urban change, as in the poem called "On the Dismantling of Millom Ironworks".[20] This poem uses long lines, whilst poems about the slowness of change in nature are always expressed by Nicholson in short lines. The poem "Shingle" ends

> the stones reside
> A while on their circuit,
> Inch by inch
> Rolling round England.[21]

The closed circuit of this slow process, emphasised by the short lines, actually creates a sense of stasis that is comfortably lacking in any tension between wind, tides and stones. Even the changes created by the dynamic of the tides in "Tide Out" are viewed in this long-term, slowed-down perspective:

> Here in the wide
>   inter-tidal lull
> The estuary suffers
>   a Pleistocene age of change.[22]

In the poem "Wall"[23] what begins as a witty metaphor of slow movement ("The wall walks the fell") ends in a literal celebration of the natural changing the unnatural. The play of sound and rhythm echoes the play of the unnatural construction as a natural being (stone as animal) and the play of the apparently static as moving. By the latter part of the poem a convincing shift has been made to see this literally: the wall "Is always on the move".

It is typical of Nicholson's whimsy that he extends this idea a little way beyond belief in the final stanza:

> They built a wall slowly,
> A day a week;
> Built it to stand,
> But not stand still.
> They built a wall to walk.

Walls shift with the land, but they fall down as they do so and need repair. The reification of "they" seems to confer the power to outwit the laws of gravity. Such easy logic is unavailable to Ted Hughes, whose poem of the same title also begins by celebrating the skill of fitting segments of stone ("syllables" here)

To the long swell of land, in the long
Press of weather.[24]

But no conceit can conceal for Hughes the cost of this exercise in understanding the dynamics of stone and land and weather. The human cost is what Hughes's wall itself ultimately represents:

Their lives went into the enclosures
Like manure. Embraced these slopes
Like summer cloud-shadows. Left
This harvest of long cemeteries.

One might argue that this last line is as much a distortion as Nicholson's. Fay Godwin's photograph opposite the poem shows a well-maintained dry-stone wall enclosing a good harvest of grass: no cemetery, but a living landscape continuing its service to later generations. But one has to admit that Hughes engages more of the tensions in the final counterbalancing of skill, labour and "manure" in the human "embracing" of "these slopes". Nicholson's yearning for permanence tempts him into exaggerating human achievement in its relationship with nature.

Alongside poems that focus upon the slowness of changes in nature those that assert the permanence of mountains. This is presented as a comforting reassurance against short-term changes. The poem "Scafell Pike" concludes with an image of the future:

No roofs, no town,
Maybe no men;
But yonder where a lather-rinse of cloud pours down
The spiked wall of sky-line, see,
Scafell Pike
Still there.[25]

Certainly the genuine admiration for "the tallest hill in England" that can be seen "between the gasworks" and "the Catholic chapel" has to be recognised here. But the utter simplicity underlying these poems represents a comfortable complacency that is an escape from not only the town but from any sense of real complexities in relating one to the other. Such is the power of the impulse towards pastoral that poetry of naive simplicity written about rocky landscapes will sooner or later be described as "geological and ultimately religious".[26] Indeed reviewers of *Sea to the West* and *Selected Poems 1940–1982*[27] found this simplicity to be seductive, leaving "everything and nothing unsaid"[28] or creating "maxims of such simplicity that they send the reader back to the poem".[29] Even Terry Eagleton's criticism was couched in an apparently unideological category of praise: "There isn't, in this volume, a great deal more than effective description."[30] If "effective description" is an innocent, neutral category it might accommodate Bill Ruddick's admiring view that Nicholson can "find comfort in natural forces"[31] in an unproblematic poetry of affirmation. Simple "effective description" for one reader can become for another "a passionate and energetic affirmation of the continuity of the processes of creation whose perspectives in so many of the poems are geological and ultimately religious".[32]

Like Nicholson, George Mackay Brown has also lived all his life where he was born, in this case in Orkney. His poetry is almost entirely set in Orkney, which he recreates as Arcadia in poems which might be called "green fables", a term which he uses in "Christmas Poem" in his latest collection, *The Wreck of the Archangel*.[33] This poem illustrates how the constants in nature for Mackay Brown are to be found in the seasons and the elements. The cycles of bread and ale at harvest home symbolise the cycle of the seasons and the unity of people with the elements of growth in nature: "We and earth and sun and corn are one." It is also characteristic of Mackay Brown that his vision is endorsed by religious belief. The simple life lived in contact with the seasons is underwritten by a hidden glory that outshines nature itself:

A wintered hovel
Hides a glory
Whiter than snowflake or silver or star.

In the telling of this "green fable" there is a typical use of an archaic word, "wintered", coupled with "hovel" to suggest an archaic vernacular. (One would not have expected a hovel to have "wintered" as animals do.) This is characteristic of this poet's form of pastoral. No one ever drinks beer in a Mackay Brown poem. Only "ale" is served in Arcadia, as in this poem. The coyness of this use of language, like the simplicity of "early/Plough-and-daffodil sun", betrays the innocent idealisation of the "green fable".

The enigmatic, symbolist manner of these fables can be seen in the apparent dialogue of "Autumn Equinox".[34] Of course a dialogue between knowers of nature, as in this poem, was a popular form of Elizabethan pastoral. In Edmund Spenser's "The Shepheardes

Calendar" two shepherds in the month of February not only try to
outdo each other with images of winter, but argue about how to cope.
Cuddie's vigorous complaint is made in vivid images:

> Ah for pittie, wil rancke Winters rage,
> These bitter blasts never ginne tasswage?
> The kene cold blowes through my beaten hyde,
> All as I were through the body gryde.
> My ragged rontes all shiver and shake,
> As doen high Towers in an earthquake.[35]

Thenot replies with equally vigorous engagement:

> Lewdly complainest thou laesie ladde,
> Of Winters wracke, for making thee sadde.
> Must not the world wend in his commun course
> From good to badd, and from badde to worse,
> From worse unto that is worst of all,
> And then returne to his former fall?[36]

This lively dialogue exposes the sham of the supposed exchange
in "Autumn Equinox" as simply a device for juxtaposing images that
do not engage or qualify each other. The effect is as much a static,
comfortable view of natural processes as in Norman Nicholson's
poetry. Poised between "ice" and "fire", Mackay Brown's view of the
autumn equinox ignores, for example, the real dynamics of storms
associated with this time of the year. These symbols simply exist to
speak for themselves in a reductive style that pretends to know more
than it says.

The problem with this style of allegory or fable is that it is so
enigmatic that its meaning is deliberately elusive. What does it actually
mean to say that the representatives of winter and summer, the
elements of "ice" and "fire", "bide together one night, gladly, in the
House of Man"? Surely this is the wrong way round. Human beings
have perceived a turning-point in nature on this day. But will sunrise
really produce a parting of these two elements, "One to the ice, one to
the cage of fire"? The reality is actually a process of change within a
continuum. One begins to feel that this poetry is not intended to bear
close examination, but to be simply accepted as the vague discourse of
symbolist fable. In this way it works as unproblematic reassuring
pastoral.

The recurrence of the same images in a reductivist style has led
some readers to ask if Mackay Brown has not been writing the same

poem over and over again. Reviewing The Wreck of the Archangel in Poetry Review, Dennis O'Driscoll guardedly raises this question: "The accusation of writing the same poem over and over is not unknown to Mackay Brown himself as a consequence of his intensive cultivation of his native ground and his tireless trawling of the waters that surround it."[37] O'Driscoll goes on to refute this charge by assertion rather than evidence. He quotes "Autumn Equinox", admiring the way "day and night are briefly reconciled and delicately balanced". Why they should need reconciling is not obvious and whether "balance" rather than "change" or even "discord" would be more appropriate to the autumn equinox is left unquestioned. The pastoral of Mackay Brown remains unchallenged here.

Sometimes this rewriting of the same material is regarded as the "magic" of his poetry. Catherine Lockerbie, literary editor of the Scotsman, comes close to exposing the repetitiveness of this poetry, but retreats in favour of its "magic":

> Nothing has changed. In a way it's his great virtue, that he doesn't change. I don't know who is Scotland's greatest writer, I don't think there is one person, but the reason I would say that he is not Scotland's greatest writer is because of that stasis . . . . For me he has always been magical and I regret that a little of that magic has worn off.[38]

The Observer writer, Peter Gillman, goes on to link this reservation from Catherine Lockerbie with "the criticism that by staying in Stromness Brown has evaded the challenges of writing about a wider world".[39] Apart from university in Edinburgh, Mackay Brown did not travel away from Orkney until, at the age of sixty-seven, he made his first visit to England in 1989. This, in itself, should not prevent a writer from engaging with the contemporary world. But in fact he has turned his back on the present. In a recent interview with David Annwn he said: "Modern Orkney has little of the stuff of poetry."[40] Annwn replied with the obvious question: "Does any time 'have poetry' except in the eye of the beholder?" Mackay Brown's response clearly indicates that his notion of poetry is based on an idyllic past: "Maybe not, but the ingredients of poetry are rarer here today than they've ever been. Too many machines, pre-packaging etcetera. Also newspapers . . . TV. Too much noise everywhere . . . ."

A revealing example of the strength and consistency of this view is that on a rare occasion when he allowed himself to write about modern concerns on Orkney, in a poem titled "Uranium", he has since tried to suppress the poem. The poem is clearly a response to local concern about test-drilling for uranium on Orkney.[41] It is a contemporary "green" poem that engages with a current environmental issue but the writer has disowned it. When I wrote to Mackay Brown asking for the published source of the poem to reference in this book, he replied: "I'd hoped that 'Uranium' poem was sunk without trace . . . . It hasn't been collected."[42] Of course, he may feel it to be a weak poem, which it is, but that simply endorses the evidence that he cannot engage with the modern world in his poetry.

In a BBC Radio 4 interview about *The Wreck of the Archangel*, Mackay Brown was asked, "Do you feel that the past is more real than the present?" His reply was, "I do. I find the present very confusing. When I write of the present it is always thirty or forty years ago or set in my childhood."[43] It is typical of Mackay Brown that he believes that "almost contemporary with us is A. E. Housman. It was a wonderful day for me when I first read *A Shropshire Lad*."[44] To regard a Georgian poet whose best known book was published in 1896 as "almost contemporary" with 1990 clearly indicates that this poet lives in the past.

Indeed the link between childhood and pastoral recurs in Mackay Brown's work:

> We were all poets, and have squandered our inheritance like the Prodigal Son. But we have kept enough back to remember how immensely rich we were once, in our childhood, when poetry flowed in unchecked through all our senses, and, like little princes who knew no other life, we accepted unquestioningly all the marvels around us – the stars, the flowers, the birds, the shells, the clouds, the waves, the people. I think it is because we cherish fragments from that immortal time that we love poetry.[45]

Much of his poetry is made up of innocent metaphors to describe nature and at times it is difficult to distinguish those seen with a child's eye from those seen from an adult perspective. Often only the title indicates a difference as in "Desert Sleepers" and its facing poem "Rackwick: A Child's Scrapbook".[46] In the latter poem the opportunity to explore the story behind the sixteen empty houses of Rackwick Bay on Hoy is only hinted at: "They say, the jar flawed/with heaviness of coins."

Mackay Brown's sense of the past is really ahistorical: "The longer we voyage among those islands, too, the more we come to recognise that the layers of history and culture cease to matter."[47] In an earlier poem about the deserted crofts in Rackwick Bay, Mackay Brown invites comparison with the Raasay poet Sorley MacLean. "Dead Fires" from *Fisherman with Ploughs*[48] opens with an echo of MacLean's "Hallaig".[49] The latter begins:

> The window is nailed and boarded
> through which I saw the West.

"Dead Fires" begins:

> At Burnmouth the door hangs from a broken hinge
> And the fire is out.
> The windows of Shore empty sockets
> And the hearth coldness.

The poem continues with a list of poignant images culminating in:

> The fire beat like a heart in each house
> From the first cornerstone
> Till they led through a sagging lintel the last old one.

"First" and "last" cleverly sum up the change from fire in the hearth and heart, to a "sagging" and now empty house.

But for MacLean the reason for depopulation is crucial. It is his own family history and that of his people. To merely name the place is to evoke the bitter memory of the Clearances. "Hallaig" also names the families whose suffering is associated with the clearance of Raasay and who have been replaced by trees:

> In Screapadal of my people
> where Norman and Big Hector were,
> their daughters and their sons are a wood
> going up beside the stream.[50]

By contrast, for Mackay Brown "the layers of history and culture cease to matter". He does not make a single reference to the Clearances anywhere in his poetry. In a life's work on Orkney no mention is made of what David Craig calls "an actual grievous history"[51] of Orkney. Instead "Dead Fires" ends with a rare, if vague, reference to a nuclear holocaust:

The poor and the good fires are all quenched.
Now, cold angel, keep the valley
From the bedlam and cinders of A Black Pentecost.

In fact Mackay Brown has written to me that "Rackwick wasn't 'cleared'; the people just left."[52] In 1851 there were 101 people in twenty-one houses. By 1895 there were seventeen crofts and in 1968 there remained only three descendants of these families.[53] The reason for this depopulation is attributed by Mackay Brown to "new altars". In his introduction to *Fishermen With Ploughs* he blames Progress: "By the middle of this century the valley was almost completely depopulated. Perhaps (the poet argues) the quality of life grows poorer as Progress multiplies its gifts on a simple community. The dwellers in islands are drawn to the new altars. The valley is drained of its people."[54]

This is presumably the "flaw" of "the heaviness of coins". Even Alan Bold, the admiring author of a monograph on Mackay Brown, is uneasy on this issue: "*Fisherman with Ploughs* is an impressive achievement, though in laying so much stress on the decline and fall of the valley of Rackwick, Brown has neglected to show us in what way the life there was once so idyllic (unless we are expected to believe that the open worship of Our Lady is the supreme happiness)."[55]

The problem with such undifferentiated ahistorical mythologising is the danger of fatalism. The whole of *Fishermen with Ploughs* is "A Poem Cycle" about the settlement of Rackwick. But its author twice uses the term "myth" in referring to his narrative in the introduction. Historical events in this named place are also mentioned in the introduction, but the emphasis is more general than specific: "Essentially their lives were unchanged; the same people appear and reappear through many generations."[56] This statement is remarkably similar to Edwin Muir's assertion that island life on Orkney "remained almost unchanged for two hundred years".[57] David Craig points out that "half the population left Orkney between 1861 and 1901 and one-third from the Rousay/Wyre/Egilsay trio in the thirty years surrounding his childhood".[58] Muir was Mackay Brown's mentor at Newbattle College, Dalkeith from 1951 to 1955, obtaining for Mackay Brown his poetic debut in the *New Statesman* in 1952. For Muir island life is an idyll in his poetry: "One foot in Eden still, I stand."[59] Mackay Brown's Arcadia forces fewer moral questions than Muir's, and there is more mythic fatalism in his nostalgia for Orkney life.

It is this fatalism that fails the poet's fellow Orcadian readers, especially the women. In the poem "Foldings"[60] the metaphor of the title constructs a mythic sense of processes that happen of themselves, as though in nature, without the exercise of human will or choice. Thus the word "ravished" can be used in this poem without any apparent moral dimension. The hard crag of experience will inevitably bring the bride to widowhood because mother and widow are enfolded within the cycles of the seasons and the contrasts of the elements. So it all appears to be all right, in the abstract mythic pattern established by the poem. Rape, marriage, widowhood, in Orkney are apparently all undifferentiated experiences. This pastoral fatalism is possible precisely because of the reductive notion of nature expressed in the "green fable" of "Christmas Poem": "We and earth and sun are one."[61]

If one tries to historically locate "Christmas Poem" or "Autumn Equinox" or "Foldings" it is obvious that they exist, not only ahistorically, but in a mythic Arcadia created by archaic and reductive language. This is the Golden Age of the generalised past when hardships are undifferentiated from joys because they replicate cycles of nature. In this life human beings are absolved of all dilemmas, moral choices (including environmental ones) and problematic desires, so long as they stay in the country and are not tempted by the money, Progress or material "gifts" associated with the city. If they are tempted, they risk "black pentecostal fire", the apocalypse, the death of nature. This is the essence of George Mackay Brown's vision, summed up by the narrative introduction to Fishermen with Ploughs. This is the vision which underlies the poetry, not only in that book, but in all his poetry to date. In the Arcadia of Orkney suffering is to be enjoyed within the inevitable cycles of nature. Sir Philip Sidney might have recognised it as not dissimilar to his own Arcadia:

Feede on my sheepe, sorrow hathe stricken sayle,
Enjoye my joyes, as you dyd taste my payne,
While our sonne shynes no clowdie greeves assaile.
    Feede on my sheepe, your Native joyes mayntayne,
    Your woll is riche: no tonge can tell my gayne.[62]

However, Seamus Heaney's nomination for the most recent continuation of the pastoral tradition in 1975 was John Montague's The Rough Field. Here there is apparently no problem of a retreat from history, nor of the creation of a mythic place. It was written over a

period of ten years (1961–71) during the latter part of which the
so-called Troubles resurfaced in the six counties of the North of
Ireland. The book incorporates, alongside the poems, prose quotations and references which keep a historical sense ever-present
throughout the text. The book has ten parts and is written in a variety
of forms and styles. In his preface to the 1990 Bloodaxe reprint
Montague cites MacDiarmid's *A Drunk Man Looks at a Thistle*[63] as his
example. The title, *The Rough Field*, the reader is told in the extensive
editor's notes to the Bloodaxe edition, "is English for the Irish *garbh
achaidh* or Garvaghey, the County Tyrone townland in which Montague was raised". In his preface Montague claims a wide frame of
reference for the text, although there can be no doubt that the overwhelming majority of his historical and contemporary references are
to the politics of Ireland:

> Although as the Ulster crisis broke, I felt as if I had been stirring a
> witch's cauldron, I never thought of the poem as tethered to any
> particular set of events. One explores an inheritance to free oneself
> and others, and if I sometimes saw the poem as taking over where
> the last bard of the O'Neills left off, the new road I describe runs
> through Normandy as well as Tyrone. And experience of agitations
> in Paris and Berkeley taught me that the violence of disputing
> factions is more than a local phenomenon. But one must start from
> home – so the poem begins where I began myself, with a Catholic
> family in the townland of Garvaghey, in the county of Tyrone, in the
> province of Ulster.[64]

In fact, Montague seems at a loss to know what to say about the
historical ghosts he raises, just as he throws up his hands in the face of
the contemporary evidence of "disputing factions". Part IX is titled "A
New Siege" and is dedicated to Bernadette Devlin. This was clearly
written when Catholic civil rights activists like her were organising the
demonstrations in Londonderry (now known as Derry) associated
with the resurgence of the Troubles in 1968. The brief dedicatory
poem ends:

> once again, it happens,
> like an old Troubles film
> run for the last time. . . .[65]

The historical reference is to the Seige of Derry in 1689 when the
Protestant garrison in the fortified town held off Jacobite troops until
the ship *Mountjoy* relieved the town.

This section begins by remembering the seige but quickly moves to contemporary "lines of defiance/lines of discord", in an image in which

> twin races petrified
> the volcanic ash
> of religious hatred[66]

The open form, without punctuation, deviates from conventional grammar in order to make sudden shifts of time and a series of juxtapositions. In 1968 protests calling for change in Ulster, Berkeley, Paris and Berlin are like "seismic waves/zigzagging through/a faulty world." The final pun here seems a little naive and inadequate to the breadth of complex political protests being touched upon. This impression is confirmed a few stanzas later when a series of glib generalisations are juxtaposed:

> lines of loss
> lines of energy
> always changing
> always returning
> A TIDE LIFTS
> THE RELIEF SHIP
> OFF THE MUD
> OVER THE BOOM
> the rough field
> of the universe
> growing, changing
> a net of energies
> crossing patterns
> weaving towards
> a new order
> a new anarchy
> always different
> always the same[67]

This begins promisingly enough, but the flux of energies in the universe are used only as abstract "crossing patterns". The relief ships can apparently arbitrarily bring "a new order" or "a new anarchy", or even, the sequencing of these lines suggests, an order that can turn into an anarchy without apparent cause. The sloppiness of "always different/always the same" exemplifies the bankruptcy of political analysis in the poem.

In fact, this is not a poetry of contemporary political engagement.

It is a poem of pastoral retreat in the face of an apparently incomprehensible present. However, three times the poet is at pains to deny this. Firstly, in Part I he argues that this is not a classical Romantic landscape:

> No Wordsworthian dream enchants me here
> With glint of glacial corrie, totemic mountain,
> But merging low hills and gravel streams,
> Oozy blackness of bog-banks, pale upland grass.[68]

This may not be a "totemic" landscape for Montague, but it is a landscape of nostalgia. In the opening of Part IV the poet revisits the landscape of his family farm:

> May, and the air is light
> On eye, on hand. As I take
> The mountain road, my former step
> Doubles mine, driving cattle
> To the upland fields. Between
> Shelving ditches of whitethorn
> They sway their burdensome
> Bodies, tempted at each turn
> By hollows of sweet grass,
> Pale clover, while memory,
> A restive sally switch, flicks
> Across their backs.[69]

This is not too far away from the tone of the "Summer" section of James Thomson's *The Seasons*:

> Or, rushing thence, in one diffusive band
> They drive the troubled flocks, by many a dog
> Compelled, to where the mazy-running brook
> Forms a deep pool, this bank abrupt and high,
> And that fair-spreading in a pebbled shore.[70]

Whether it is "abrupt and high" or "fair-spreading" most details evoke a sensuous well-being. But Montague denies that he is describing an idyll: "A high, stony place – bogstreams,/Not milk and honey – but our own."[71] The giveaway is a moment when the poet reveals that what he is searching for is

> a lost (slow herds of cattle
>   roving over
> soft meadow, dark bogland)
>   pastoral rhythm.[72]

That this rhythm is actually described as a fiddle tune's suggesting the "pain of/a lost . . . pastoral rhythm" only compounds the whimsy of the conceit. Stan Smith accuses the poetry of Heaney and Montague of speaking, "at times, with the tone of a shell-shocked Georgianism that could easily be mistaken for indifference before the ugly realities of life, and death, in Ulster".[73]

"Indifference" is obviously the wrong word for Montague's uncomprehending anguish in The Rough Field and in Chapter 5 I shall argue that it is inaccurate for Heaney too. One might understand the reason for the accusation of Georgianism when Montague declares that he is seeking a "lost pastoral rhythm" in the "pain" of a fiddle tune. But what makes "indifference" so wide of the mark is the context of the loss of language from which the image of the fiddle tune first emerges in the book. Part IV is titled "A Severed Head". This is a metaphor for the loss of the Irish language, described with moving detail and depth in the fractured poetry. In this book the poet "stumbles over lost/syllables of an old order". Somehow the fiddle music has retained that memory of "an old order" and the writing about it evokes a history in images that rise as the fiddle modulates from "hornpipe or reel to warm/us up well" into "the slow climb of a lament":

> & a shattered procession
> of anonymous suffering
> files through the brain:
> burnt houses, pillaged farms,
> a province in flames.[74]

"Shell-shocked Georgianism" is surely too glib to account for the long pull of tensions in this section of the poem.

In the Epilogue of The Rough Field Montague indicates an awareness of the danger of pastoralism: "Only a sentimentalist would wish/to see such degradation again."[75] "Yet something mourns", the poem continues, and is immediately back into consciously expressed pastoral leading to envious evocations of Samuel Palmer's paintings and Goldsmith's The Deserted Village. In fact, it is with the County Tyrone equivalent of the latter that the poem ends:

> Our finally lost dream of man at home
> in a rural setting! A giant hand
> as we pass by, reaches down
> to grasp the fields we gazed upon

Harsh landscape that haunts me,
well and stone, in the bleak moors of dream
with all my circling a failure to return
to what is already going

going

GONE[76]

But it has not "GONE", that "finally lost dream of man at home/in a rural setting". Changed it must be, and "at home" was always problematic for each younger generation. It is a feature of the pastoral golden age that it has always just gone, yet poem after poem in Seamus Heaney's Seeing Things[77] affirms that, despite as Montague rightly points out, there are "Fewer hands, bigger markets, larger farms", a connectedness with nature is still available in Ireland and it cannot be disconnected from memory. In the poem "xlii" from the "Squarings" section of Seeing Things[78] awareness of change has heightened appreciation of nature for the present generation in this poem, rather than producing the fatalistic sense of irretrievable loss with which Montague concludes The Rough Field.

Seamus Deane attempts to retrieve positive qualities in The Rough Field, suggesting that where Montague returns and finds qualities of the past broken "out of their brokenness [he] tries to recompose the wholeness of feeling which they once represented".[79] A sharper analysis is John Wilson Foster's account of The Rough Field:

> The Ulster Catholic writer has lived so long with the imagery of land-decay and land-loss that he has become addicted to it . . . What he wants is not progress, a forward-looking reversal of decay through agricultural improvement, but rather a return, the recovery of a politico-spiritual impossibility – a mythic landscape of beauty and plenitude that is pre-Partition, pre-Civil War, pre-Famine, pre-Plantation and pre-Tudor.[80]

The landscape of The Rough Field is not mythic as is the island Arcadia in the poetry of Mackay Brown: a real landscape reduced to its generalised elements. Montague is insistent on particularising the landscape of County Tyrone. This is a "harsh landscape that haunts me", more with a sense of "failure to return" than as a "mythic landscape of beauty". Its "plenitude" was gleaned by the "degradation" of "heavy tasks". But it does finally represent a notion of nature as pastoral escape from the present discord. What Palmer, Chagall and Goldsmith "commemorate" for Montague is

> a world where action had been wrung
> through painstaking years to ritual.
>
> Acknowledged when the priest blessed
> the green tipped corn, or Protestant
> lugged pale turnip, swollen marrow
> to robe the kirk for Thanksgiving.[81]

Here are seasonal rituals which retain difference but function in unison. This is the classic pastoral desire for a countryside "where, tho' all things differ, all agree".[82]

R. S. Thomas does offer a landscape of religious escape. Albeit in bleak and melancholic poetry, from a poet riven with doubt, suspicious of his God's indifference, it is a poetry that is pastoral in function rather than style. Thomas is the only contemporary candidate named by the editors of the The Penguin Book of English Pastoral Verse as a possible writer in the pastoral tradition today.[83] It is typical of the editors' use of the term "English" that they appear not to have noticed that he is Welsh: a Welsh speaker who writes specifically about a Welsh landscape.

R. S. Thomas has had a long and changing poetic career. Colin Meir tells us that, "under the influence of Patrick Kavanagh's The Great Hunger (1942), Thomas turned from merely descriptive verse like 'Cyclamen' (published in the Dublin Magazine in 1939 and collected in The Stones of the Field, 1946) and found both subject and theme in his native Wales".[84] But there has been a further important shift from the interest in nature and people in Selected Poems 1946–1968[85] to his search for God in Later Poems 1972–1982,[86] which continues to the present in Counterpoint.[87]

It is easy to see why R. S. Thomas should find an affinity with Kavanagh's anti-hero Maguire, the Monaghan farmer, and to also find in Kavanagh's anti-Romantic descriptions of landscape, a model for his own wet, bleak hills. Thomas made his early reputation through poems like "A Peasant" and "Welsh Landscape" which Barrell and Bull may have in mind when they refer to Thomas's "pessimism". He is a poet of paradoxes and each of these poems can be described as offering, ultimately, a pastoral vision, almost against much of the poem's apparent evidence. The opening of "A Peasant"[88] presents an ordinary man of bald hills who is nevertheless, given the poem's title, a representative figure, later to be called a "prototype". The images of both man and landscape that follow are unremittingly negative in a linked manner. This linkage is important because the man comes to be presented a few lines later as himself an animal living amongst the elements. He is first "half-witted", then completely "vacant" in his mind. Finally he is described as "enduring like a tree under the curious stars". Man and nature are one, but in a perversely pastoral making of a mythic hero out of the material of an anti-hero. This "peasant" is at one with nature at the expense of his human consciousness, in contrast to Ted Hughes's description of the farmer enduring atrocious conditions at work in "A Monument":

> And this is where I remember you,
> Skullraked with thorns, sodden, tireless,
> Hauling bedded feet free, floundering away
> To check alignments, returning, hammering a staple
> Into the soaked stake-oak, a careful tattoo
> Precise to the tenth of an inch,
> Under December downpour, mid-afternoon
> Dark as twilight, using your life up.[89]

It is the detail of this that conveys a conscious determination that this is the opposite of Thomas's half-witted animalistic hill-farmer. Precision of alignment here is typical of the careful and caring human responsibility for his stock that distinguishes Hughes's from Thomas's farmer. Even though Hughes's poem is a "monument", like the fence itself, to a good farmer, it demonstrates that the degree of consciousness necessary to do the job must render Thomas's "peasant" an exaggeration in his "stark naturalness". The evidence justifying the epithet "enduring like a tree" is described rather than assumed in Hughes's poem. But Hughes is not tempted to such a heroic, pastoral posture; his last phrase is "using your life up". The poignancy is all the more powerful.

In 1963 Thomas wrote, "the potential audience of a poet is one of town dwellers, who are mostly out of touch, if not sympathy, with nature. Their contact with it is modified by the machine. This is tending to deprive country-rooted words of their relevance."[90] Thomas has a hatred for the "Machine", which he sometimes spells with a capital M,[91] that is parallel to Mackay Brown's dislike of "Progress".

"Welsh Landscape"[92] evokes a culture that is to be understood through nature and is located in the past, beyond "the noisy tractor/ and hum of the machine". A history of "strife" here not only overlays nature, "dyeing the immaculate rivers", but seems to remake nature everywhere in Wales. All river courses are apparently affected. The people may ultimately be "impotent" in this poem, "sick with inbreeding", but the landscape, which is the subject of the poem, is a powerful presence of the past. The pastoral nostalgia of this landscape, which has no continuing dynamics of change or disputes, is a wilfully bleak construction of melancholy: a reluctant pastoral. The wilfulness of Thomas's early bleak representation of the Welsh landscape is best illustrated by the way in which the weather seems to have improved in *Later Poems 1972–1982*. Whilst it may have been true that recorded hours of sunlight on "the bald Welsh hills" gave a few hours "perhaps once a week",[93] *Later Poems* does seem to notice them more in poems such as "The Bright Field", "The Moor", and "That Place".

The two poems which conclude *Selected Poems 1946–1968* anticipate a more personal inner life of enquiry in Thomas's contemplation of nature. The poem titled "That" presents nature as an impersonal "that", giving nothing but "this blank indifference" to the poet who complains about

the neutrality of its answers, if they can be called, answers
These grey skies, these wet fields,
With the wind's winding-sheet upon them.[94]

But such a vision of nature can be used, as it is in the next stanza, to confirm a religious necessity for suffering: "The shadow of the tree falls/On our acres like a crucifixion." Such a vision can then turn the "bird singing in the branches" into a religious source of presumably divine suffering, "Hammering its notes home/One by one into our brief flesh". If this is good, albeit painful, it is hard to avoid the term "pessimistic . . . pastoral" used by Barrell and Bull.

At the turn of a page, however, birds are presented as the source of uplift, "after the bitter/Migrations".[95] It is not the poet's house that they nest in, he says, but his mind. This implies some inward moral discipline that, despite bitter experiences, is able to maintain a capacity to "receive" them. The suggestion is that this demands more than just alert wondering observation. It is a pastoral of an inner "possession" of nature that characteristically sets itself against the science of "facts" and the recordings that any ornithologist knows will provide the evidence for the protection of the very birds that Thomas admires. These birds ignore "outward changes" in the poet, but only a pastoralist can ignore "outward changes" in nesting sites and in influences on "the bitter migrations". Indeed, "outward changes" may be altering the meaning of poetry itself. Jonathan Bate makes the point that if, due to increased winds following continued global warming, swallows are prevented from returning to Britain each year, some poems will have lost their meaning for younger readers: "Keats's ode 'To Autumn' is predicated upon the following spring's return; the poem will look very different if there is soon an autumn when 'gathering swallows twitter in the skies' for the last time."[96] Now, more than ever before, bird-watchers like Thomas need to open themselves to the scientific evidence to which they should be contributing. But the science Thomas comes to be interested in is confined to abstract concepts.

From *Later Poems* onwards Thomas has been explicit about his quest to define God in poetry, embracing, in the process, the concepts of science: "genes and molecules", "cells and chromosomes". In "The Absence" in *Frequencies*[97] he writes, "I modernise the anachronism/of my language, but he is no more here/than before." In the poem "Emerging", from *Laboratories of the Spirit*,[98] God is now to be found, not in nature, which is rejected in a remarkable phrase, but in the abstractions of the mind:

> Emerging
> from the adolescence of nature
> into the adult geometry
> of the mind. I begin to recognise
> you anew, God of form and number.

This explicit search for God had begun in nature in "The Moor" from the earlier collection *Pietà*.[99] This poem is a retreat into the senses that leaves behind the mind ("Not listened to"; "no prayers said") and regains an unproblematic being, "simple and poor", to whom grace, like bread, is then generously given. It would be hard to find a better example of religious pastoral, unless it were "The Bright Field"[100] in which the poet "turns aside", in a Georgian gesture, to a moment of sunlight on a small field:

> Life is not hurrying
> on to a receding future, nor hankering after
> an imagined past. It is the turning
> aside like Moses to the miracle
> of the lit bush.

Thus, despite the bleakness of the early poems, nature becomes in Thomas's poetry the idyll that is being resisted. In fact, in "The Moon in Lleyn", nature worship has become religion:

> In cities that
> have outgrown their promise people
> are becoming pilgrims
> again, if not to this place,
> then to the recreation of it
> in their own spirits.[101]

"This place" is significantly both a church and the Lleyn peninsula. Nature has become a church and can be "recreated" in human spirit. Just as the moor is a church for Thomas, so a church can contain, even in the city, a sense of eternity glimpsed in nature. Poems such as "The Moor", "The Bright Field" and "The Moon in Lleyn" represent a modern version of Milton's Eden:

> So little knows
> Any, but God alone, to value right
> The good before him, but perverts best things
> To worst abuse, or to their meanest use.
> Beneath him with new wonder now he views
> To all delight of human sense expos'd
> In narrow room Natures whole wealth, yea more,
> A Heav'n on Earth: for blissful Paradise
> Of God the Garden was, by him in the East
> Of Eden planted.[102]

Despite the difficulty of "valuing right/The good before him", the "narrow room" can be glimpsed as the Heaven-on-Earth of "Natures whole wealth". Despite the bleakness of Thomas's Welsh landscape and the apparent bleakness of the culture that grows out of contact with it, the later poetry can find idealised sightings of eternity to be "recreated" in the human spirit.

For Roger Sales, "reconstruction is the most important of the famous five Rs" that are the elements of the pastoral: "*refuge, reflection, rescue, requiem and reconstruction*":[103] "Economic distances are more important than geographical or temporal ones. Before you become too nostalgic about the merry old days of rural England, it is worth thinking about which groups have a vested interest in such nostalgia."[104] If one substitutes for "merry" the word "bleak", and for "England", "Wales", the question becomes an interesting one for the

49

poetry of R. S. Thomas. He has chosen to retreat from the early poetry's concern about rural landscape and culture into a personal search for an unexpected Paradise that might be found in that land-scape after all. In a reflective poem in *Frequencies*, "The Small Country",[105] Thomas accuses himself of fear of hubris in daring to identify Wales with "the kingdom", but now accepts that "the pro-mised/land was here all the time."

The elusiveness of "the promised land" has so soured the poetry of *Counterpoint* that nature can only remind Thomas of his frustration:

> The way the brain resembles
> a wood, impenetrable thicket
> in which thought is held fast by the horns,
> a sacrifice to language.[106]

Indeed this seems to be a fair representation of Thomas's own sacrifice of thought in his vague language of "the machine" (still present in his current work), "mathematics" in nature, and in his equally vague hints at references to genetic engineering, acid rain and radiation:

> Only
> Satan beams down,
> poisoning with fertilisers
> the place where the child
> lay.[107]

Such fatalism simply throws up its hands in the face of the desecration of the "promised land".

But in his prose writing in Welsh, Thomas has continued to develop his concern for the nation in an international context. He is an activist for both the Welsh language and CND, for example. He "opposes the poll tax and privatisation on the grounds of their evident social injustice", John Barnie, the editor of *Planet*[108] tells us in a review of Thomas's prose book, *Bluyddyn yn Llyn*.[109] In a passage of reflection upon the elected representatives of the State, John Barnie translates for us the following:

> What interests do these have in nature and its ancient and won-derful order? But we're in authority to protect you from the enemy, they say. Friends, I don't need you to tell me who the enemy is. It's you, even so for that you are prepared to contaminate the earth and the environment for your own profit.[110]

That nothing of this has emerged in the collected poetry[111] leaves it open to the accusation of reluctant pastoral, which can be used by those who have a vested interest in nostalgia, as Roger Sales suggests.

So in conclusion one must say that, certainly by the criteria of a number of writers on the pastoral, including Sales, and in direct comparison with the classic pastoral texts, versions of pastoral have been written by contemporary poets in every country of our archipelago. Like Pope's use of Windsor Forest, Norman Nicholson's poetry constructed a refuge in the comfortable constants of the English Lake District, ignoring the kind of tensions that might have interested a poet like Ted Hughes. George Mackay Brown's poetry constructs an Orkney Arcadia amongst the constants of the seasons and the elements that echoes Sydney's *Arcadia*. He attempts to rescue a way of life from the threat of Progress. His reflective, backward-looking poetry does not attempt to bring insights from local history to bear on the present, as in the poetry of Sorley MacLean. John Montague's *The Rough Field*, like Goldsmith's *The Deserted Village*, is a requiem which Heaney was right to nominate as pastoral poetry. R. S. Thomas's reconstruction of Milton's Eden, will, in the final chapter of this book, be compared with the less escapist achievements of Gillian Clarke writing about nature from contemporary Wales.

But can it be convincingly shown that the whole work of MacLean, Heaney and Hughes has avoided the pastoral? Before answering that question one might expect that the easier case to make would be for an anti-pastoral poet such as Patrick Kavanagh in *The Great Hunger*.

Notes

1 John Barrell and John Bull eds, London: Allen Lane, 1974, p. 432.
2 ibid.
3 New Haven: Yale University Press, 1960.
4 in G. Gregory ed., *Elizabethan Critical Essays*, Oxford University Press, 1904, II, p. 39.
5 *Pastoral*, London: Methuen, 1971, p. 8.
6 Bryan Loughrey ed., *The Pastoral Mode*, London: Macmillan, 1984, p. 181.
7 *The Penguin Book of English Pastoral Verse*, p. 4.
8 Dublin: The Dolmen Press, 1972, revised edition Newcastle upon Tyne: Bloodaxe, 1989.
9 *The Penguin Book of English Pastoral Verse*, p. 432.
10 *Sea to the West*, London: Faber & Faber, 1981, p. 30.

11 *Times Literary Supplement*, 3 Jul. 1981, p. 759.
12 See Chapter 6 for a discussion of this poem.
13 H. Davis ed., *Pope: Poetical Works*, Oxford University Press, 1966, p. 37.
14 *Pastoral*, p. 75.
15 *English Literature in History 1780–1830: Pastoral and Politics*, London: Hutchinson, 1983, p. 15.
16 *Some Versions of Pastoral*, London: Chatto & Windus, 1935, p. 23.
17 Marshall Berman, *All That Is Solid Melts Into Air: the Experience of Modernity*, New York: Simon & Schuster, 1982, p. 324.
18 In *The Pastoral Mode*, p. 154.
19 p. 13.
20 p. 49.
21 p. 23.
22 p. 26.
23 p. 15.
24 *Remains of Elmet*, London: Faber & Faber, 1979, p. 33.
25 *Sea To The West*, p. 12.
26 Matt Simpson, *London Magazine*, July 1984, p. 33.
27 London: Faber & Faber, 1982.
28 Andrew Motion, *Times Literary Supplement*, 10 Dec. 1982, p. 1376.
29 Alan Hollinghurst, *London Review of Books*, 18 Feb. 1982, p. 20.
30 *Stand*, Vol. 23, No. 2, p. 63.
31 *Critical Quarterly*, Vol. 24, No. 2, p. 59.
32 Matt Simpson, *London Magazine*, July 1984, p. 33.
33 London: John Murray, 1989, p. 104.
34 p. 88.
35 (1579) in *The Penguin Book of English Pastoral Verse*, p. 28.
36 ibid.
37 *Poetry Review*, Vol. 80, No. 2, p. 44.
38 *Observer*, 3 Sept. 1989, p. 59.
39 ibid.
40 "Correspondences", *Poetry Wales*, Vol. 27, No. 2, p. 19.
41 "the South of Scotland Electricity Board set about establishing a claim to uranium in Orkney. Landowners were visited by agents of the Board in the early summer of 1976 and were asked to sign an agreement whereby for the next seven years the Electricity Board would have the sole right – 'to explore and search for uranium by whatever means the Board may deem necessary'." Marjorie Linklater goes on to document the (thus far) successful Anti-Uranium Campaign of the 1970s in "Uranium: A Questionable Commodity", a chapter in William P. L. Thomson ed., *Orkney Heritage*, Kirkwall: Orkney Heritage Society, 1981, pp. 7–21.
42 Letter to the present author, 9 Jun. 1991. The poem is quoted in full in my Ph.D. thesis, *Beyond Pastoral Poetry: Notions of Nature in Poetry 1942–1992*, Lancaster University.
43 "Kaleidoscope" programme, BBC Radio 4, 8 Jun. 1989.
44 *Chapman*, No. 60, p. 29.
45 ibid., p. 30.
46 *The Wreck of the Archangel*, pp. 54, 55.

47 *Chapman*, No. 60, p. 28.
48 London: Chatto & Windus, 1971, p. 76.
49 *From Wood to Ridge*, Manchester; Carcanet, 1989, p. 227.
50 ibid.
51 *On the Crofters' Trail*, London: Jonathan Cape, 1990, p. 327.
52 Letter to the present author, 9 Jun. 1991.
53 R. Miller and S. Luther, *Eday and Hoy: A Development Survey*, Department of Geography, University of Glasgow, 1968.
54 *Fishermen with Ploughs*, p. 1.
55 *George Mackay Brown*, Edinburgh: Oliver & Boyd, 1978, p. 40.
56 *Fishermen with Ploughs*, p. 1.
57 *The Estate of Poetry*, London: Hogarth Press, 1962, p. 9.
58 *On the Crofters' Trail*, p. 329.
59 "One Foot in Eden", *Selected Poems*, London: Faber & Faber, 1965, p. 80.
60 *Fishermen with Ploughs*, p. 50.
61 *The Wreck of the Archangel*, p. 104.
62 (1590) in *The Penguin Book of English Pastoral Verse*, p. 38.
63 (1926) in M. Grieve and W. R. Aitken eds, *The Complete Poems of Hugh MacDiarmid*, Vol. I, Harmondsworth: Penguin, 1985, p. 83ff.
64 *The Rough Field*, p. vii.
65 p. 71.
66 p. 72.
67 p. 75.
68 p. 11.
69 p. 33.
70 (1727) in *The Penguin Book of English Pastoral Verse*, p. 303.
71 p. 40.
72 p. 44.
73 *The Inviolable Voice*, Dublin: Gill & Macmillan Humanities Press, 1982, p. 189.
74 p. 38.
75 p. 82.
76 p. 83.
77 London: Faber & Faber, 1991.
78 p. 102.
79 *Celtic Revivals*, London: Faber & Faber, 1985, p. 147.
80 "The Landscape of the Planter and the Gael in the poetry of John Hewitt and John Montague", *Canadian Journal of Irish Studies*, Vol. 1, No. 2, Nov. 1975, quoted by Edna Longley, *Poetry in the Wars*, p. 191.
81 *The Rough Field*, p. 82.
82 H. Davis ed., *Pope: Poetical Works*, p. 37.
83 p. 432.
84 P. Jones and M. Schmidt eds, *British Poetry since 1970: a Critical Survey*, Manchester: Carcanet, 1980, p. 1.
85 St Albans: Granada, 1973.
86 London: Macmillan, 1983.
87 Newcastle Upon Tyne: Bloodaxe, 1990.
88 *Selected Poems*, p. 3.
89 *Moortown Diary*, London: Faber & Faber, 1989, p. 55.

90 A. E. Dyson, *Three Contemporary Poets: Thom Gunn, Ted Hughes, R. S. Thomas*, London: Macmillan, 1990, p. 218.

91 See, for example, "Once", in H'M, London: Macmillan, 1972, p. 1.

92 *Selected Poems 1946–1968*, p. 9.

93 "A Peasant", *Selected Poems 1946–1968*, p. 9.

94 p. 129.

95 p. 130.

95 *Romantic Ecology*, Wordsworth and the Environmental Tradition, London: Routledge, 1991, p. 2.

97 London: Macmillan, 1978, p. 48.

98 London: Macmillan, 1975, p. 1. Not to be confused with the poem of the same title in *Frequencies*. It is the *Frequencies* poem which is collected in *Later Poems*.

99 London: Rupert Hart-Davis, 1966. This poem is in *Later Poems*, p. 97.

100 p. 81.

101 ibid., p. 66.

102 (1667) in *The Penguin Book of English Pastoral Verse*, p. 193.

103 *English Literature in History 1780–1830: Pastoral and Politics*, p. 17.

104 ibid.

105 p. 19.

106 p. 43. All poems in *Counterpoint* are untitled.

107 p. 29.

108 No. 86, Apr./May 1991.

109 Gwasg Gwynedd, 1991.

110 p. 74.

111 A bitter little book of twelve political poems, *What Is a Welshman?*, Llandybie: Christopher Davies, 1974, is represented by only one poem in *Later Poems 1972–1982*, and that is the least political.

3

The anti-pastoral tradition
and Patrick Kavanagh's
The Great Hunger

KAVANAGH'S long poem in fourteen parts is concerned with
the inward hunger of a Monaghan farmer whose emotional life has
been stunted by local forms of "respectability and righteousness".[1] It is
a bitter and moving poem which charts with telling detail the effects
upon Patrick Maguire, "the old peasant", of the repressions and false
hopes engendered in him by the twin authorities of his mother and
the Catholic Church.

Just as the poetry is stylistically torn between authentic practical
detail and portentous melodrama, so too the poet is caught in the
tension between the revelation of false hope offered by the mother
"when she praised the man who made a field his bride"[2] and the
recognition that the farmer can at times be genuinely "lost in the
passion that never needs a wife",[3] that is, his connection with his land
and its processes. There lies the central tension of the anti-pastoral
tradition: how to find a voice that does not lose sight of authentic
connectedness with nature, in the process of exposing the language of
the idyll. *The Great Hunger* is characteristic of a tradition which includes
Goldsmith's *The Deserted Village*, Crabbe's *The Village* and writers who,
like Kavanagh, experienced nature as workers: Stephen Duck and
John Clare.

The poem is, as Heaney puts it, "a poem of its own place and
time"[4] about a pre-war small farmer in County Monaghan. Yet it is
remarkable to discover how many of Patrick Kavanagh's preoccupations and problems echo those found in eighteenth-century
anti-pastoral poetry. In order to establish this point in detail I want to
briefly indicate the terms of the anti-pastoral dialectic in the poetry of
Goldsmith and Crabbe before showing how Kavanagh "fights his own

corner" in the manner of Duck and Clare. If *The Great Hunger* will ultimately be shown to be a flawed work, the reasons for this may perhaps be more readily understood by reference to the linguistic tensions in Duck and the social pressures on Clare.

Kavanagh's fellow-Irishman, Oliver Goldsmith, wrote *The Deserted Village*[5] in order to engage with the pressures of his own particular place and time. Enclosure of the commons and the consequent depopulation of villages was taking place in England as well as in Ireland in the mid-eighteenth century. Goldsmith's "Auburn", his newly deserted village, is both a literary construct of a rural repository of community values, and an authentic place in which the writer wished to retire, knowing its detail from his youth in Ireland. For Goldsmith the precise location of place is less important than the effects of economic changes in agriculture that have now altered it:

> One only master grasps the whole domain,
> And half a tillage stints thy smiling plain;
> No more thy glassy brook reflects the day,
> But choked with sedges, works its weedy way.[6]

The local details of the changes to the land work as concrete images for economic effects. The "stinting" of the plain and the "choking" of the brook represent a change in feeling which will be developed in human detail as the poem develops. Raymond Williams was unconvinced by these images:

> But the actual history, in which the destruction of the old social relations was accompanied by an increased use and fertility of the land, is overridden by the imaginative process in which, when the pastoral order is destroyed, creation is "stinted", the brook is "choked", the cry of the bittern is "hollow", the lapwing's cries "unvaried". This creation of a "desert" landscape is an imaginative rather than a social process; it is what the new order does to the poet, not to the land.[7]

There are two points to be made in reply to this. Goldsmith is not claiming that "creation" is stinted, but that monoculture has stinted the diversity of previous land-use by more than one master. John Clare also uses the word "desert", twice in the poem "Remembrances",[8] to describe the change that Enclosure had brought to the land and its people. I see no reason, therefore, to disbelieve the contemporary detail that the plough had reduced grassy hillocks to a "desert" of levelled monoculture.

But the important point is that we are dealing here with an artistic expression of social history. Goldsmith is offering images of a moment in history, not just for their historical documentation, which, as Clare confirms, is more accurate to village experience than Williams's general overview allows, but because these images evoke the very feeling of that experience for those it affects directly. The verbs "stints" and "choked" are the powerful signifiers, just as "desert" also signifies "unpeopled". What the new order does to the poet, returning to end his days in his native village, it has also done to the inhabitants of that landscape. For Goldsmith these images have significance beyond the nostalgic response to changing land-use. They represent what people have done to people. Here is the importance of the way Goldsmith's poetry urgently, though often melodramatically, seeks to convey the bitterness of those dispossessed by enclosure, clouded as this might be by the poem's dramatic pastoral structure of return and regret on personal terms.

Goldsmith quickly gets beyond this, in his introductory section, to a sharp political use of the Augustan couplet. Indeed for Goldsmith's poem the real focus is upon a loss in terms of an ideology. There is a new callousness behind the new commercial approach to agriculture:

> But times are alter'd; trade's unfeeling train
> Usurp the land and dispossess the swain;
> Along the lawn, where scatter'd hamlets rose,
> Unwieldy wealth and cumbrous pomp repose;
> And every want to opulence allied,
> And every pang that folly pays to pride.

What Goldsmith is punching home here rather heavily with his alliteration and rhyming opposites ("unfeeling train"/"swain"; "hamlets rose"/"pomp repose") is the supplanting of village values by the culture of exploitation. An ideology based upon people has been replaced by one based upon efficient use of the land. Like Patrick Kavanagh, Goldsmith is interested in the way a particular ideology can be located in place through a particular view of nature. The new attitude to the land is summed up by Goldsmith in a couplet which, changing metaphor into metonymy, assumes that the fate of the land includes the fate of its workers:

> Ill fares the land, to hast'ning ills a prey,
> Where wealth accumulates, and men decay.

The starkness of "men decay" has the metonymic effect of treating men as natural plants which are uncared for and "when once destroy'd, can never be supplied". So for Goldsmith the notion of nature at work on the landscape, which is unfeeling in relation to it and unwieldy in its use of it, is also a notion of humanity.[9] In Goldsmith's view it follows that wealth derived from such an attitude leads inevitably to "pomp", "opulence", and "pride".

But Goldsmith's alternative notion of nature is his own poetic downfall. As might have been hinted at earlier by "smiling plain" and "glassy brook", Goldsmith's alternative is expressed in an archetype of pastoral poetry: nostalgic, idealised, unproblematic.

> A time there was, ere England's griefs began,
> When every rood of ground maintain'd its man;
> For him light labour spread her wholesome store,
> Just gave what life requir'd, but gave no more.

"Light labour" is a phrase we must later put against the evidence of "Streams [of] Sweat" in Stephen Duck's poetry.[10] But here again is the classical pastoral of nature giving just enough for happy poverty. Austerity is the moral basis of the humanity of Goldsmith's famous portraits of the schoolmaster and parson at the heart of *The Deserted Village*. It is also the basis of his Augustan notion of poetry:

> And thou, sweet Poetry, thou loveliest maid,
> Still first to fly where sensual joys invade.[11]

So the poem ends with a farewell to poetry itself, in the belief that Goldsmith's pastoralisation of "sweet Auburn" has been a last exercise of restraint and integrity. Williams's explanation of this paradox is to see Goldsmith as trapped poetically in a pastoral tradition which he cannot now get beyond because the new social order negates a "new relationship and imagination": "Yet to be a poet is, ironically, to be a pastoral poet: the social condition of poetry – it is as far as Goldsmith gets – is the idealised pastoral economy. The destruction of one is, or is made to stand for, the destruction of the other."[12] This problem is important in relation to *The Great Hunger* because it is about tensions between form and content, between intention and tone, and about the cultural limitations upon language when referring to nature, values and labour.

Goldsmith left himself open to Crabbe's accusation that he did not know what he was talking about and was in the old position of the privileged poet pastoralising the poor. Thirteen years after *The Deserted Village*, George Crabbe published *The Village* as a direct anti-pastoral reply to Goldsmith:

> Yes, thus the Muses sing of happy swains,
> Because the Muses never knew their pains:
> They boast their peasants' pipes; but peasants now
> Resign their pipes and plod behind the plough;
> And few, amid the rural-tribe, have time
> To number syllables, and play with rhyme;
> Save honest DUCK, what son of verse could share
> The poet's rapture and the peasant's care?[13]

The contrast in this last line indicates that Crabbe is going to distort in the opposite direction, denying that there is any music at all in his village, that only the worker himself can have any credibility as a writer about the country, and that the only choice is between "the poet's rapture and the peasant's care". It is true that Crabbe's own verse does have some humour at the expense of the language of the classical pastoral:

> Can poets soothe you, when you pine for bread,
> By winding myrtles round your ruin'd shed?[14]

But Crabbe, like Goldsmith, can also be utterly serious in his savouring of a melancholy scene for his late eighteenth-century readership.[15]

Clearly the anti-pastoral tradition is itself caught in a tension between notions of reality and poetic conventions, between authenticity and the temptation for the poet to become "Bard" as Crabbe puts it: "I paint the Cot,/As Truth will paint it, and as Bards will not."[16] The assumption is that he is not himself a "Bard" when evoking rural depression in the image of tolling bells or moping owls. This tension will resurface in the work of Patrick Kavanagh, who has the bardic presence of Yeats looking over his shoulder.

Kavanagh wants to both counter the pastoral and represent the moments of joy in working the land in a more ambitious project than *The Village*. Kavanagh seeks to engage with the dialectic at the heart of the anti-pastoral tradition whether it is expressed between Crabbe and Goldsmith or within *The Deserted Village* itself. For those who do not have the pastoral vision open to them, precisely because they do not see the land from a position of privilege, the land is both a joy and a trap. The anti-pastoral tradition shows again and again that the problem is to find a language that can hold that balance. This is the challenge taken up by the Monaghan small-farmer, Patrick Kavanagh, in 1942.

After their son failed as a hired hand, Kavanagh's parents bought an extra three acres to add to the four already attached to the house and the two rented from a nearby estate.[17] The subject of The Great Hunger is a Monaghan small-farmer who lives with his mother, working their farm, until she dies when he is sixty-five. This is not to suggest that The Great Hunger is autobiographical in a simple sense, but to indicate that Patrick Kavanagh would satisfy Crabbe's required credentials for his project. He sought to expose the unproblematic idealised view of the Irish peasantry popular in the Irish Literary Revival, begun by Yeats and Synge in the first two decades of the century and persisting in Kavanagh's time.[18]

It is in the penultimate Part XIII of Patrick Kavanagh's poem The Great Hunger that he parodies the Revivalist pastoral: "The peasant has no worries/In his little lyrical fields."[19] Were this section to be the opening of Kavanagh's poem it would appear to be a straw castle easily demolished, a reductio ad absurdum of Sidney's Arcadia of "careless" swains and of Pope's biblical Eden in "Windsor Forest". But placed near the end of the poem, although its reductiveness may still prevent its being recognised as a serious attitude, every line now rebounds with irony from the earlier evidence of the poem.

The Great Hunger of the title refers, not to the potato famine of the 1840s, but to the emotional and sexual hunger of a County Monaghan potato-farmer of the 1930s.[20] The effect of borrowing this historically located phrase is to suggest a parallel which renders the case of Patrick Maguire symbolic of a hunger felt "in every corner of this land", as the poem's final line claims. Similarly Maguire's sexual hunger is symptomatic of a hunger for the release from repression of his sense of himself as part of nature.

The poem explores the perceived pressures of Catholicism and "townland" culture on the peasant who worries about how he missed getting a wife. His "little lyrical fields" of the pastoral view in Part XIII are actually presented in Part I as "the grip of irregular fields". That grip is to be revealed as the trap of the man "who made a field his bride". Rather than "loving fresh women" like "fresh food", as the Revivalist travellers think in Part XIII, his guilt and fear reduce him to a distorted mistrust of his own natural sexuality: "He was suspicious in his youth as a rat near strange bread,/When girls laughed."[21] In fact his elderly mother is his resented mistress: "She had a venomous drawl/And a wizened face like moth-eaten leatherette."[22] This kind of description substitutes for narrative incidents that might provide the reader with evidence for the mother's power over her son.

But the bitterest irony is the notion that religion apparently endorses Patrick Maguire's existence as being in some kind of harmony with nature in an innocence before the Fall. The word of God for him, however, is sin and it alienates his spirit from his land. Part of the project of the poem is to show that the people of this Catholic rural community sense that really earth "does not believe/In an unearthly law"[23] that represses them, however much they impose religious images on nature. Maguire's discovery of this deception comes whilst facing his own death, and is therefore too late. His ultimate unity with his land comes at the moment of silence: "The tongue in his mouth is the root of a yew."[24] Clearly Kavanagh is writing a bitter anti-pastoral, however complicated that stance might be by a necessary recognition of what is indeed, at times, the lyrical quality of fields.

This tension between the bitter and the lyrical in anti-pastoral was first faced, not by Goldsmith or Crabbe, but by Stephen Duck, the Wiltshire farm worker who in *The Thresher's Labour* of 1736 wrote,

> No Fountains murmur here, no Lamkins play,
> No Linnets warble, and no Fields look gay;
> 'Tis all a gloomy, melancholy Scene,
> Fit only to provoke the Muse's Spleen.[25]

Stephen Duck uses the language of Pope ("the Muse's Spleen") to parody the pastoral vision of those who do not work the fields they poeticise as "gay". His anti-pastoral expression of the thresher's labour cannot avoid the classical language of the pastoral if he is to gain acceptance as a poet in the Augustan age:

> Now in the Air our knotty Weapons fly,
> And now with equal Force descend from high;
> Down one, one up, so well they keep the Time,
> The Cyclops' Hammers could no truer chime;
> Nor with more heavy Strokes could Aetna groan,
> When Vulcan forg'd the Arms for Thetis' Son.
> In briny Streams our Sweat descends apace,
> Drops from our Locks, or trickles down our Face.[26]

61

It is characteristic of Stephen Duck that he follows a series of classical references with the practical detail of the unpastoral reality of what he is writing about: hard work and sweat. Patrick Kavanagh knows in similar physical detail the work of a small-farmer, and also shares the insecurity of a writer over-eager to gain credibility as a poet having an unliterary background. In the fourteen parts of *The Great Hunger* Kavanagh uses different registers of language with varying degrees of success. He moves in and out of the voice of narrator and the voice of Maguire. He is at times rhyming, at times conversational, at times addressing the reader and at other times his muse, "Imagination". Indeed the opening of the poem is typical of the strange mixture of tones Kavanagh can use within one dominant register. In this case Kavanagh is addressing the reader whom he draws in to share his vision on the fourth line with the assumption that "we watch". This opening tone, which is part invocation, part deflation, part apocalyptic, part empirical, is established in the first line: "Clay is the word and clay is the flesh."

This apocalyptic opening line, balancing the abstract "word" against the material "flesh", is itself at odds with the deflation of the potato-gatherers as "mechanised scarecrows" that follows. The biblical is brought hard up against the anti-romantic language in a way that seems to work because of the link through "clay" and its literally down-to-earth associations. Similarly, although less successfully, the Yeatsian construction, "Book of Death", is used in a sentence setting out on an apparently empirical project for the epic poem: "Is there anything we can prove/Of life as it is broken-backed over the Book/Of Death?" At first "broken-backed" seems to be presenting the physical evidence of Stephen Duck, but the worker's image leads through alliteration to a sub-Yeatsian reaching for significance in a heavy-handed symbolism. Kavanagh seems to sense this in his need to deflate that abstraction again in his return to the physical evidence of crows killing worms, and gulls like old newspapers. These are the farmer's concrete unromantic images of death and of cynical depression.

However, there is a deftness in the last word of the line in which gulls are "blown clear of the hedges, luckily". This suggests not only the depressed spirit the gulls represent, but their physical movement. One is reminded of the same effect in Hughes's poem "Wind" in which a gull "bent like an iron bar slowly".[27] The essential difference is that Hughes is celebrating an awe-inspiring control in the face of powerful forces, whilst for Kavanagh the gulls represent an attitude of an opposite kind: it is only by good luck that men like Maguire might be said to be "blown clear of the hedges". When a few lines later Maguire is shown boasting of his negotiation of the obstacles of life, the distancing of the writer is clearly evident. Here the image of Maguire shifts from the temporary freedom of a horse from its halter, to the nets set for a rabbit where it will not see them as it runs for a gap. Maguire believes he can run free of the halter and avoid the nets of experience. He "pretended to his soul/That children are tedious in the hurrying fields of April."[28] Yet this is the man who, we are told in the twelfth line of the poem, had "promised marriage to himself" before Hallowe'en. So he has not, in fact, escaped the nets. He is rationalising his emotional and sexual frustration, claiming that he is instead "Lost in the passion that never needs a wife". He pretends that he "lives that his little fields may stay fertile". The effect of this is to affirm a natural connection felt by the farmer between the processes at work in himself and those in his fields.

At the same time these lines express Maguire's disconnection, for all his having "made the field his bride". His passion is like that of his horses and his fertility is like that of his fields; his own slow decay is like that of organic material with which his fields are fertilised. Yet, despite his "mud-gloved fingers" and his "clay-wattled moustache" he is alienated from the natural processes he lives and works amongst. Here lies the force of his bitterness.

The bitterness of a man alienated from his own land connects Kavanagh's poetry with that of John Clare, in, for example, Clare's poem "The Lament of Swordy Well".[29] Kavanagh conveys the feel of this in an early evocation of the physical work itself which begins " 'Move forward the basket and hold it steady.' "[30] It is this kind of practical detail and the authenticity of voice, including the use of dialect in "graip", that also connect with Clare. The full development of the sense of disillusion in this passage is actually more convincing than Kavanagh's following abstract poeticising of a man whose "spirit/ Is a wet sack flapping about the knees of time."

Maguire's source of alienation derives from Catholicism mediated by his mother. Her praising "the man who made a field his bride" is responsible for Maguire's feeling "the grip, O the grip of irregular fields! No man escapes." The grip upon him is actually that of his mother, "tall, hard as a Protestant spire". Part II of the poem indicates Maguire's childlike devotion to his mother and their farm until she died when he was sixty-five. What begins as a parody of nursery-rhyme verse leads to images of the sexual impotence of Maguire: "His face in a mist/And two stones in his fist/And an impotent worm on his thigh."[31] This becomes a metaphor for his unnatural disconnection from the forces of recreation and decay amongst which he lives.

But "For the strangled impulse there is no redemption."[32] The force of the poet's comment suggests a double deprivation of both sex and redemption. This is made the more poignant by the suggestion that redemption is a deception anyway. Throughout the poem religion is shown to be simple superstition. His sister "curses the cat between her devotions".[33] Kavanagh exposes the need for religion as the congregation rises to leave: "Five hundred hearts were hungry for life." Here is one of the rare moments in the sequence when Kavanagh indicates the scale of the hunger for life and its channelling into the Church's repressive "living in Christ". At this moment Maguire's great hunger is representative of that in 500 neighbours.

Maguire's problem is that he does not himself see that others find a way of recognising that this religion is an impossibility whilst following its rituals. His mother's advice is the lie that confession copes with sexuality. "And all the while she was setting up the lie/She trusted in Nature that never deceives."

Maguire does not follow his own nature but believes in sin, without the practical compromise provided here by confession. Kavanagh seems to be presenting us with a man dominated by his conscience rather than realising that others make a compromise in practice. The concept of sin complicates his instinctive knowledge that actually, in an existential sense, nature never does deceive. In the lines which follow the poet comments on the unspoken way in which this conflict is resolved for others: "Religion's walls expand to the push of nature./Morality yields to sense."

"Sense" here implies not only "common sense" but "the senses", that is, not only expanding the verbal walls of religious morality, but recognising the physical inevitability of "soft thighs spread". But this "yielding to sense" is not understood, apparently, by this literal-minded man who works the little tillage fields. He is confounded by the religious construction of mystery. Maguire, says Kavanagh, "read the symbol too sharply and turned/From the five simple doors of sense."[34] The religious puzzle of symbols has so confused Maguire that he cannot trust his own senses and his own common sense.

Indeed, it is Kavanagh's ability to unify common-sense detail through sensory experience into glimpses of *potential* affirmation of connection with nature that gives his poem about disconnection such pathos. In a single stanza, for example, in Part III, there is a movement from sexual imagery in ploughing, to neighbourly rivalry, which ends on an evocation of pantheism: "These men know God the Father in a tree."[35]

In the process of showing how Christianity has appropriated from these men an ancient pantheism, Kavanagh is celebrating visionary moments that perceive the great forces of the seasons in a way that is potentially enlarging. But this passage is not a celebration of natural regeneration, nor is it pagan tree-worship. It is the overlaying of a naturally special moment with Christian symbolism.

For these men it does nevertheless remain a moment of connection between their sense of awe and their knowledge of nature. The irony is that the religious construction of their experience, which demands that it is expressed in religious terms, is the very culture which is responsible for alienating their own natures from the nature they experience in their work. Thus the potential moment of connectedness through awe at natural beauty is deflected into "the lie" which Maguire's mother perpetuated for him of simple, idealised "Nature that never deceives". But the everyday awareness of these men that a unity with the forces they work among is necessary and natural makes Maguire's inner alienation all the more difficult to comprehend. The last lines of Part IV sum up Maguire's state. His fantasies of taking strength from his being part of the Tree of Life remain as fantasies whilst he is bowed down by the everyday fight against "weeds" that seem even to ensnare him in their wet sensual twining.

One might ask why this should be so for Maguire, whilst other men apparently find that "Religion's walls expand to the push of nature"? If "morality yields to sense", why not in Maguire's "little tillage fields"? Indeed how can it be that Maguire the farmer can turn "from the five simple doors of sense"? Kavanagh's presentation of Maguire here seems to rest on a literal-mindedness that is at odds with the practical compromises of the contradictions between religion and nature that Kavanagh has so clearly exposed. Kavanagh's wilful straining of his presentation of Maguire is evident in his asking the reader to perceive Maguire as not feeling the very things that give his situation its poignancy.

In the summarising passage at the end of Part IV, the Church appears to be blamed for Maguire's cowardice. The analysis of the repression, mystification and alienation created by the Church, and the mother's mediation of it, is brilliantly achieved by the poetry. But ultimately Kavanagh uses the Church as an excuse for the fatalism with which he presents Maguire. Once again the anti-pastoral poetry suffers from an over-straining of its case.

Ironically the set-piece anti-pastoral of Part XIII is superb parody, although it, too, finally raises again the central problem of Kavanagh's presentation of Maguire. Here it is a question of voice, as the language moves from that of narrator to the travellers and back again. There is no problem in the simple comedy of the traveller's idea of the renewal of connectedness with nature: "The travellers touch the roots of the grass and feel renewed/When they grasp the steering wheels again."[36] "Touch" and "grasp" are deftly chosen verbs for the contrast of "roots of the grass" and "steering wheel". But the superficiality of the pastoral travellers extends to the ancient unproblematic view of the peasant's relationship with the clay. The poet over-simplifies the travellers.

Of course Kavanagh is specifically parodying the pastoral expression of the Irish Literary Revival. Yeats had written that,

> John Synge, I and Augusta Gregory, thought
> All that we did, all that we said or sang
> Must come from contact with the soil.[37]

Kavanagh appears to have had these words in mind when he parodies the travellers' idealisation of the peasant: "There is the source from which all cultures rise." In the passage which follows, the use of the word "clay" rather than Yeats's word "soil" brings up against Yeats's romantic, softer, general term, the particular experience of Maguire for whom "Clay is the word and clay is the flesh." This is sharply focused poetic parody, which is continued to a point where the tone shifts the irony against Maguire's life rather than the literary establishment's view of it. But in the passage which follows the voice finally shifts to one that Kavanagh himself takes over to make his own point. At first the voice of the travellers comes uncomfortably close to his own when the travellers salute "without irony" the peasant's being "half a vegetable" that nevertheless has the capacity to see when "the cataract yields". The peasant's desire for "conscious joy" and "intensity" of feeling that are patronised by the travellers are exactly what Kavanagh has had Maguire hungering for. The travellers' word "breed" for the way the peasant would view sexual relationships in the heightened moment of perception when "the cataract yields", is exactly the way that Kavanagh has himself presented Maguire's feelings towards young girls ("fillies in season"). There is indeed a sense in which Kavanagh himself presents Maguire as "half a vegetable", or "only one remove from the beasts he drives", in the travellers' words.

This is what is ultimately unconvincing at the heart of *The Great Hunger* and it is based on the poem's crucial flaw of pessimistic fatalism. The problem can be traced to the recurring suggestion that Maguire's sense of love is limited to the stirrings of animal appetite, the very image that Kavanagh parodies in the opening of Part XIII. In this way the poet limits his enquiry into how Maguire becomes alienated from nature by implying, perhaps more than he realises, that Maguire's own nature has not only been repressed and distorted, but is, in itself, already fundamentally limited. This then becomes an underlying element in a circular argument that is asserted by simple statements of closure. Part XIII continues from the mention of "the desire to breed" in language that we have come to recognise as the narrator's voice talking about Maguire when he says, "No escape, no escape."

The fatalism of this is intended, I think, to be that in Maguire's mind. In effect it is also the position of the poet on his subject. Kavanagh's motivation is the presentation of Maguire's anguish in a way that avoids heroic alternatives. In his desire to deflate the pastoral view of the peasant, Kavanagh, like Crabbe before him, errs on the opposite side, despite wishing to resist sub-Yeatsian melodrama in describing Maguire's death: "No mad hooves galloping in the sky." Once again the very image that is most authentic – that of a sick horse seeking a clean place to die – is also unfortunate in emphasising Maguire's animal nature, and in doing so to emphasise his fatalistic weakness rather than any potential instinctive strength.

One would like to believe, with Seamus Heaney, that images which indicate that Maguire is capable of fulfilment are given equal counterpointing emphasis with the images of his frustration. But Heaney's argument in his major essay on *The Great Hunger* is unconvincing: "The poem accumulates a number of incidents in which the fallow/fertile and the repression/fulfilment contrasts are dramatized, and simultaneously it establishes the prevailing atmosphere of futility in which these incidents occur."[38] Fulfilment remains a matter of willfully denied potential in the poem. Indeed, a reading of *The Great Hunger* would leave a reader who accepted Kavanagh's presentation of

Maguire as representative of a culture, wondering where the body of Irish love songs has come from, or, indeed, Kavanagh's own celebratory lyric "Inniskeen Road: July Evening".[39]

The final irony of Maguire's lack of expression of whatever potential the poet allows him is that in death he imagines a practical connectedness with the earth. The Church allows him an afterlife which his imagination treats in a characteristically pragmatic way. He will know the quality of clay and the names of the roots underground. If the humour of this is at Maguire's expense, and is consistent with Kavanagh's image of Maguire as simple-minded, it is affectionate as much because of the loss of this satisfaction in reality. The joke that this will never happen, of course, is tinged with an awareness that the connectedness that Maguire's knowledge might seem to give him, has in fact never been fulfilled.

The poem thus justifies the bitterness of its final images of loss and closure. Kavanagh's evocation of the metaphysical hunger of Maguire, in borrowing for its title the famous Great Hunger of the 1840s is, in the poem's final images, generalised into a metaphor for the state of a national culture. That hunger screams as an "apocalypse of clay" in the final line, "In every corner of this land."

Seamus Heaney's comment on the final lines is significant in revealing both criticism and recognition, suggesting that the lines are both flawed and necessary:

> It is a loving portrait which Kavanagh was to reject because "it lacks the nobility and repose of poetry". It is true that there are strident moments, especially at the end, . . . yet I do not feel that the apostrophizing of the Imagination at the beginning and the end involves a loss of repose . . . If *The Great Hunger* did not exist, a greater hunger would, the hunger of a culture for its own image and expression.[40]

That desire to make a literary impact which results in an over-straining of language is itself, as Heaney hints, a feature of the culture's expression, just as it was for the Hardy who used the "President of the Immortals",[41] classical allusions and occasionally pompous prose in his eagerness to impress as a newly middle-class novelist from the peasant community. In fact, the story of Kavanagh's literary career might seem remarkably similar to that of Stephen Duck and John Clare in being artistically weakened by acceptance into the literary establishment.[42] Actually Kavanagh's case is one of self-destruction rather than of acceptance and rejection.

Kavanagh's later response to the interest of the Vice Squad in *The Great Hunger* was to accept it as confirmation of artistic weakness in the poem: "There is something wrong with a work of art, some kinetic vulgarity in it when it is visible to policemen."[43] Kavanagh's ultimate rejection of *The Great Hunger* simply confirms that the vague despair which dominates the poem was, in part, a projection of his own neurosis on to the tensions of the townland culture which he explores through Maguire. He is himself caught between his knowledge of the complexities of that rural culture and his romantic notion of "the nobility and repose of poetry".[44]

The temptations to grandness of fatalistic abstract language and to pastoralise within the anti-pastoral indicate not only the persistent power of conventions in the sense that we have few alternative models of discourse about the country experience, but are a feature of the duality of that experience. Patrick Kavanagh shows, in *The Great Hunger*, a farmer who is aware of what he contributes to his fields at the same time as feeling their grip on him in a cycle of unending hard work. He can see the fruits of "the Tree of Life", yet feels that he is alienated from that tree. He knows he is, in many practical ways, a part of nature, connected to his land, its seasons, and his animals, yet sees that he is disconnected by the frustration of his own fulfilment. He does not see the process whereby the Church connects guilt with the lie of the pastoral – the simple assertion that "Nature never deceives" and the promise of "God the Father in a tree".

That Kavanagh's bitter satire and fatalistic pessimism are derived from outrage and compassion turns a flawed work into an important one. The challenge he set himself, to present "an old peasant who can neither be damned nor glorified", was always going to be difficult if he really cared about the effects of the Church's distortion of human vitality through its pastoralisation of nature. If he himself erred on the side of fatalistic despair in his presentation of Maguire he is closer to Crabbe's anti-pastoral than to Goldsmith's nostalgia. But what he achieves is a more subtle, more detailed exploration of the way a twentieth-century national culture has alienated land workers from their own inner nature and from their land. *The Great Hunger* is a moving example, out of its own place and time, of the strengths and some of the difficulties of the anti-pastoral tradition.

Notes

1 Patrick Kavanagh, *Collected Poems*, London: Martin Brian & O'Keefe, 1972, p. 48.
2 ibid., p. 35.
3 ibid., p. 34.
4 *Preoccupations*, London: Faber & Faber, 1980, p. 126.
5 First published in 1770.
6 In John Barrell and John Bull eds, *The Penguin Book of English Pastoral Verse*, London: Allen Lane, 1974, p. 392.
7 *The Country and the City*, London: Chatto & Windus, 1973, p. 100.
8 E. Robinson and G. Summerfield eds, *Selected Poems and Prose of John Clare*, Oxford University Press, 1967, p. 175.
9 This is a point that will recur in this book, particularly in Chapter 7 in relation to poems by Debjani Chatterjee and David Craig.
10 Barrell and Bull, *The Penguin Book of English Pastoral Verse*, p. 386.
11 A. Dobson ed., *The Poetical Works of Oliver Goldsmith*, London: Bell, 1895, p. 41.
12 *The Country and the City*, p. 99.
13 First published in 1783. J. Lucas ed., *A Selection from George Crabbe*, London: Longman, 1967, p. 43.
14 ibid., p. 44.
15 "The bell tolls late, the moping owl flies round,/Fear marks the flight and magnifies the sound." ibid., p. 52.
16 ibid., p. 44.
17 Darcy O'Brien, *Patrick Kavanagh*, Bucknell University Press, 1975, p. 37.
18 "Kavanagh was fond of calling the Literary Renaissance 'a thorough-going English-bred lie'." O'Brien, *Patrick Kavanagh*, p. 23. Antoinette Quinn's book *Patrick Kavanagh: Born-Again Romantic*, Dublin: Gill & Macmillan, 1993, relates the development of Kavanagh's work to his relationship with the Literary Revival.
19 *Collected Poems*, p. 52.
20 Antoinette Quinn points out the irony that social historians can now see that "the infrequency or belatedness of marriages in twentieth century rural Ireland was a consequence of the Famine". *Patrick Kavanagh: Born-Again Romantic*, p. 139.
21 *Collected Poems*, p. 35.
22 ibid., p. 37.
23 ibid., p. 55.
24 ibid.
25 In *The Penguin Book of English Pastoral Verse*, p. 386.
26 ibid. p. 385.
27 *The Hawk in the Rain*, London: Faber & Faber, 1957, p. 40.
28 ibid.
29 *The Penguin Book of English Pastoral Verse*, p. 415.
30 *Collected Poems*, p. 35.
31 ibid., p. 37.
32 ibid., p. 39.
33 ibid., p. 41.
34 ibid.

35 ibid., p. 38.

36 ibid., p. 52.

37 "The Municipal Gallery Re-Visited", *Collected Poems*, London: Macmillan, 1950, Papermac edition, 1982, p. 369.

38 *Preoccupations*, p. 125.

39 ibid., p. 19.

40 *Preoccupations*, pp. 125–6.

41 *Tess of the d'Urbervilles*, London: Macmillan, 1967 edition, p. 446.

42 "He was treated as the literate peasant he had been rather than as the highly talented poet he believed he was in the process of becoming." John Nemo, *Patrick Kavanagh*, London: George Prior, 1979, p. 79.

43 *Collected Poems*, p. xiv.

44 Heaney was quoting Kavanagh from *Self-Portrait*, Dublin: Dolmen Press, 1964, p. 24.

4

A culture of kinship and place: the poetry of Sorley MacLean

IT IS SADLY characteristic of literary criticism in Britain that a major European poet who lives in Scotland has been almost totally neglected by English commentators on contemporary poetry. Now in his eighties, Sorley MacLean has been recognised in Scotland by the publication of a collection of critical essays on his work[1] and the collection of his prose writing.[2] But from England there persists a critical silence, which is perhaps the more remarkable when one considers the number of monographs by English writers prepared to comment on a poet such as Seamus Heaney, whose work also comes from a subtle and complex non-English culture. This may partly be a symptom of the apparent assumption that Scottish literature is best left to Scottish critics, although there are signs that this attitude is weakening in relation to Hugh MacDiarmid.

But part of the explanation for the English neglect of the work of MacLean must be that he writes in Gaelic, although his own translations have been available in the dual-language *Spring Tide and Neap Tide: Selected Poems 1932–72* since 1977.[3] In North America more recently *Poems 1932–82*[4] appeared with texts only in English, and in 1989 the English publisher, Carcanet, produced *From Wood to Ridge: Collected Poems in Gaelic and English*.[5] The latter contains nothing more recent than the poem "Screapadal",[6] but it has sixteen previously uncollected texts and a brief introduction by MacLean himself. There can certainly no longer be any excuse for the critical neglect of Sorley MacLean's poetry south of the border.

Somhairle MacGill-Eain, Sorley MacLean was born in 1911 on the island of Raasay which lies between Skye and the mainland just north of the Kyle of Lochalsh. Three factors influenced his poetic development. His family were tradition-bearers of Gaelic song, music and poetry. Also linguistically important was the influence of Free Presbyterianism which had a stronghold on Raasay after seceding from the Free Church of Scotland in 1893. Thirdly, having gone to university in the early 1930s, MacLean became a Marxist. The Gaelic scholar John MacInnes points out that "Sorley MacLean was not the only Free Presbyterian Marxist on Raasay"[7] In 1934 MacLean met Hugh MacDiarmid whose *First Hymn To Lenin And Other Poems* had been published in 1931. In 1935 MacLean made a visit to MacDiarmid on Whalsay, Shetland. By May 1940 MacLean was writing to MacDiarmid, "Names like Lenin, Connolly, John MacLean etc. are more to me than the names of any poets."[8]

After writing poems in English and Gaelic during his teens, MacLean made a decision whilst still a student to write only in Gaelic because "I realised that my Gaelic stuff was better."[9] John MacInnes suggests that "Gaelic is not only a dialect; it is not even a minor language ... modern Gaelic is really a major medieval European language" capable of coping with "the intellectual activities of the modern scientific world ... as Professor Ronkin has shown in Mathematics or Professor Thomson in Biology".[10] A reader of MacLean's poetry in translation will obviously miss important rhythms, rhymes, assonance, diction and cultural associations – the subtle interplay between convention and innovation that is a feature of MacLean's Gaelic poetry. But with some help from Gaelic-speaking writers, the English reader may receive some of the power of feeling and thinking in MacLean's own translations. John MacInnes writes,

> Personally, and in spite of the author's modest disclaimer, I regard these translations as poems in their own right. Of course they make a very different impression from the originals. Perhaps in English they do not administer the same shock of modernity, or because they are easier, or for some other related reason, bilingual readers may occasionally prefer the translation.[11]

This chapter represents an attempt by an English writer to take up the challenge of evaluating the achievement of MacLean's translations, especially in relation to the development of his particular frame of reference to the natural world.

To an English reader MacLean may seem to be a pastoral poet whose notion of nature is tied by language to traditional Gaelic concepts of place and kinship. In fact he has taken the Gaelic pastoral tradition into an international concern for the future of human beings and the earth they inhabit. The case of the long poem "The Cuillin" provides an interesting insight into the features of MacLean's verse and his poetic project. MacLean's celebration of place in this poem uses a traditional form to link local history with the contemporary politics of 1939. But its starting-point is very much within the world of Gaelic culture, the *Gaidhealtachd*:

> I see the noble island in its storm-showers
> as Mairi Mhor saw in her yearning,
> and in the breaking of mist from the Garsven's head
> creeping over desolate summits,
> there rises before me the plight of my kindred,
> the woeful history of the lovely island.[12]

The publishing history of this poem indicates the pull of the pastoral in Gaelic poetry. This long poem of seven parts was written during 1939, but was not included in *Selected Poems 1932–72* and remained unpublished in its present form until *From Wood to Ridge* was published in 1989.[13] A shorter version was published in America in *Poems 1932–1982*. But it is remarkable that MacLean was satisfied to let the poem be represented by this shorter version for a North American audience in 1987 when he must have been preparing for publication, in a revised translation, the text which began appearing in the summer 1987 issue of *Chapman*. Clearly he had for many years suppressed the poem and then preferred "The Cuillin" to be read only in those parts (released over the years to magazines) which make up the shorter version.

A comparison reveals the shorter version, published for an American and Canadian audience, to be a backward-looking historical poem, whereas in his preface to the poem in *From Wood to Ridge* MacLean explains that the poem was actually conceived as a contemporary Marxist complaint against "the idea of the conquest of the whole of Europe by Nazi-Fascism without a war in which Britain would not be immediately involved but which would ultimately make Britain a Fascist state".[14]

What had been a poetic Marxist response to the historical moment in 1939 using the traditional Gaelic form of the "praise-song" (*Moladh*) had been reduced to a conventional nostalgic complaint, albeit a remarkably powerful one, by MacLean himself. He admits that by the time he came to publish parts of "The Cuillin" after the war, "the behaviour of the Russian Government to the Polish insurrection of 1944 made me politically as well as aesthetically disgusted with most of it". This feeling seems to have persisted until the preparation of his dual-language collected poems, From Wood to Ridge.

This might appear to be yet another case of the temptation towards the pastoral having suppressed the radical use of the poetic tradition that MacLean had actually made in 1939. This would be too extreme a view and a misreading of the cultural frames of reference upon which "The Cuillin" draws. Traditional Gaelic pastorals are different from "The Cuillin" in at least two important respects.

Derick Thomson suggests that eighteenth-century Gaelic poets were influenced by the developments of English pastoral.[15] For example, Mac Mhaighstir Alasdair, who wrote descriptive verse in the form of songs to Summer and Winter, was following James Thomson's The Seasons.[16] Mac Mlaighstir Alasdair actually wrote verse for the Jacobite cause with the same vigour as his pastorals. The praise-poem for a bard's patron and the patron's lands, which had been strong in the clan system for centuries, is not all that different in function from Pope's "Windsor Forest" which ends with definitive pastoral functionalism:

Rich Industry sits smiling on the plains,
And peace and plenty tell, a STUART reigns.[17]

MacLean's praise-song for the Cuillins differs from this traditional pastoral, even in its non-Marxist form, in that its tone is one of tension derived from personal engagement with what is being praised. The valuing of detailed description is still there, but it is not depersonalised or complacent. Indeed the poem quickly places the emphasis on the personal struggle of ascent. Then, just when the climb is generating a sense of personal achievement, more waves of gabbro "break on the struggle's head". The explicit reference to struggle here anticipates the wider paradox of the following stanza. Personal struggle with the Cuillin is transposed to evoke "the woeful history of the lovely island". Here lies the second way in which "The Cuillin" differs from conventional pastoral. The poem presents the past, not as an idyllic golden age, but as a history of struggle which has a continuity in the present.

What might appear conventionally melancholic in the manner of the worst kind of pastoral, is, in fact, for the Gaelic reader a sharply political point:

> I see the noble island in its storm-showers
> as Mairi Mhor saw in her yearning.[18]

The cultural frame of reference would assume a knowledge that Mairi Mhor nan Oran (Big Mary of the Songs) was the nineteenth-century Skye singer who was legendary for her compositions in support of land-reform. Derick Thomson describes her as a travelling political activist: "It has been said that her songs contributed significantly to the victory of the popular land-law reform candidates in the Highlands in 1885 and 1886, and she was indeed the bard of that movement."[19] This is the core of the notion of kinship for MacLean in "The Cuillin". It is an identification with the politics of the poor, located in the culture of place.

In Part VI we hear the voice of the ghost of a girl whom Douglas Sealy describes as kidnapped in Gesto on Skye in 1739 and sold to the Carolinas as a slave:

> It is not the death of chiefs
> that ever pained me
> but the hard lot of those I loved.[20]

She was sold by her own chief, who, even before the Forty-five rising, had already become an "anglified" landlord.[21] In MacLean's poem glory is not located in clan history but in the spirit that the Cuillins come to represent in the poem: a spirit that, in the final line of the poem, rises "on the other side of sorrow".[22]

So the edited version of "The Cuillin" is a poem that looks backward to an incident that Douglas Sealy claims to be the precursor of the Clearances on Skye. The poet makes a strong personal identification with suffering, in order to evoke the spirit of the Cuillins for the reader in the present. MacLean avoids falling into the Gaelic pastoral convention of the praise-song by his emphasis on suffering in the precise historical conditions of place.

It is important to recognise the resonances of MacLean's iconography of place. There are two aspects to this. Firstly the power of place-names as evocations of historical suffering, still potent and alive in present Gaelic culture. The stories of the clearing of specific places are still alive in striking detail throughout the Highlands and Gaelic Canada, as David Craig's book, *On the Crofters' Trail*,[23] clearly shows. Secondly the dramatically physical nature of those places provides an imagery of contrasts which might appear melodramatic elsewhere, especially in the hands of a symbolist like MacLean. But it is local history that is located in the physicality of place, a local history that is often expanded to represent international historical forces. A phrase like "a nightmare on the fields"[24] might seem a rather forced abstraction, but in this context and in this language it refers to a well-remembered history of atrocities perpetrated, in MacLean's view, by a European capitalist ideology.

Quite clearly the poetry takes as a springboard not only the language, but the shared assumptions of the *Gaidhealtachd*, the people's knowledge of what happened at places within their culture's community. There are therefore two audiences for this poetry: those who share that knowledge and those who have to pick up not only the knowledge, but its cultural significance.

In part VII of "The Cuillin" the rock produces a black ooze which is used as an image that generalises suffering.[25] So far, in the edited version, this suffering has been specifically that of the Clearances, although the vague listing of the misery as past, future, long and lasting "of millions" might well give some unease to the reader. In fact when Sorley MacLean wrote about the "black ooze on the rock face" in 1939 he had already defined his "nightmare" in the latter section of Part II of "The Cuillin" which was not published until 1988.[26] However, in this fuller text discussion of the Clearances is followed by a broad sweep of references to Spain and beyond. The peasants of Minginish are linked to an international vision in which "the humble of every land/were deceived by ruling-class, State and Civil Law".[27] The current absence of leaders on Skye is deplored with a shared guilt. There is a vision of the island losing its people in the present. The physical struggle of the writer climbing the Cuillin, with which the poem opened, can now be seen as anticipating a political turmoil in the mind of the poet viewing this historical moment:

Another day this upon the mountains
and great Scotland under the doom of beasts:
her thousands of poor exploited,
beguiled to a laughing-stock,
flattered, doctored and anointed
by the nobles and godly bourgeois
who make a bourgeois of Christ.

Another day this upon the mountains
and our choice Scotland a porridge of filth;
England and France together
smothered in the same dung-heap;

> great Germany a delirium of falsehood
> and Spain a graveyard where valour lies;
> and the rulers of Poland
> a laughing-stock of Europe.[28]

The desperate bitterness of this, and its feeling of a void in Scotland of any potential alternative, requires a forceful resistance from a socialist who believes in the possibility of social change. This is provided by the image of the Cuillin, particularly in the closing stanzas of the poem. Here images of the mountain range are asked to carry as much as one could possibly imagine a natural image ever being asked to carry in any poem in any language. The image of the Cuillin represents nothing less than the spirit of potential resistance to the momentum of European Fascism in December 1939! Yet it is a tentative, hardly formed, gentle ghost upon the mountains that MacLean sees.[29] It is the spirit of a gentle lover, but it is also "the ghost of a bare naked brain" as one might expect to be required by the Marxist seeking a source of resistance to Fascism; it is "the naked ghost of a heart", but on the following line it is also "a spectre going alone in thought".

The Cuillin, a familiar image of place, has become a symbolic reminder of human capacities for love and for thought that can enable people to themselves "rise on the other side of sorrow". This raises questions about MacLean's poetic method, the nature of his assumptions about symbolism and the poetic context within which his poetry is to be read. But before considering these questions and their relevance to the major poems of MacLean's achievement it might be helpful to draw together points that have arisen so far from a consideration of "The Cuillin".

In the edited version Sorley MacLean produced what might have been expected of a Gaelic writer: a poem which explores an image of place in the form of the praise-song to connect himself through kinship with the history of his culture, and the Clearances in particular (despite his only detailed example coming from a century before the major period of clearance). His dominant image of the mountain as a repository of natural forces becomes representative of human qualities needed to revive Scotland from its demoralisation. In doing this he avoids the traps of Gaelic pastoral poetry through the detail of his initial personal, physical struggle in climbing the mountain, and through the implicit reference to Skye's cultural history in a poetry reverberating with associations of place-names and people for Gaelic readers.

The poem MacLean had actually written in 1939 was, in fact, a radically new kind of poem for Gaelic poetry. John MacInnes has outlined, as a Gaelic-speaker, the technical ways in which Sorley MacLean revolutionised Gaelic poetry. "Somhairle MacGill-Eain," he writes, "restored to Gaelic poetry the scope and amplitude of a mature adult voice. His work is not only the product of his own genius but is shaped, controlled, energised by tradition."[30] Whilst most of his arguments refer to Gaelic diction, metre, and rhyme, MacInnes does make the following point: "MacGill-Eain may be the 'Bard of his people', as he has been described, but one must understand that this is a specialised use of the word 'bard'. In medieval and later Gaelic society the bard was a fairly simple praise-singer."[31]

But this praise-song to the Cuillin was most radical in that it was inspired by the example of Hugh MacDiarmid's *A Drunk Man Looks At The Thistle*. In an interview MacLean has said that he believed *The Drunk Man* to be "the greatest long poem of the century that I have read . . . It converted me to the belief that the long medley with lyric peaks was the great form for our age."[32] "The Cuillin" emerged from that belief:

> It was in Mull in 1938 that I conceived the idea of writing a very long poem, 10,000 words or so, on the human condition, radiating from the history of Skye and the West Highlands to Europe and what I knew of the rest of the world. Its symbolism was to be, mostly, native symbolism. I started it in Edinburgh in the summer of 1939. The idea came from *The Drunk Man*.[33]

All that remains as evidence of *The Drunk Man's* influence is the notion of length and scope. There is in "The Cuillin" none of MacDiarmid's modernist movements between styles and MacLean himself came to feel that "The Cuillin" was "a crude declamatory poem",[34] partly attributable to the fact that he "didn't have the *vis comica* that MacDiarmid had so magnificently, so wonderfully".[35] His feelings of the poem's ultimate failure evidently persist today so that the most complete text remains only "what I think tolerable of it".[36] In 1940 it was politically impossible to publish "The Cuillin" and the events of Stalinism further compounded MacLean's aesthetic dissatisfaction with political disgust. So MacLean apparently came to regard the poem as salvageable within a restricted field of reference.

MacLean's use of "lyric peaks" within the long poem hints at another modern Gaelic use of language that he has extended. Iain Crichton Smith reminded me recently that at Edinburgh University, as a student of English Literature, Sorley MacLean was influenced there by Herbert Grierson, the Donne scholar, just before MacLean made the decision to write poetry only in Gaelic. It is clear that MacLean's symbolism can easily be related to that of Donne. MacLean himself acknowledges this in his Preface to *From Wood to Ridge*.[37] In "The Cuillin" one can see that the way in which a "black ooze on the rock face" becomes an extended metaphor in an elaborated symbolic structure has some echoes of Donne's method. But is this unusual within mid-twentieth-century Gaelic poetry?

Iain Crichton Smith himself makes strong use of nature symbolism in his Gaelic poetry, nowhere more directly than in the remarkable poem "Going Home", quoted here in his own translation:

Tomorrow I shall go home to my island
trying to put a world into forgetfulness.
I will lift a fistful of its earth in my hands
or I will sit on a hillock of the mind
watching "the shepherd at his sheep".

There will arise (I presume) a thrush.
A dawn or two will break.
There will be a boat lying in the glitter
of the western sun: and water running
through the world of similes of my intelligence.

But I will be thinking (in spite of that)
of the great fire at the back of our thoughts,
Nagasaki and Hiroshima,
and I will hear in a room by myself
a ghost or two ceaselessly moving,

the ghost of each error, the ghost of each guilt,
the ghost of each time I walked past
a wounded man on a stony road,
the ghost of nothingness scrutinising
my dumb room with distant face,

till the island becomes an ark
rising and falling on a great sea
and I not knowing whether the dove will return
and men talking and talking to each other
and the rainbow of forgiveness in their tears.[38]

Here is a Gaelic poet considering his island and its natural qualities in relation to modern weapons that would destroy nature itself. Sorley MacLean takes this a stage further in describing the weapon-carrying nuclear submarines as supplanting nature in his poem "Screapadal". It is also interesting to note the modernist way in which Crichton Smith wittily parodies the pastoral which he has evoked in the opening stanza of the poem with his sense of retreat to forgetfulness in a natural Eden "watching 'the shepherd at his sheep' ": "There will arise (I presume) a thrush." The self-conscious intrusion of the parenthesis, drawing attention to the writer as the creator of the image, also draws attention to its apparent cliched pastoral simplicity. By contrast, what seems quite unselfconscious is the directness of nature symbolism in Gaelic. "A hillock of the mind" contains both the physical place and the mental activity going on there whilst visually affirming the naturalness of that abstract activity. Similarly "water running/through the world of similes of my intelligence" asserts the naturalness of the poet's fluent thinking through images.

It is tempting to wonder whether in a culture so much dominated by the language of the Bible (referred to directly at the beginning and the end of "Going Home"), any nature imagery takes on symbolic significance, especially since the crofting activities of Highland culture echo so many of the symbols of the Bible's peasant iconography (" 'the shepherd at his sheep' "). In Donald MacAulay's short Gaelic poem "For Pasternak, For Example . . .", he says of Pasternak, "you have understood their inadequacy –/that they consign all seed for milling".[39] Anyone from a peasant culture knows the need for some seed not to be turned into bread but reserved for generating more seed. This practical basis of the poem is entirely secular. But in the Gaelic poem this imagery renders Pasternak a writer with a religious aura for MacAulay.

Derick Thomson writes of the twentieth-century renaissance in Gaelic poetry that "the new poetry is also characterised by its use of images and symbols".[40] Yet one only has to turn back a few pages in his book to see Mairi Mhor nan Oran (the Big Mary of the Songs referred to by Sorley MacLean in "The Cuillin") using symbols in a manner that makes a direct connection with MacLean's descriptive symbolism:

> But change has come upon the clouds,
> on the hills and on the fields,
> where once kindly people lived
> now there are "big sheep" and lambs.[41]

A physical change may well be seen on hills and fields, but any change on the clouds is symbolically suggesting darkness over Skye as a consequence of the Clearances for the "big sheep".

The boldness and the enigma of MacLean's symbolism may well be characteristic of twentieth-century Gaelic poets, as Thomson suggests, although MacLean is probably distinctive in being more bold and more enigmatic than any other contemporary Gaelic poet in his use of nature symbolism, his sense of place, and his political exploration of his kinship with the history of that place. As an antidote to an English reader's possible feeling of the ponderousness, if not the heavy-handedness with which MacLean burdens his central symbols, I want, finally, to establish an awareness of weighty symbolism as traditional in Gaelic poetry and prose. (In an oral tradition there is less separation in their deployment.)

The Church is the centre of the continuity of Gaelic prose, both in the extempore sermons carried through oral tradition, and in the training of writers. The Established Church of Scotland in the *Gaidhealtachd* drew its ministers from the landlord class and at the time of the Clearances the Evangelical Movement offered an alternative. "Its poets", writes John MacInnes, "made the first powerful attack on the injustices perpetrated by the landlord class, one of whom opprobriously described this Calvinist Revival as 'the peasant religion' ".[42]

Here the radical anti-Establishment fervour connects with the poetry of Big Mary of the Songs and shows its influence, "especially in the largely unpublished poem 'The Cuillin'' ', writes MacInnes. MacInnes quotes Sorley MacLean's testimony to the influence of Evangelical prose:

> Even as late as the 1920s it was quite common to hear some minister or elder quoting richly, by oral tradition, from sermons or prayers delivered 70 or 100 years before. Such quotations made it quite plain that in frankness, sincerity and psychological insight, expressed with an astonishing wealth of imagery and illustration, sometimes sonorously eloquent with the incomparable resonances of the Gaelic language and sometimes racily colloquial, Gaelic once had a great prose.

It is clear that "The Cuillin", attempting to follow Hugh MacDiarmid's example of linguistic variety, ranges from the "sonorously eloquent" to the racily bitter colloquial of political disgust. But it is a range in tone rather than styles. The poem's "wealth of imagery" derives from its central, evolving symbol which is finally expressed as "a Cuillin trinity":[43] the mountain, "ancient Scotland" and "mankind". This trinity characterises what MacInnes calls "the connection, and disjunction, between the Marxist view of history and the world view, in the Gaelic Evangelical context, of history and its meaning, as that has been interpreted in Christian thought".[44]

Is the Cuillin ultimately, then, a symbol of transcendence as its religious language might suggest, or is it an image that, in the more complete version, successfully evokes the lessons of history on Skye for the future of the human species? In fact, MacLean seems to intend the symbol to work in both ways at once, as the transcendent spirit and as socialist future. The result, even in the longer version, is a final disappointing vagueness in the conclusion to an ambitious but uneven achievement. One suspects that in the tensions contributing to the expression of a Free Presbyterian Marxist, "sonorousness" has substituted for "eloquence" in the poem's (present) last lines:

> Beyond the lochs of the blood of the children of men,
> beyond the frailty of plain and the labour of the mountain,
> beyond poverty, consumption, fever, agony,
> beyond hardship, wrong, tyranny, distress,
> beyond misery, despair, hatred, treachery,
> beyond guilt and defilement; watchful,
> heroic, the Cuillin is seen
> rising on the other side of sorrow.[45]

It appears that one of the sources of MacLean's linguistic richness may have also been the major influence in the ultimate failure of "The Cuillin". Indeed the tension between "sonorousness" and "eloquence", between rant and real detail, between religion and history, between transcendence and politics, may in itself represent a stage in the development of a culture. Recent Gaelic-speaking critical opinion endorses a view of "The Cuillin" as a flawed achievement in these terms: "It is easy to see why MacDiarmid welcomed the poem with such enthusiasm, but reading it now it is the interludes between the political tirades that come off best."[46]

But how does MacLean handle nature symbolism elsewhere, in his early lyric verse, for example? It is characteristic of Sorley MacLean that he can begin a poem about choosing between staying with a girl, or fighting in the Spanish Civil War, "The Choice", in the apparently simple diction of a song. His use of imagery enables him to represent his reason, which is his subject, by the place in which he is thinking. There is a metonymy whereby "the sea" comes to stand for his personified mind. The poem begins,

> I walked with my reason
> out beside the sea.
> We were together but it was
> keeping a little distance from me.[47]

The "beside" becomes "together" before being qualified by the visual image of "a little distance". Without direct comparison, the poet's sense of alienation from his own reason has been represented by metonymic association with the place where thoughts can be sorted out.

The Marxist is also quite aware that his reason is a product of nature and in facing this same personal dilemma in the poem "Prayer", achieves by the end of the poem a clear-sighted notion of the source of his problem:

> Since the blame will not be put on gods,
> who are only the shadow of desire,
> and to avoid the man Christ,
> I do not feel kindly towards Nature,
> which has given me the clear whole understanding,
> the single brain and the split heart.[48]

MacLean refuses to conceive of "Nature" as a god to whom appeal might be made, as by a pantheist perhaps, or as fate in the sense of a future already predestined. It is simply that in his particular case the process of nature has produced a strong emotional desire for two irreconcilable things, together with an intelligence that enables him to consider the dilemma, but not to resolve it; "The single brain and the split heart" remain. It is no consolation that his suffering is "natural", but it is important to recognise that its source is in the organic realm rather than the superstitious. The poem "Prayer" is a rejection of prayer. Nature is a practical process that has to be accepted, confronted directly and lived through.

This rationalist attitude towards nature is the key to the achievement of MacLean's greatest poems, "The Woods of Raasay", "Screapadal", and most importantly, "Hallaig". It is a concept of nature which enables him to deal with the mystery of experiences of the heart without sentimentality or vagueness, despite some temptations in that direction from Gaelic culture.

It is John MacInnes again who traces the sentimentalising of Gaelic poetry to "English Romanticism, especially from 1872 when compulsory education (in English only) was imposed".[49] MacInnes recognises the "Romantic sensibility" in "Hallaig" in a positive sense, but it is already clear that MacLean, in these early lyrics, is obviously more of a Marxist than a pantheist. Indeed, despite the influence of the Church on his language he deliberately chooses in "Prayer" "to avoid the man Christ". Thus MacLean the Marxist can use nature images as metaphor (the sea washes in and out like a dialogue), metonymy (the sea standing for reason by association) and primal reality (nature as the producer of one's reason) in a way that rejects the metaphysical whilst drawing on the language of an intensely religious culture.

MacLean is, then, a lyric rationalist and this is possible for two reasons that are evident in "The Woods of Raasay". Written a year later than "The Cuillin", this poem echoes two of its features: the celebration of the physical detail of specific places and the way those places act as the repository of the history of a people of which the poet is a voice. The tensions in nature are the reflections of tensions in the individual and in society.

It might at first appear that "The Woods of Raasay" is indeed a condensed Gaelic parallel to The Prelude in the way that body and mind have been formed by place:

> I took your banners
>   and wrapped them round me.
>   I took your yellow
>   and green banners,
>   I clothed pampered
>   volatile thoughts:
>   I clothed them in your
>   yellow and red banners.[50]

Nature has not so much "ministered" to the poet here: the poet has himself been active in the verbs "took" and "wrapped". However, the effect of learning from the qualities of the wood might appear to be the same as it could be for Wordsworth. Indeed, the poem reflects, structurally, the notion of being "foster'd alike by beauty and fear".[51] The third stanza celebrates positive gifts in the image of the trees as victorious helmets. But when this idea is returned to later, "the helmet of the serene" is followed by "helmets of pride/maiming me with unrest".[52]

At this moment the eight-line stanza form, intoning the qualities of the wood in short lines, is replaced by four-line stanzas of longer lines, which are themselves eventually disrupted by eight-line and six-line stanzas as MacLean pursues his "unrest". His "pride" in the wood has to also engage with less beautiful elements in it. These come to be represented by the presence of the adder. His "pride" also reminds him of the history of his people who know these woods and are buried beside them. The phrase "You gave me helmets" really means "You gave me reminders of . . ." because the reference to helmets is to MacLean's ancestors (among whom is "Ruain Beag of the glittering helmet" in "Elegy for Calum I. MacLean"[53]). Their serenity was also accompanied by pride, "the pride that led the MacLeans to their 'leirchreach', their destruction, and not only at Inverkeithing", writes Douglas Sealy.[54]

It becomes clear that what undoubtedly begins as "a richly assonantal and rhythmically hypnotic paean to the woods",[55] as Douglas Sealy says of the Gaelic text, is also a strongly symbolist text. Thus the adder's presence in the wood, which is associated with the fire-dragon of Sgur nan Gillean and the graves of "the men of Raasay returned", comes to symbolise "the venom of the cry of pain in the love-making" – the anguish that is an inevitable cost of love and beauty.

The recognition of this paradox is central to the work of MacLean and is reflected in the two-part structure of this poem. Moreover it is present not only in the texture of the imagery of the poem ("the pursued man vehement in pursuit") but in the philosophical enquiry of the poem which strikes at the heart of the notion of the praise-poem itself:

> What is the meaning of worshipping Nature
> because the wood is part of it?

Here might appear to be a direct challenge to the Romantics, as well as to the very tradition which is one of the major forms of Gaelic culture. The rhythmic pattern of building accumulations of praised charac-teristics is implicitly criticised as inadequate to accommodate the unrest that must follow.

At this point the poem comes close to wilful pessimism. Love,

heroism and hope are all seen as worthless because they have produced anguish. But this is merely asserted symbolically against the
beauty of the wood. The adder, or "serpent" as it is commonly called
in the islands, is a biblical and biological source of harm to human
beings and an obviously accurate symbol of evil in the woods. But
how the Cuillin wall can be seen to be "knocked down" is hard to
imagine. Similarly the heroism that the Cuillin symbolises in this
poem is not historically specific. But in the final three stanzas MacLean
re-engages his dialectic by considering the unpredictable forces at
play in love as natural and capable of partial understanding through
their parallels in nature.

The remarkably rational, poignant ending of "The Woods of
Raasay" is both an affirmation and a detraction. Science knows more
about woods than it does about "the crooked veering of the heart".
Yet "the subtlety of the bends/with which [the heart] loses its course"
are themselves affirmingly a natural process like the course of a river,
or the crooked growth of a branch:

> The way of the sap is known,
>   oozing up to its work,
>   the wine that is always new and living,
>   unconscious, untaught.
>
> There is no knowledge of the course
>   of the crooked veering of the heart,
>   and there is no knowledge of the damage
>   to which its aim unwittingly comes.
>
> There is no knowledge, no knowledge,
>   of the final end of each pursuit,
>   nor of the subtlety of the bends
>   with which it loses its course.[56]

This final moment, with its awe at "subtlety", does not seem to me
to be that of a poem of unqualified despair, as it is for Douglas Sealy,
"where human endeavour is seen to be without hope and without
direction".[57] This may have been the poet's intention, with the density
of words like "crooked", "damage" and "loses". But the assertion of
mystery is as powerful as the "sap" imagery is affirmative. Sexuality and
the woods have been unified in profound, if still problematic images.
It would surely be irrational to expect to know "the final end of each
pursuit", and for the intelligent, self-aware poet, the knowledge that
"damage" is possible is a prerequisite for its avoidance. It is also a

preparation for its acceptance if it is ultimately unavoidable. In fact the form of the traditional praise-song (*Moladh*) has been used to create a dispraise (*Miomholadh*) for the conventional assumptions of the praise-song. In the knowledge of the heart, scientific rationalism is not, ironically, a useful alternative for the Marxist, although a clear-eyed recognition of that fact and wonder at the heart's veering and bending provide a better starting-point for coping than uncritical nature worship. It is characteristic of Sorley MacLean's honest intelligence that the rationalist, having done his best, must still confront a mystery.

Seamus Heaney, in his Introduction to *Sorley MacLean: Critical Essays* finds these same undercurrents in MacLean's "Hallaig". Heaney emphasises the undercurrent that works against the surface evidence: "a sense of loss became a sense of scope, and what might have been a pious elegy became a rich and strange ode to melancholy".[58] Indeed Heaney goes further in a statement about the poem's sense of history which not only appears to contradict the celebration of melancholy, but which says much about Heaney's own valuing of nostalgia: "The naming of people and places gives it a foundation in history and a foothold in bardic tradition, but there is also a visionary objectivity about the point of view whereby the sorrowful recognitions are transposed into a paradisal key."

Can an "ode to melancholy" and "sorrowful recognitions" become a "paradisal" vision? It might be possible for Keats or for Heaney, but MacLean's "Hallaig", for all its symbolic mysteriousness, is a tougher poem than Heaney's description of it. It is a love poem that takes its starting point in subdued political outrage: it begins with an empty home and ends with "a vehement bullet" of love. All ghosts in the centre of the poem are recognisable as the historical people of that place and their contemporary successors, anchored to earth not only by place-names but by references to "Sabbath", "congregation", and "the endless walk" to the kirk that is so recognisable an image in the island culture.

This is not to deny the magical power with which the poem moves through the political and the personal, evoked immediately in its opening lines:

The window is nailed and boarded
through which I saw the West
and my love is at the Burn of Hallaig,
a birch tree, and she has always been.[59]

John MacInnes explains that "between 1852 and 1854 the entire population of twelve townships, ninety-four families in all, were driven from their homes" on Raasay.[60] The opening reference is not just a historical evocation, but a politically emotive touching of a raw nerve to a Gaelic speaker. It was the Scottish landlord, George Rainy, a Highland son of a minister father, who cleared Raasay, and who planted the pines in the south-west of the island.

The birch tree thus represents: firstly, "my love", a potentially healing force that will come with "a vehement bullet" at the end of the poem; secondly, island girls in general, past and present, walking in silence to Clachan (the village with the church) but returning without the inhibitions of obedience, "their laughter a mist in my ears" (a phrase which derives its magic from the rhetorical device of describing a sound by a visual image); thirdly, the indigenous culture which was wiped out in two years by the minister's son, the "great pietist of Screapadal"; and fourthly, the indigenous woods as opposed to the introduced. Hence one can see the remarkable way in which nature imagery, in Gaelic poetry at its best, can perfectly easily integrate the political and the personal: the love of place and the love of a woman are both present at once in the image of the birch trees. Both must be defended by "a vehement bullet . . . from the gun of Love".[61] Only such passionate strength in the living can overcome the injustice and grief that has been left by time. "The deer of time" will be prevented from further ravaging this place by the power of the writer's love for the place, a love that can be symbolised by the power of the bullet that

> will strike the deer that goes dizzily,
> sniffing at the grass-grown ruined homes;
> his eye will freeze in the wood,
> his blood will not be traced while I live.

The power here is surely that of a defiant love of place rather than "paradisal melancholy" as Heaney would have it. The continuity that connects poet, people and place is the unifying and ultimately affirmative achievement of "Hallaig". Only an apolitical reading of the poem could produce Heaney's description of it. This connectedness is achieved through a remarkably subtle and dense use of nature imagery that was made possible by Romanticism. John MacInnes confirms that in "Hallaig" MacLean has achieved a fusion of an English Romantic sensibility with the traditional feeling for nature located in place in Gaelic poetry: "What Sorley MacLean has done here, as elsewhere in his poetry, is to fuse these disparate elements of two cultures in an utterly new statement which is emotionally subtle and powerful, unsentimental and wholly Gaelic."[62]

"Hallaig" is indeed MacLean's greatest achievement in the breadth of elements which it integrates in a poem generating passionate resilience out of a bitter awareness of the personal and political. But MacLean's final poem in *From Wood to Ridge*, "Screapadal",[63] represents an interesting development of the poet's use of nature imagery, although the poem's symbolic subtlety is more limited. The poem ultimately remains a praise-song carrying a simple but important warning.

"Screapadal" takes the politics of the nineteenth century of "Hallaig" into the twentieth century of Hiroshima. In many ways "Screapadal" is the counterpoint of "Hallaig". Geographically, the ruined township lies at the opposite end of Creag Mheircil, the two-mile long former sea-cliff on the east side of Raasay. The poem shares the praise-poem form with "Hallaig", but adopts a more direct style. It makes explicit more of the historical background to "Hallaig", but deals with the threat of the ultimate clearance – "an leirsgrios", the holocaust of nuclear war. If "Hallaig" is a poem of both outrage and affirmation, "Screapadal" is a warning that the social forces that produced the Clearances could produce the holocaust.

The force of bitterness against Rainy rises again at the mention of each place celebrated in the poem. It is an indication of how much the Gaelic mind values nature not only for its own sake, but as a location of community, as an indicator of that community's organic con- nectedness. One feels this particularly in the loving familiarity of the writer's intimate knowledge of the place in the fifth stanza. It is a mark of Rainy's lack of connection with the place that he would have cleared its beauty too if it had been necessary:

> Rainy left Screapadal without people,
> with no houses or cattle, only sheep,
> but he left Screapadal beautiful;
> in his time he could do nothing else.[64]

But the "greed and social pride" that produced "Rainy's bad deed" is present in the world and could destroy even the beauty of this place.[65]

The most remarkable achievement of this poem lies in the use of nature imagery for a new effect in Gaelic poetry:

A seal would lift its head
and a basking-shark its sail,
but today in the sea-sound
a submarine lifts its turret
and its black sleek back
threatening the thing that would make
dross of wood, of meadows and of rocks
that would leave Screapadal without beauty
just as it was left without people.

The shift is not only from seal to submarine, but from contemporary threat back to history, as though nothing has been learned in spite of "Rainy's bad deed".

A similar movement is made later in the poem from the tower of Castle Rock to the conning towers of the submarines from Faslane using the Sound of Raasay for testing in the deepest sea-channel in the Hebrides. Worse than death by hunger and famine, as in the past, would be "the death of the great heat and the smoke". Rockets and bombs can rise like "the poisonous bracken". Both nature and the "little remnant of people/in the Island of the Big Men" are vulnerable to destruction by the holocaust.

The sombre formality of the Gaelic praise-poem lends a seriousness to the caring for people and place that is interwoven through the Gaelic sensibility of the poem. Although Iain Crichton Smith is well-known for "bringing Hiroshima into a number of his poems",[66] one senses here that the Gaelic language is being strained in confronting this now familiar contemporary presence for the people of Raasay. John MacInnes says that MacLean has never produced a neologism in Gaelic,[67] but he says that MacLean "has invented his own diction" and "there are times when he appears to be pushing Gaelic to its limits".[68] The culture is, in this poem, engaging with new dangers in an old poetic form. Innovations in the use of nature imagery demand innovation in language to confront new threats to people and place.

It is Sorley MacLean, writing in Gaelic, who provides a fine example of the possibility for modern poetry to go beyond both the pastoral and the anti-pastoral. When the "black sleek back" in the Sound is not that of a seal but a nuclear submarine, nature poetry has arrived at the position of taking a responsibility for nature in all its forms. For Sorley MacLean as a poet I suspect that the concept of "nature poetry" does not exist. He can write nothing else, not because there is nothing else, but because there are no other images for what he values. "Nature poetry" is a construct which can only be applied outside Gaelic culture. His achievement, in "Screapadal" for example, is unique. His poetic notion of nature is characteristic of contemporary Gaelic poetry, innovating out of a tradition in a minority, but certainly not a minor, European language.

Notes

1 R. J. Ross and J. Hendry eds, *Sorley MacLean: Critical Essays*, Edinburgh: Scottish Academic Press, 1986.
2 W. Gillies ed., *Ris a' Bhruthaich: The Criticism and Prose Writings of Sorley MacLean*, Stornoway: Acair, 1985.
3 Edinburgh: Canongate.
4 Philadelphia: Iona Foundation, 1987.
5 All quotations are from this text.
6 First published in *Cencrastus*, No. 7, winter 1981–82 and collected in *From Wood to Ridge*.
7 *Cencrastus*, No. 7, p. 16.
8 Quoted in *Sorley MacLean: Critical Essays*, p. 94.
9 Interview with Angus Nicolson, *Studies in Scottish Literature*, No. 14, 1979, p. 25.
10 *Cencrastus*, No. 7, p. 15.
11 *Sorley MacLean: Critical Essays*, p. 138.
12 *From Wood to Ridge*, p. 67.
13 After serial publication in *Chapman*, Nos. 50–57, summer 1987–summer 1989.
14 p. 63.
15 *An Introduction to Gaelic Poetry*, London: Gollancz, 1977, p. 157.
16 (1727) in John Barrell and John Bull eds, *The Penguin Book of English Pastoral Verse*, London: Allen Lane, 1974, pp. 303–13.
17 ibid., p. 276.
18 *From Wood to Ridge*, p. 67.
19 *An Introduction to Gaelic Poetry*, p. 245.
20 *From Wood to Ridge*, p. 107.
21 *Sorley MacLean: Critical Essays*, p. 59.
22 *From Wood to Ridge*, p. 131.
23 London: Jonathan Cape, 1990.
24 *From Wood to Ridge*, p. 81.
25 ibid., p. 127.
26 *Chapman*, No. 52, spring 1988.
27 *From Wood to Ridge*, p. 81.
28 ibid., p. 83.
29 ibid., p. 129.
30 *Sorley MacLean: Critical Essays*, p. 137.
31 ibid., p. 138.
32 Angus Nicolson interview, *Studies in Scottish Literature*, p. 27.
33 *Ris a' Bhruthaich*, p. 11.

34 Letter to MacDiarmid, 12 May 1940, quoted in *Sorley MacLean: Critical Essays*, p. 96.

35 Interview with R. J. Ross, quoted in *Sorley MacLean: Critical Essays*, p. 96.

36 From *Wood to Ridge*, p. 63. A further 780 lines remain unpublished from this unfinished project, according to Douglas Sealy, *Chapman*, No. 60, spring 1991, p. 88.

37 ibid., p. xiv.

38 D. MacAulay ed., *Modern Scottish Gaelic Poems*, Edinburgh: Canongate, 1976, p. 174.

39 ibid., p. 192.

40 *An Introduction to Gaelic Poetry*, p. 283.

41 ibid., p. 246.

42 *Cencrastus*, No. 7, p. 15.

43 From *Wood to Ridge*, p. 127.

44 *Cencrastus*, No. 7, p. 16.

45 From *Wood to Ridge*, p. 131.

46 D. Sealy, *Chapman*, No. 60, p. 88.

47 From *Wood to Ridge*, p. 23.

48 ibid., p. 21.

49 " 'Hallaig': a note", *Calcagus*, No. 2, 1975, p. 32.

50 From *Wood to Ridge*, p. 171.

51 *The Prelude*, 1805, Book I, line 306.

52 From *Wood to Ridge*, p. 175.

53 ibid., p. 265.

54 *Sorley MacLean: Critical Essays*, p. 65.

55 ibid.

56 From *Wood to Ridge*, p. 183.

57 *Sorley MacLean: Critical Essays*, p. 66.

58 ibid., p. 3.

59 From *Wood to Ridge*, p. 227.

60 *Calcagus*, No 2. p. 29.

61 From *Wood to Ridge*, p. 231.

62 *Calcagus*, No 2. p. 32.

63 First published in *Cencrastus*, No. 7, pp. 18–19. The poem is particularly well presented in Tim Neat's film "Hallaig".

64 From *Wood to Ridge*, p. 307.

65 The misprint "green" in the final stanza has been allowed to stand in all three published versions of the poem. That "greed", also used earlier in the poem, is the correct word here was affirmed by MacLean in an unpublished conversation with David Craig.

66 *An Introduction to Gaelic Poetry*, p. 267.

67 *Sorley MacLean: Critical Essays*, p. 145.

68 ibid., p. 152.

5

"Art a paradigm of earth": the poetry of Seamus Heaney

IN HIS review of *Station Island* Blake Morrison describes Heaney's verse in that collection as "superstitious, pantheistic, even mystical".[1] Morrison quotes the poem "Making Strange" in which a voice "came out of the field across the road/saying, 'Be adept and be dialect' ". This voice, Morrison suggests, is not a literary convention. It is not the voice of a specific ghost, as are many of the other voices in *Station Island*. It is the voice of nature speaking directly to the poet out of his familiar fields. This is not, in other words, a personification of the voice of dialect, but, in Wordsworth's terms, one of nature's "Severer interventions, ministry/More palpable"[2] than has been in evidence much since *The Prelude*. Heaney might well be thought of as himself too ironic a poet to be caught in such a crudely pantheistic posture. But is Heaney, as Morrison hints, the modern inheritor of Wordsworth? What would that mean in stylistic, philosophical and political terms, for a contemporary poet writing out of the experience of the island of Ireland?

There is much in Heaney's collection of prose, *The Government of the Tongue*, that makes the case for poetry as an engagement with political reality in terms that are redolent of Wordsworth. The emphasis is on poetry that fortifies "our inclination to credit promptings of our intuitive being".[3] A central notion is that of a knowledge "in the first recesses of ourselves, in the shyest, pre-social part of our nature".[4] Heaney quotes Anna Swir to exemplify his conception of inspiration: "A poet becomes then an antenna capturing the voices of the world, a medium expressing his own subconscious and the collective subconscious."[5]

It is interesting to observe the poet at work as critic endorsing concepts that are elaborated perhaps most famously in The Prelude, Book II.[6] But if Heaney is a pantheist in the Wordsworthian sense, it will be in the post-Wordsworth form of having absorbed the concepts, rather than in imitating the discourse. To see Heaney as a religious worshipper of Nature would be to expect too much earnestness and too little irony. I want to argue that, in a fundamental sense, Heaney's poetry has gone beyond the pantheism of the Romantics by having taken it for granted. His understanding of the Troubles, of marriage, of his inner self, is dominated by an assumption of his unity with nature, even as he explores what that relationship means. The case for Heaney as the inheritor of Wordsworth lies perhaps most clearly in the poetry of Field Work,[7] as Blake Morrison claims in his discussion of the "Glanmore Sonnets". The issue is not only conceptual, of course, but resolves itself into a question about style. It might, therefore, be helpful to briefly observe how far Heaney has come in his poetic development by the time of Field Work. A revealing way of doing this is to briefly summarise his changing uses of the first person in relation to nature in each of the previous collections.

The gradual development of his vision of connectedness with nature can be observed in the shift from evocation in the first two volumes, to exploration of connections between forces in Wintering Out,[8] to mythic experimentation in North.[9] This can be represented first by the writer as the observer of "The Diviner" in Death of a Naturalist.[10] The water-spirit's feminine voice itself is evoked in the poem that carries her name, "Undine", in Door Into the Dark.[11] The male in this poem simply cleaned the drains: "And I ran quick for him, cleaned out my rust." In Wintering Out the writer goes on an imaginary journey to see "The Tollund Man" whom the earth-goddess has more ambivalently captured and preserved as bridegroom. Through the course of the poem Heaney comes to identify with this "bridegroom". An imaginative exploration of forces at work in the history and the bogs of Jutland, "the old man-killing parishes", has found a connection with the Six Counties and a familiar discomfort for the writer by the end of the poem: "I will feel lost,/Unhappy and at home."

North develops the discoveries of this earlier exploration into something resembling a poetic experiment: what are the political implications of the comforting and discomforting elements in Heaney's knowledge as himself "bridegroom to the goddess"? What, in the tribal context in which Heaney finds himself, are the implications of his connectedness with nature in its violent as well as its fertile forces? Stylistically this is the result of a shift from "I-the observer" in "The Diviner", to "I-the directly evoked voice" in "Undine", to "I-the mythic explorer" of "The Tollund Man", to the ironically dramatised voice of the earth-goddess herself in "The Bog Queen" in North.[12]

The raising of this preserved body, "the Bog Queen", is against the violence of sacrilege that is her delivery; against the "bribe" from the Protestant peer's wife who wanted to possess her hair; against the very divisions of different kinds of knowledge and power represented by her being placed, by the poet, "between turf-face and demesne wall". Despite "hacked bone, skull-ware" (these wrenched Norse constructions are typical of the linguistic part of the project of North) the goddess is brought to the surface world of human affairs where turf-bank opposes demesne wall and metal spade stands against soft "coomb". The denatured people (associated with demesne wall and spade) are divided from their own natures in North, and are at war with themselves.

At the end of "The Bog Queen" we are left with "small gleams on the bank" as tokens of her presence. In 1983 I wrote, with Neil Roberts, "the queen rises out of the bog to resume a role in history which Heaney leaves for the reader's sense of history to judge".[13] By Field Work Heaney had already absorbed these small gleams of the goddess into his reflections upon his own place in relation to the living history of Ireland as he was experiencing it. The "I" of Field Work is remarkably unified with the spirit of the Bog Queen, throughout the elegies as much as the marriage poems.

Heaney's vision in Field Work works from the confident assumption of connectedness with the feminine forces of the natural world. This assumption is expressed in the assured style of reference to nature in these poems that also characteristically question, uncomfortably, the role of the writer himself. Tensions in the self, the tribe and territory are raised and resolved through assumptions about language. A. Alvarez questions Heaney's style in Field Work: "Unless, of course, the point is other than what it seems: Heaney is not rural and sturdy and domestic, with his feet firmly planted in the Irish mud, but is instead an ornamentalist, a word collector, a connoisseur of fine language for its own sake."[14] This is the classic challenge to the poet as a pastoralist rather one with his "feet firmly planted in Irish mud". How does Field Work appear when read with this challenge in mind?

The title of the book is Heaney's daring response to the accusation of pastoral retreat from the tensions of Ulster. In 1972 Heaney gave up university teaching "to discover if I could be a full-time writer"[15] and moved with his family from Belfast to Glanmore in County Wicklow. "Ulster Poet Moves South" ran the headline in one newspaper in the Republic.[16] The very public debate about Heaney's supposed pastoral retreat is answered in the title of Field Work by a recognition that the move was from city to fields, but asserts that these are workings, the full-time work of a writer, committed to this domestic enterprise. Heaney has said:

> I think the centre of the book is the "Glanmore Sonnets", which are about living in Glanmore, but also about choice and commitment, and they were able – perhaps for the first time – able to bring it some of the contingencies. They were very close to the actual concerns of day-to-day, and I think in them I learned something of how to speak in the first person out of the self.[17]

"Sonnet IX"[18] provides the evidence of the day-to-day in the form of a black rat. Heaney's wife asks, " 'Did we come to the wilderness for this?' " and the poem answers with an image of the "burnished bay tree at the gate". Yet why should the question be answered by a "classical" image? Is this the only model imaginable? This "burnished bay tree" is in reality "hung with the reek of silage". The possible humour of bathos in this is outdone by the even more self-mocking reference to Sir Philip Sidney's classic treatise in "What is my apology for poetry?" Despite the joke of Heaney's owing an apology to his wife for bringing her to this unpastoral retreat for him to write poetry, the question is also intended to be taken seriously, if we are to understand the final image as its answer: "Your face/Haunts like a new moon glimpsed through tangled glass." "Haunts" is not a joke, nor is the image of his wife's white face.

The full horror of this experience, which is claimed by this final image, has been dissipated by using the opportunity for literary wit about pastoral expectations. The result is to distort anti-romantic material into an artefact as arch as a pastoral poem created purely for literary effect. In this poem Alvarez's suggestion has come dangerously close to the mark – the writer as "ornamentalist", the very writer whose coming into adulthood was signified by the necessary killing of pests such as rats in "The Early Purges".[19]

Perhaps the antidote to such self-conscious distortion is to be found in a different discipline in Field Work which resists and rejects notions of the classical pastoral. Such a discipline evolves from having learned, like Wordsworth, to accept nature's "ministry" of both beauty and fear. Indeed one possible reading of "Sonnet IX" would be to see the "new moon" of his wife's pale face at the end of the poem as indicating her new knowledge of the stare of the rat: that "infected fruit" is also natural, and rather more serious in reality than the poetic-sounding ornamental simile Heaney is indulging in here. To accept an affinity with nature is not only to accept the "water-snakes", but like the Ancient Mariner, to "bless them unaware".[20] But the basis of Heaney's affinity to nature is located in Wordsworth rather than Coleridge.

In the remarkable climax of "Home at Grasmere", Wordsworth struggles to express the biological basis of his metaphysic. The human mind ought to be able to comprehend its connection with nature because it is formed by nature to fit the natural world:

> Speaking of nothing more than what we are –
> How exquisitely the individual Mind
> (And the progressive powers perhaps no less
> Of the whole species) to the external world
> Is fitted; and how exquisitely too –
> Theme this but little heard of among men –
> The external world is fitted to the mind;
> And the creation (by no lower name
> Can it be called) which they with blended might
> Accomplish.[21]

This passage really explains why it is that Heaney thinks through nature imagery; why he seeks to bring to the surface "pre-social" knowledge that is pagan and located often in place; and how he can suggest that art is "a paradigm of earth".[22] These are the three distinctive themes underpinning Heaney's assumption of a connectedness with nature in Field Work: the human as organic and animal; the pagan elements of tribal culture; and the notion of art as finding expression for the earth itself.

Although Heaney later considered doing postgraduate research on Wordsworth's educational ideas,[23] his early education had alienated him from his own experience of nature. Certainly contemporary poetry did not make that connection until

> I remember the day I opened Ted Hughes's Lupercal in the Belfast University Library. [There was] a poem called "View of a Pig" and in

my childhood we'd killed pigs on the farm, and I'd seen pigs shaved, hung up, and so on .... Suddenly the matter of contemporary poetry was the material of my own life. I had had some notion that modern poetry was far beyond the likes of me – there was Eliot and so on – so I got this thrill out of trusting my own background, and I started a year later, I think [to write poetry].[24]

Many critics refer, like Neil Corcoran, to Heaney's "reciprocal relationship with Nature".[25] I see no reason to avoid describing this relationship as one that assumes a unity with nature, although admittedly a unity that is at times under strain, as in "Sonnet IX". One of the "creations", as Wordsworth dares to call them, that the mind and nature accomplish "with blended might",[26] is a celebration of life under the strain of coping with death: the elegy. There are four in *Field Work* and each one provides examples of Heaney's thinking through nature imagery, exploring the assumption that human life is organically unified with the natural world. At the simplest level this could be illustrated by Heaney's use of a bestiary that is familiar, mysterious and mythologised, as he says of the subject of "The Skunk". This bestiary actually represents people: just as his wife is jokingly, lovingly the skunk in that poem, Heaney is himself the sandmartin in the poem that follows it in *Field Work*. In "Casualty" the cliché "he drank like a fish" is used to represent the fisherman as himself a fish "naturally/ Swimming towards the lure/of warm lit-up places", only to be killed by a pub bombing during an IRA-imposed curfew for Bloody Sunday. In *Field Work* Heaney has not turned his back on news from Ulster, but taken comfort from the natures of those who have died. Sean O'Riada, on one occasion a guest conductor of the Ulster Orchestra, is remembered in images not only of sight, but of sound:

> O gannet smacking through scales!
> Minnow of light.
> Wader of assonance.[27]

He also fished with Heaney and each of the images in these three lines are of creatures fishing (the visual image of gannet and heron resembling the white and black of a conductor) or of a fish turning into light with the whole shoal, just as a conductor turns sound to colour through the unified movement of bows in an orchestra. These are not mere ornamentations, but witty celebrations of a vitality now lost.

"The high moments of Wordsworth's poetry", Heaney argues in his essay on Wordsworth and Yeats, "occur when the verse has carried us forward . . . to a kind of suspended motion . . . a prolonged moment of equilibrium during which we feel ourselves to be conductors of the palpable energies of earth and sky".[28]

His point is that this form of poetry is not cognitive but musical in the way it generates and conveys its force. There is a danger here of implying that only orchestrated, architectural verse such as Wordsworth's can achieve an evocation of natural energies. Is it not also true that lyric verse such as Heaney's can put the reader in touch with "the energies of earth and sky" through the potency of metaphor charged with the elemental emotional energy of, say, a song of grief for the dead? The force of the life of Robert Lowell is evoked in this way in the poem that is simply titled "Elegy".[29]

This poem is a daring example of Heaney's usage of the organic juxtaposed with the man-made in metaphors which only just manage to avoid becoming disastrously mixed by the very boldness of Heaney's wholeness of vision. The frame of reference is assumed to be that of a unified universe, complete with its infected fruit. The drive of the poem, which is addressed directly to Lowell ("you . . . rode on the swaying tiller/of yourself") characterises him as firstly a dolphin, then "helmsman, netsman, *retiarius*", then a night ferry and finally the owner of "fish-darting eyes". Heaney's poem might well itself be described, like Lowell, as having "the course set wilfully across/the ungovernable and dangerous". Heaney casts himself as the timorous child at the end of the poem, yet he is surely bold in his range of metaphor, for how can Lowell be fish, fisherman and boat? The answer is perhaps to be found in three elements of the poem which reflect Heaney's assumption, implied here, that in Wordsworth's words, Lowell might "roam/An equal among mightiest energies".[30]

First there is the force of Lowell's life, established not just in the bold verbs ("You drank America"; "you bullied out/heart-hammering blank sonnets") but in that distinctive construction which appears early in the poem: "you . . . rode on the swaying tiller/of yourself". This formulation is a feature of Heaney's verse which suggests remarkable wholeness and self-possession. In this case "riding" the tiller is an unforced, vibrant acceptance of his own nature that dared to explore it in poems about mental illness. Lowell is indeed both fish and fisherman.

Secondly, the pairings that recur throughout the poem on complementary or contradictory forces ("timorous or bold"; "art's/deliberate, peremptory/love and arrogance"; "ungovernable and dangerous"; "opulent and restorative") are accepted as parts of the whole, however admittedly contradictory they may be. Indeed Lowell wilfully sets course into these dangerous areas, knowing both sides of the experience: "That hand. Warding and grooming/and amphibious".[31] "Amphibious" sums up that self-integrated duality of Lowell as both fish and fisherman once again.

Thirdly, in addition to the energy of the verbs and the paradoxes there is the framing dramatic tension of the wind and rain threatening the geranium, apparently whilst the poem is being written. This image of vulnerability, introduced at the opening and at the end of the poem, is a reminder of the risk in Lowell's boldness. The echoes of Lowell's own poems within "Elegy" ("Two a.m., seaboard weather") also serve as reminders of his "dangerous course". The poem ends with "the fish-dart of your eyes", conveying the friendly presumption of Lowell's "risking, 'I'll pray for you' ". Who then, is being represented by "the geranium *tremens*"? It is Heaney, the child who cannot be shielded by prayers made by the father-figure. But it is also Lowell, the bold but vulnerable explorer of "the ungovernable and dangerous". This connection with Lowell would seem to be reinforced by the joke on *delirium tremens*, the affliction of those who "drink America".

The point is that, as well as setting up direct metaphors such as "your dorsal nib", Heaney can also simply reintroduce the windowsill geranium as "*tremens*" to have it make a subtle connection between Lowell and himself. The grammar of the final sentence suggests that the connection between "child" and "father" poets is as "restorative" as the bay tree or the summertime. And there is that "bay tree/by the gate at Glanmore" again. For Heaney, like MacLean, personal and social meanings are located in the natural forms of place.

In his explanation of the poem "Hercules and Antaeus" from *North*, Heaney describes what it is to be denatured, to be cut off from the meanings invested in your own native earth:

> The Hercules–Antaeus thing came to seem like a myth of colonisation almost – that Antaeus is a native, an earth-grubber, in touch with the ground, and you get this intelligent and superior interloper who debilitates the native by raising him, taking him out of his culture, his element, and leaving him without force. You could think about Ireland in those terms.[32]

This tension seems to underlie "The Toome Road" where the

coloniser's armoured cars are ironically camouflaged with broken alder branches and desecrate the speaker's sense of his "rights-of-way". He invokes a litany of material possessions that mark his territory as Antaeus the "earth-grubber", the farmer living amongst a network of neighbours always ready for "the bringer of bad news" who "by being expected, might be kept distant". The superstition in this underground of pagan resistance leaves one feeling that the mysterious "untoppled omphalos" is vibrant with wider dimensions than simply "the navel of nationalist Irish feeling" that Neil Corcoran suggests:[33] the armoured cars have set vibrating a primitive, invisible sense of the desecration of territory and its values that are rooted in the natural cycles of this place. These modern successors to the Roman charioteers are known by the speaker to also be participants in those cycles. If they did but know it, they too are "Sowers of seed, erectors of headstones", as the grammar suggests.

The word "omphalos" is open to the charge of having a rather self-conscious mysticism about it. But the Greek word for the navel of the earth is used here to represent a Celtic sense of place against that of the colonialists. Heaney has argued that it was the Romans who first, in his words, "reduced"' the Celtic gods "to the likenesses of living men and women; before that, the deities remained shrouded in the living matrices of stones and trees, immanent in the natural world".[34] Heaney finds it significant that in the Ireland of the Druids "the poet is connected with the mysteries of the grove, and the poetic imagination is linked with the barbaric life of the wood, with Oisin rather than with Patrick". Heaney goes on in this talk on "Early Irish Nature Poetry" to refer to Sweeney as an example of such a "poet". It does not need the evidence of Heaney's identification with Sweeney in the "Sweeney Redivivus" part of Station Island to see that Heaney regards himself as writing in this tradition of what he suggests are the "green men" poets. Those who are observers of a tendency to re-run the Celtic Revival would find much to criticise in this radio talk. But in it Heaney is attempting to find out how his vision of nature can be importantly restorative in the face of the present tribal tensions. The evidence is there throughout Field Work and nowhere more strongly pagan and religious than in the "Triptych" sequence.

The sequence begins and ends with images of military "profanity". The first image is that of the Nationalist killers of Christopher Ewart-Biggs after whose killing in July 1976 the first poem was written. The last image is that of a British helicopter "shadowing our march at

Newry". Between these images – the first recalling the "founders" of Ireland, the last a modern reference to the start of the most recent Troubles – there is a counter-movement backwards towards a primitive religious attitude. It is present in the characteristic litany of images of place in the first poem, "After a Killing", which later materialises into "a stone house by a pier", where "we might dwell among ourselves" in the simplest way, accepting the discipline of "scoured light", and finding significance in orchids as "survivor flowers". Finally an image that comes straight out of a poem by Patrick Kavanagh carries authenticity in having the mud still on it and only hints, by its climactic placing, at its acting as a pagan token, a tribal gift to set against the killing:

> And to-day a girl walks in home to us
> Carrying a basket full of new potatoes,
> Three tight green cabbages, and carrots
> With the tops and mould still fresh on them.

This is a positive ending. The emphasis on "fresh", a token from the green world, hints, through "tops and mould", at the force of growing that has been brought into the home. The Sibyl of the second poem in "Triptych" says, "My people think money/And talk weather. Oil-rigs lull their future." Hers is the voice of the contemporary Irish people, but her voice is not heard. The ground is "tented by an impious augury". People who should feel at home in this island share a little of Caliban's alienation in the poem's last line. Nothing short of a miracle is needed: "Unless the helmeted and bleeding tree/Can green and open buds . . .". The Sibyl is the priestess who gives voice to the prophecy of Apollo. (Is the helmeted and bleeding tree a Greek warrior image overlaid upon a Celtic pantheistic one?) The nymphs she refers to are not the dryads which appear in the poem "Field Work". Under this colonial Greco-Roman culture there lies an earlier religion which is the subject of the third poem, "At the Water's Edge". But this too has gone dead: the "god-eyed, sex-mouthed stone" on the earliest Irish holy island is now "a stoup for rain water". As a result of this historically backward journey through the sequence, Heaney rediscovers the basic natural humility of pagan religion:

> Everything in me
> Wanted to bow down, to offer up,
> To go barefoot, foetal and penitential,

> And pray at the water's edge.
> How we crept before we walked!

Unfortunately the Sibyl's prophecy has been fulfilled: her people have apparently changed their posture ("I think our very form is bound to change") under the colonial presence. That creeping is not, in fact, a religious attitude of humility, "forgiveness" and awe, such as that of a Celtic pantheist "at the water's edge", but an image of the Newry marchers cowed and humiliated by a British army helicopter. No wonder this third poem ends with the suggestion that these have been "irrevocable steps". So too were the steps of the two killers, who walked the hill in the first poem's opening lines.

That "creeping" at Newry in 1972 has generated the opposite of the stance which Heaney has discovered to be fundamental to Irish political, social and personal regeneration: the humility and strength of feeling connected to the organic processes located in meanings attributed to place and objects from the earliest stages of the culture. Of course the "Triptych" sequence is not dogmatic. The poems leave the possibilities implicit, but it is from these images that the poems derive their power, images which go a stage beyond awestruck worship to an articulation of unity.

Heaney concluded his essay "The Sense of Place" by asserting that it is to "the stable element, the land itself, that we must look for continuity".[35] His sense of "the land" here is not just territory and the meanings invested in knowing place, but of "the way the surface of the earth can be accepted into and be a steadying influence upon the quiet depths of the mind". His model is again Wordsworth because "Wordsworth was perhaps the first man to articulate the nature that becomes available to the feelings through dwelling in one dear perpetual place." The "Glanmore Sonnets" not only take their name from Heaney's chosen place of exile, but that place comes to represent his enquiry into the role of the poet and the nature of poetry. Blake Morrison has drawn attention to the way the image of ploughing the earth, as a metaphor for poetic composition in the first of the Glanmore Sonnets, is derived from Heaney's interest in Wordsworth's method of composition by pacing the ground "chaunting", as Hazlitt put it.[36]

The context in which the "Glanmore Sonnets" were written is revealed in Sonnet III where Heaney finds himself guilty of drawing a direct parallel between Wordsworth's situation and his own at

Glanmore. Heaney took his family to Glanmore, County Wicklow, in July 1972, four months after that "irrevocable" creeping at Newry. As I have said, for many observers Glanmore represented Heaney's pastoral retreat from the Troubles. Heaney himself comes close to admitting this in his definition of "pastoral" as "beautified" when he says that he thinks "of the countryside where we live in Wicklow as being pastoral rather than rural, trying to impose notions of a beautified landscape on the word, in order to keep 'rural' for the unselfconscious face of raggle-taggle farmland".[37]

The "Glanmore Sonnets" are selfconscious, but it seems to me, pace Morrison,[38] that they are self-conscious about *avoiding* becoming pastoral in that falsely "beautified", escapist sense. Take, for example, Heaney's comments introducing a reading of Sonnet III at the Cheltenham Literature Festival on 16 October 1982:

> This was the first of the sonnets to be written. I had moved to Wicklow to discover if I could be a full-time writer . . . if I was a writer. All the poems had been coming in a narrow, cramped, tense form on the page. This poem was the first freeing from that. The first two lines came out of the hills and sounded too comfortable, iambic, English even. So I got them at a distance with the next eight lines. I had been to Dove Cottage to do a TV programme and was struck by the similarity of structure with our cottage in Wicklow. Those last six lines came later.[39]

It is important to realise that the third line of Sonnet III is intended to sound a note of warning about the first two:

> This evening the cuckoo and the corncrake
> (So much, too much) consorted at twilight.
> It was all crepuscular and iambic.[40]

But the tension has already been established in the "too much" which prefaces the tendency to beautify what is latent in that third alliteration, "consorted". A hint of humour actually prevents "consorted" from taking itself seriously as a pastoralisation: cuckoo and corncrake cannot consort in the biological sense. So it really does not need the obvious evidence later in the poem that Heaney is attempting to express the lessons of what he refers to in Sonnet II as "the hedge-school of Glanmore" whilst avoiding the temptation to pastoralise. The rigour of "this strange loneliness I've brought us to" is used throughout Field Work to undercut pastoral romanticism as quickly as the voice of Heaney's wife at the mention of the similar loneliness of Dorothy and William: " 'You're not going to compare us two . . .?' "

The iambic, for all it is "too comfortable . . . English even"[41] to Heaney's ear is, of course, intended to refer to the rhythm of the voice of cuckoo and corncrake. In fact the call of the cuckoo is a trochee, and that of the corncrake is a spondee! But crepuscular is exactly the right word for the corncrake's call, "creeping" at dusk to hear it, as you must. The poetic term "iambic" is an attempt to suggest an organic continuum between, on the one hand the poet's art, and on the other hand natural rhythms heard and felt at Glanmore. Every poem in the sonnet sequence deploys sensuous language to connect with natural energies, often with a reflexive reference to the way language is making that connection.

This discovery of the way language connects with the land is Heaney's mode of responding to the pressures and tensions in contemporary Ireland. It is the source of stable continuity that underlies both the elegies and the marriage poems. The sonnets are his most intense discoveries of rhythms that place those feelings and tensions within a natural framework. The first sonnet – listening, feeling, tasting, smelling the land – finds a "dream grain" of poetry that is in tune with the rhythm of working the land (that is, field work):

> Now the good life could be to cross a field
> And art a paradigm of earth new from the lathe
> Of ploughs. My lea is deeply tilled.

The notion of "paradigm" works two ways here, giving and taking: giving expression to the earth itself and taking a pattern for the poem from earth's rhythms. Sensuous texture, rhythm and poetic form are to be taken from "the lathe/Of ploughs". This giving and taking is present in both the passive and active notions contained in the sentence, "My lea is deeply tilled." The notion of the poet's "lathe" of ploughs recognises a process of re-making. It affirms a connection through the process of making metaphors and sounds in poetry. As Heaney writes in Sonnet I: "Old ploughsocks gorge the subsoil of each sense."

Thus we find in the second sonnet a remarkable expression of art achieving its form through a discipline described in the second line of the poem as the equivalent of "Words entering almost the sense of touch." In this case it is a sculptor

> hankering after stone
> That connived with the chisel, as if the grain
> Remembered what the mallet tapped to know.[42]

This kind of knowledge is achieved in Sonnet III in which, after his wife's bringing him down to earth, the writer listens again:

> Outside a rustling and twig-combing breeze
> Refreshes and relents. Is cadences.[43]

The poem thus recovers from its potentially pastoral start, with its falsely "iambic" corncrake, to catch the simple cadences that "refresh" and "relent".

This cadence of the spirit is one example of Heaney's discoveries from the land that can be set against the rites of North and the North of Ireland. What "refreshes and relents" is caught through the art process and expressed in poetic cadences by listening directly to the cadences in nature. Here Heaney is what he claims Wordsworth to be: "conductor of the palpable energies of earth and sky",[44] not just instinctively finding metaphors for people in other creatures, or conducting the energies of place, but in the discovery of the purpose of art-making for his context of killings and bigotry. What dominates Field Work more than the tensions of pastoral and anti-pastoral, or the question of the writer's role in the "wilderness", is the sensuous warmth and compassion that underlie poems of both grief and love. It is Heaney's various ways of drawing strength from a unity with nature that always gives the best poems in Field Work their distinctive quality.

The danger of this use of nature is that images can be assumed to be potent icons of nature in contexts that do not substantiate their meaning adequately. The bay tree could be asserted to be restorative simply because it is a presence of nature. Without the words "opulent" and "full" it would have an idealised pastoral function (as indeed it does when it is described as "classical"). In a remarkable poem in Station Island Heaney accuses himself of having pastoralised in just this way in a poem in Field Work. "The Strand at Lough Beg" from Field Work was written in memory of Colum McCartney, a cousin of Heaney's who was shot dead one night while driving home in County Armagh.[45] At the end of the poem Heaney imagines himself kneeling to

> gather up cold handfuls of the dew
> To wash you, cousin. I dab you clean with moss

Fine as the drizzle out of a low cloud.
I lift you under the arms and lay you flat.
With rushes that shoot green again, I plait
Green scapulars to wear over your shroud.[46]

Despite its obvious echoing of the lines from Dante's *Purgatorio* quoted as the poem's epigraph, the activeness of this grieving, together with the practical use of the natural materials to hand, surely save this concluding image from posing as a classical scene from a pastoral text. But in the title sequence of *Station Island* the ghost of Colum McCartney makes a bitter attack on the writer of the concluding lines of "The Strand at Lough Beg":

"You confused evasion and artistic tact.
The Protestant who shot me through the head
I accuse directly, but indirectly, you
who now atone perhaps upon this bed
for the way you whitewashed ugliness and drew
the lovely blinds of the *Purgatorio*
and saccharined my death with morning dew."[47]

The courage of the Seamus Heaney is breathtaking here, not only because of the poignancy of his guilt, spoken aloud, but because this is a direct challenge to his use of nature in *Field Work*. The gesture which I have justified as a practical act of grief is accused of being a self-indulgent, self-deceiving literary gesture. In this *Station Island* poem Heaney simply lets the challenge stand, as one of the series of penitential self-accusations of pastoral evasion made through voices from the past in the "Station Island" sequence. But one ought to consider in which poems "whitewash" or "saccharine" is really applied, and those in which this challenge can be rebuffed. Has a word like "omphalos", for example, actually been used to end "The Toome Road" with an aura of classical mysticism in an archly literary gesture? I have argued that the text has provided its definition as a primitive notion of territory *before* the word is used to conclude the poem. The Greek has been given an Ulster context that is deep enough to stand against the image of the intruding armoured car. In *Station Island* there is a similar poem which attempts a similar achievement but fails, in my view. It provides an example of Heaney's capacity for a token use of natural images in his later poetry.

It appears that the young Heaney's personal "omphalos" was an old hollow tree. In a 1978 radio talk Heaney describes how, hidden in the tree, he felt himself to be "a little Cerunnos pivoting a world of antlers".[48] The poet as green man, "connected with the mysteries of the grove",[49] might have got a little carried away here (as is sometimes the case in Heaney's prose writings). In the *Station Island* poem, "In the Beech", written supposedly in the voice of Sweeney the exiled king who has been turned into a bird, the tree of the title is clearly the one in which

> the school-leaver discovered peace
> to touch himself in the reek of churned-up mud.
> And the tree itself a strangeness and a comfort.[50]

The tree represents personal growth, presented with the characteristic ambivalence of "strangeness" and "comfort". But a political dimension is introduced through this very tree as the boy feels the vibration of advancing tanks. By the end of the poem the tree has to represent a depth of knowledge that is simply set in juxtaposition to another image of English military supremacy that suddenly appears from nowhere in the form of a low-flying aircraft. This "tree of knowledge" has hardly earned its opposition as political "boundary tree" on the childhood evidence in the poem.

In "The First Kingdom", which follows "In The Beech", an anti-romantic description is given of a kingdom before a revealing question is raised:

> And if my rights to it all came only
> by their acclamation, what was it worth?

This is precisely the problem with Heaney's use of "my tree of knowledge". It is an acclamation, an assertion of depth that, in the poem, goes no further than the personal knowledge of a school-leaver. If this is a joke about sexual self-knowledge it is being required to carry a lot of political weight in juxtaposition to an aircraft and tanks! "Boundary tree" has not been invested with evidence of the community's sense of territory as the Toome Road has. In "In the Beech" the writer is falling back on the technique of juxtaposing images rather than exploring their contradictions and relations. Edna Longley noted this tendency in relation to the use of images in *North*: "Heaney seems to regard a symbol or myth as sufficiently emblematic in itself: 'beauty' pleading with 'rage' within the icon of 'The Grauballe Man' – Man and poem synonymous – rather than through any kind of dialectic."[51]

This is a limitation in Heaney's use of the domestic tokens presented in Part One of *Station Island*, in "Shelf Life", for example, or "The Sandpit". There are moments when natural images make a deeper connection with experience within the evidence of a poem, in the delicate undersounds of the discovery of nature shared with a child in "Changes", or in the brilliant making of a metaphor in "A Hazel Stick for Catherine Ann": "the very stick we might cut/from your family tree".[52]

But at a political level, Heaney in *Station Island* has come down to postures which are merely "superstitious . . . even mystical", in Blake Morrison's words.[53] The pantheist, instead of shaping his art from feeling the forces of natural forms, becomes the pastoralist, nostalgically asserting the mysterious, idealised, symbolic power of the old images. This can elevate equivocation into a style of poetic practice. In "Sandstone Keepsake" in *Station Island* a stone, red with the blood of literary and historic associations, carries a symbolic weight against the internment camp on the other side of the river. It really won't do to make a virtue out of this pastoral stance by claiming, as Neil Corcoran does, that this poem "seems more ironically assured of the poet's peripheral status".[54] This is to make a style out of equivocation.

The best advice Heaney gives himself through the voices of the past in "Station Island" is that which, unlike many that advocate swimming clear of engagement, finds a natural image for a way forward. The voice of William Carleton interrupts a familiar litany of natural images (alders, mushrooms, dung in grass, "the melt of shells corrupting") to comment upon Heaney's preceding list of images.

> "All this is like a trout kept in a spring
> or maggots sown in wounds –
> another life that cleans our element.
>
> We are earthworms of the earth, and all that
> has gone through us is what will be our trace."[55]

Here is a demand to confront corruption ("the melt of shells", internment camps, the interrogator, the killer, the tanks) through natural images that represent organic processes of dissolution. These images, considered with the discipline of one who knows that these natural processes are at work in human beings, can act as a "cleansing". The process that Heaney identified elsewhere in *Station Island* in the image of "a stone swirled under a cascade,/Eroded and eroding its bed",[56] is accepted and confronted with all the attendant artistic and political risks. These must surely be greater than is suggested by the notion of experience simply passing through us to leave our trace as history or poetry. A commitment to art might draw upon the pre-social, but cannot be a-social in its mediation of it. Unfortunately at least two admirers of Heaney feel that this is the direction Heaney is taking and are enthusiastic about it. John Haffenden speaks of Heaney as rising "above contemporary political and religious struggles"[57] in the final section of *Station Island*, which includes "In the Beech". In the same issue of *The Yearbook of English Studies* Neil Corcoran anticipates *The Haw Lantern* by quoting a line from the already published poem, "The Spoonbait": "I look forward to a poetry which may seem 'Risen and free and spooling out of nowhere'."[58]

Poems, of course, do not come " 'spooling out of nowhere' ". In the poem "The Spoonbait", Heaney is making an image for the soul at the moment of death – perhaps the ultimate escapist activity for the poet. I have tried to show how Heaney has avoided, in *Field Work* particularly, the temptation to indulge in image-making which falsifies the tensions and contradictions of his experience by adopting the discipline of what I have called "the vision of Wordsworth". Through his unifying deployment of natural images in his mode of thinking, in his drawing upon social energies deriving from a sense of place, and through his notion of art itself working through sounds and rhythms that are natural forces within poetic shapings, Heaney is the contemporary inheritor of Wordsworth's legacy. His awareness of the risks he takes – to "whitewash ugliness", to "saccharine" death – does not absolve him from his lapses. But his achievement is to turn his vision, in his best poems, rigorously upon his own experience of the Troubles, his marriage and himself as a writer. As self-aware participant in these processes Heaney takes strength and confidence, in his examination of them, from his own unity with nature, however inadequate a mediator he might at times consider himself to be. That fundamental, stylistically expressed, assumption of connectedness has shown Heaney's best work to be a fine example of what might be called "contemporary post-pastoral poetry".

Notes

1 *Times Literary Supplement*, 19 Oct. 1984, p. 1191.
2 *The Prelude*, 1805, Book I, lines 370–1.

3 *The Government of the Tongue*, London, Faber & Faber, 1988, p. 106.

4 ibid., p. 107.

5 ibid., p. 93.

6 *The Prelude*, 1805, Book II, lines 262–77.

7 London: Faber & Faber, 1979.

8 London: Faber & Faber, 1972.

9 London: Faber & Faber, 1975.

10 London: Faber & Faber, 1966, p. 36.

11 London: Faber & Faber, 1969, p. 34.

12 p. 34.

13 K. Sagar ed., *The Achievement of Ted Hughes*, Manchester University Press, 1983, p. 96.

14 "A Fine Way With the Language", *New York Review of Books*, 6 Mar. 1980, p. 16.

15 Recorded by the present author at Heaney's Cheltenham Literature Festival reading, 16 Oct. 1982.

16 B. Morrison, *Seamus Heaney*, London: Methuen, 1982, p. 72.

17 John Haffenden ed., *Viewpoints*, London: Faber & Faber, 1981, p. 72.

18 *Field Work*, p. 41.

19 *Death of a Naturalist*, p. 23.

20 S. T. Coleridge, "The Rime of the Ancient Mariner", Part IV, line 287.

21 Lines 1005–14.

22 *Field Work*, p. 33.

23 Neil Corcoran, *Seamus Heaney*, London: Faber & Faber, 1986, p. 20.

24 *Ploughshares*, Vol. 5, No. 3, 1979, p. 14.

25 C. Rawson ed., *The Yearbook of English Studies*, Modern Humanities Research Association, 1987, p. 125.

26 "Home at Grasmere", line 1013.

27 *Field Work*, p. 30.

28 *Preoccupations*, p. 65.

29 *Field Work*, p. 31.

30 "The Excursion", Book IV.

31 *Field Work*, p. 32.

32 Haffenden, *Viewpoints*, p. 70.

33 *Seamus Heaney*, p. 134.

34 *Preoccupations*, p. 186.

35 *Preoccupations*, p. 149.

36 Quoted in *Preoccupations*, p. 65.

37 ibid., p. 173.

38 *Seamus Heaney*, p. 85.

39 Recorded by the present author.

40 *Field Work*, p. 35.

41 Cheltenham Literature Festival reading, 16 Oct. 1982.

42 ibid.

43 ibid., p. 35.

44 *Preoccupations*, p. 65.

45 Michael Parker, *Seamus Heaney: The Making of the Poet*, London: Macmillan, 1993, p. 160. This is currently the best source of information about the background to the poems.

46 *Field Work*, p. 18.
47 *Station Island*, p. 83.
48 "Omphalos", *Preoccupations*, p. 18.
49 ibid., p. 186.
50 *Station Island*, London: Faber & Faber, 1984, p. 100.
51 *Poetry in the Wars*, Newcastle upon Tyne: Bloodaxe, 1986, p. 156.
52 *Station Island*, p. 42.
53 B. Morrison, *Times Literary Supplement*, 19 Oct. 1984.
54 *Seamus Heaney*, p. 158.
55 *Station Island*, p. 66.
56 ibid., p. 86.
57 *The Yearbook of English Studies*, p. 116.
58 ibid., p. 127.

6
Laureate of nature: the poetry of Ted Hughes

WHEN the newly-appointed Poet Laureate is quickly presented with his first opportunity to produce a poem for a royal christening and he comes up with a long poem about a rainstorm in Devon, something interesting is happening in the culture. The new symbolic shaman of the tribe, as Heaney characterised the appointment,[1] was a poet whose notion of the significance of nature was so strongly developed that he could risk irreverence by invoking, for this royal occasion, a "drenching" that could be experienced by any non-Royal any summer in England. "Rain-Charm for the Duchy: A Blessed, Devout Drench for the Christening of Prince Harry",[2] is a celebration of the rivers of Devon, each described in intimate detail as they receive a sudden rainfall after five months' drought. As "rain didn't so much fall as collapse", the poet writes in the poem, "I was thinking . . .

> of the Lyn's twin gorges, clearing their throats, deepening their
> voices, beginning to hear each other
> Rehearse forgotten riffles.

But the Royal Family also have to read of the less pleasant evidence of

> the Okement, nudging her detergent bottles, tugging at her nylon
> stockings, starting to trundle her Pepsi-Cola cans.

Indeed, the only suggestion within the poem that it was written for this royal religious occasion comes near the end:

> I imagined the two moors
> The two stone-age hands
> Cupped and brimming, raised like an offering –

However, that dash indicates that this offering of water filling the Devon rivers is not for Prince Harry, but for what are actually revealed, in the final stanza, to be

> The salmon, deep in the thunder, lit
> And again lit, with glimpses of quenchings,
> Twisting their glints in the suspense,
> Biting at the stir, beginning to move.

Here then is a litany of rivers, skilfully described, in both their beauty and their pollution, which culminates in a celebration of salmon beginning to move back up to their spawning-pools in these rivers. In itself this is a well-crafted, celebratory but unremarkable poem which escapes pastoral comfortableness. However, to a non-royalist reader of Hughes's early poems, the poem's simple celebration of nature in the service of a royal christening might produce some unease on at least two counts. The poem's lack of any contextualising awareness of the death of salmon in the process that is "beginning to move", or of any qualification of the poem's simple celebration, might begin to seem like pastoral after all, as the function of the poem is to confirm the social status quo. Here nature is used by the poet to suggest that all's well in the natural and social world. Indeed, the natural world includes the feudal order of royalty endorsed by religion, although only the poem's title is explicit in asserting the poem's symbolic function. The implicit image of Devon's two great moors "raised like an offering" side-steps its feudal and religious function by being directed in the poem towards the salmon. In effect, by the conclusion of the poem, with its forward-looking promise of "beginning to move", the salmon, too, have been "offered" in this "Rain-Charm" for the future of a royal child. To the matter of salmon and the Poet Laureate I shall return in considering *River*,[3] but what is the source of Ted Hughes's confident belief in his conception of nature as appropriate for this social purpose? And what are the origins and antecedents of his particular vision of nature?

Hughes began as an anti-pastoralist, having more in common with Blake in the earliest conception of his project than his linguistic imitations of Gerard Manley Hopkins might have suggested. Indeed Hughes's central accusation against comfortable attitudes to nature in his first collection, *The Hawk In The Rain*, was actually expressed in an image that is the same as a key image of Blake's. The poem "Egg-Head" can be seen, in retrospect, to have been something of a manifesto poem. Many critics will find it strange, considering the poem's appalling climactic pastiche of Hopkins, that "Egg-Head" is collected in *Selected Poems 1957–1981*.[4] The poem begins with images that are ironic pastoralisms – that is, potentially powerful images, prettified by the form of their expression:

> A leaf's otherness,
> The whaled monstered sea-bottom, eagled peaks
> And stars that hang over hurtling endlessness,
>   With manslaughtering shocks
> Are let in on his sense.[5]

The bathos of "manslaughtering" indicates that the only shocks which the egghead lets in are safely defused by his perception of them. If "otherness" evokes Lawrence, it is not the really manslaughtering otherness of a mountain lion, or a jaguar, that is "let in" by the egghead, but a leaf's. This first collection opens with a title-poem in which the writer, in contrast to the egghead, is "Bloodily grabbed dazed last-moment-counting"[6] by his letting in on his sense an apprehension of "the master-/Fulcrum of violence where the hawk hangs still". The influence of Hopkins may, again, render this poem melodramatic, but it indicates that Hughes intends "a leaf's otherness" to be the soft option. The evidence of this poem, together with "Jaguar", would also support a suspicion that "eagled peaks" is being presented in "Egg-Head" as a pastoralism. One would expect Hughes's interest to be in the eagle, but the egghead's perception turns the noun into an adjective describing the peak as prettily "eagled". Similarly the sea-bottom is coyly "whaled", and even "monstered", as if the real monster of a whale were not marvel enough.

If the reader had not already read the earlier poems in *The Hawk In The Rain* before coming to "Egg-Head", these opening images might well have an attraction in their linguistic inventiveness. Indeed it is the function of a pastoral to be a seductive-sounding, distorting disengagement from reality. But the reader might be alerted by "manslaughtering" and "are let in" to the direction of the poem's argument and the dominant ironic tone that comes to be established in the following lines:

> So many a one has dared to be struck dead
> Peeping through his fingers at the world's ends,
>   Or at an ant's head.

For Blake too, the problem of human dislocation from the natural world was expressed as one of perception and his ultimate image of this, in *The Marriage of Heaven and Hell*, was precisely that of Hughes in "Egg-Head":

> But first the notion that man has a body distinct from his soul is to be expunged. This I shall do by printing in the infernal method by corrosives, which in Hell are salutary and medicinal, melting apparent surfaces away, and displaying the infinite which was hid.
>
> If the doors of perception were cleansed everything would appear to man as it is – infinite.
>
> For man has closed himself up, till he sees all things through narrow chinks of his cavern.[7]

Blake's emphasis is on the self-imprisonment of selective perception. A self-protective tendency has led people to retreat behind the narrow chinks of a cavern of their own making. Blake is describing the process of making what he called in the poem "London", "mind-forged manacles".[8] Hughes describes precisely the same process in his image of "the eggshell head" which provides a perfect definition of the pastoral: an apparent engagement with the natural world which protectively, "prudently", excludes uncomfortable forces and their tensions. In "Egg-Head" the logic of this is self-destructive since the forces themselves will not be suppressed by being ignored. This egg's chemistry of complacency and arrogance produces a man/cockerel who "trumpet[s] his own ear dead" in an overdose of Gerard Manley Hopkins that appears to get rather beyond the control of the poet in the poem's contorted climactic sentence. The strange vehemence of this ending also has something in common with Blake's choice of corrosives for "salutary" cleansing purposes. Indeed the characterisation of human arrogance as a cockerel anticipates, in the first collection, Hughes's later putting a cockerel on trial for his complacency in *Cave Birds*.[9]

But almost last in the line of alliteration and compound words is "the whelm of the sun", itself a forceful Anglo-Saxon conception. This is what has been so easily dismissed by the complacent assumption that this "braggart-browed" man can "oppose" his eye to it. "Whelm" links back to the poem's central images of sun and earth where the verbs "flash" and "bolt" suggest a force that is both creative and destructive. To "receive" these forces can be life-giving, indeed essential, although to the egghead it is clear that they are perceived as

117

destructive. Here Hughes hints at his own project in ironic contrast to that of the egghead. Like Blake, Hughes seeks to look with cleansed perception upon the "fearful symmetry"[10] of creative–destructive forces. Like Blake, Hughes is aware from the outset that those forces are also at work within human nature as well as in external nature, hence the presence in *The Hawk In The Rain* of that group of awful poems satirising women who are hiding from passion ("Parlour-Piece", "Secretary", "Soliloquy of a Misanthrope") and men who are passionately predatory ("The Dove Breeder", "Fallgrief's Girl-Friends").

Indeed, problems arise in reading the first two collections because Hughes writes "cleansing" anti-pastoral poems at the same time as "seeing" celebratory poems. The long-running critical debate over the poem "Hawk Roosting",[11] for example, is a result of uncertainty about whether its tone is wholly ironic or partly admiring. The fact that there are twenty-one assertions of the first-person singular in "Hawk Roosting" should indicate that this hawk has more in common with the " 'I am' " of "Egg-Head". But the poem does raise some complex issues surrounding Hughes's notion of nature in the early poetry. The matter is complicated by Hughes's denial that this is a fascist voice: "Actually what I had in mind was that in this hawk Nature is thinking. Simply Nature."[12]

First of all this poem clearly is, at one level, a human voice speaking. The hawk is a persona by which the writer wittily builds the self-deception of this violent voice to the irony of the final line: "I am going to keep things like this."[13] This is a voice which is obviously fascist: "No arguments assert my right:/The sun is behind me." A natural moral order is claimed simply by sitting in front of the sun. "Egg-Head" indicated that complacency and arrogance distort human vision of nature. This is clearly what is being parodied through the hawk in "Hawk Roosting":

> It took the whole of Creation
> To produce my foot, my each feather:
> Now I hold Creation in my foot.

So what can Hughes mean when he says that "in this hawk Nature is thinking"? Neil Roberts and I have argued that Hughes shows us a creature "rehearsing its own necessary blindness"[14] to the possibility of its own death. The one path of its flight "is direct/Through the bones of the living". The hawk can have no sense of himself in a cycle that includes his own death. The poem illustrates the way the "thinking" of nature in the hawk excludes what human beings can think. The effect is to emphasise the difference between the necessarily limited perception of the hawk and the responsibility of the potentially larger perception of human beings (except when they are being as fascist as a hawk). The implications of difference and responsibility will need to be examined further, but the point to establish here is that Hughes's notion of nature is consistently one that challenges domineering human perceptions of nature. The determination to "cleanse the doors of perception" in anti-pastoral poems persists in Hughes's work well beyond the early poems.

"Glimpse", in Crow, cuts short Crow's trembling pastoral lyric with "the touch of a leaf's edge at his throat".[15] But for Crow, one lesson is not enough, and the desire for the comfort of pastoral is hard to stop:

> Speechless he continued to stare at the leaves
> Through the god's head instantly substituted.[16]

In the *Cave Birds* poem, "A Green Mother", the pastoral idyll of the earth as heaven is given a new slant in the opening suggestion that "The earth is a busy hive of heavens."[17] The dead cockerel protagonist, to whom this is addressed, is introduced to some of the processes at work in this "hive of heavens":

> And here is the heaven of the worm –
> A forgiving God.
> Little of you will be rejected –
> Which the angels of the flowers will gladly collect.

The sort of "god's head" vision of "Glimpse" is undermined here by using the language of that idyllic vision to describe what it tends to ignore: the worm's consumption of dead matter. A number of poems in *Remains of Elmet* show nature reclaiming the sites of failed pastoral ventures. "Lumb Chimneys" finally salvages a positive image out of an unpretty process of industrial decay in which "Nothing really cares. But soil deepens":

> Before these chimneys can flower again
> They must fall into the only future, into earth.[18]

The emphasis of this and other anti-pastoral poems is on the acceptance of the death process everywhere within life. This has led to the accusation that Hughes is preoccupied with the forces of death and violence. It has been true that at times distortions have occurred in the opposite direction and can still occur. *Wolfwatching* opens with the poem "Sparrow Hawk" in which Hughes is guilty of melodramatic overkill in describing this bird as a warrior:

> Those eyes in their helmet
> Still wired direct
> To the nuclear core – they alone
>
> Laser the lark-shaped hole
> In the lark's song.[19]

"Helmet" is a strong visual image, but quite what "the nuclear core" is doing here is unclear and seems to be an over-reaching effect.[20] But what this poem attempts to celebrate is the quiet, delicate presence of a necessary killer at home in the wood, counterbalancing the dove of the last page of the collection. What would later be called "ecology" had already provided Blake with the symbolic imperative that the lamb requires the tiger. Hughes has now taken this imperative further on several fronts, including the practical front which leads from farming to green politics.[21] Further evidence that Hughes has adopted something of Blake's corrosive method of cleansing pastoral perceptions is provided by his public readings from the farming poems in *Moortown*,[22] now collected in *Moortown Diary*. In a new note on the poem "Little Red Twin" Hughes writes: "The bulk of these pieces, I'm aware, concern the nursing if not the emergency hospital side of animal husbandry. All sheep, lambs and calves are patients: something in them all is making a steady effort to die. That is the farmer's impression."[23] It is clear from the last sentence that Hughes is mediating for a non-farming readership.

Some of these poems describe horrific farming procedures. In a note on the poem "Dehorning" he remembers "what a shattering effect the operation had on me, though I am not squeamish".[24] Yet he reads at every public opportunity the poem "February 17th", in which a lamb, strangled in the process of being born, has to have its head cut off in order to save the mother. Such a poem might well have "a shattering effect" on any audience, but on a commercial tape Hughes makes a defence of this practice in his introduction to a reading of the poem: "Once I read this in a hall full of university students and one member of the audience rebuked me for reading what he called 'a disgusting piece of horror writing'. We either have a will to examine what happens or we have a will to evade it."[25] Philosophically this is sound anti-pastoralism. Cosy cultural associations with lambs have been put into the perspective of real tensions between life and death for a sheep-farmer. Only an anti-pastoral propagandist, however, would impose on a live audience proven disturbing material which originates in what the writer himself has obviously found to be a shattering experience. This has indeed been corrosive cleansing for largely urban, poetry-reading audiences.

But if "cleansing" poems have gone alongside "seeing" poems, what is it that is distinctive about Hughes's vision of nature when he has got beyond an anti-pastoral mode of writing? The comprehensiveness of Ted Hughes's poetry can be indicated by six interrelated features, some of which have already been touched upon. These six qualities might provide a definition of what I have called a "post-pastoral poetry". This is not to suggest that Hughes's work is without tendencies in the direction of pastoral, too, at times. So it will be necessary to ask of more recent poetry whether it does not, in some of the *River* poems in particular, slip into pastoral mode. But there is a remarkable consistency in the development of the six key elements of the post-pastoral project of Ted Hughes.

Firstly, then, a central feature of the notion of nature in the best of Hughes's poetry is the dynamic tension of elemental forces. What fascinates Hughes about the otter, for example, is its ability to survive on both land and water, yet it cannot be wholly at home in either element. The otter

> Gallops along land he no longer belongs to;
> Re-enters the water by melting.
> Of neither water nor land.[26]

It is typical of early Hughes poems that he is explicit about the dynamic of processes he wants the reader to perceive in the poem's images:

> The otter belongs
>
> In double robbery and concealment –
> From water that nourishes and drowns, and from land
> That gave him his length and the mouth of the hound.

The paradoxes of binary opposites here analyse a complex series of interactions representing nature as both giving and taking. Survival is not taken for granted. It requires of the otter both robbery and concealment on both land and water which, in their own way, both

"nourish and drown". For all this brilliantly dense suggestion of paradoxes, the poem is strongest when images evoke the mystery of life
outflanking death, as in the lines that follow those above: "He keeps fat
in the limpid integument/Reflections live on." The suggestion here is
that we only see reflections on the surface of a life that "keeps fat"
within what appears limpid.

It is interesting to contrast a more recent poem that celebrates a
life lived in that integument. In "Little Whale Song", from *Wolfwatching*,
the dynamics of nature are presented with a slightly different
emphasis and effect. Whales

> Amplify the whisper
> Of currents and airs, of sea-peoples
> And planetary manoeuvres,
> Of seasons, of shores, and of their own
>
> Moon-lifted incantation, as they dance
> Through the original Earth-drama.[27]

More relaxed, even a little loose ("of seasons, of shores . . ."), this
poem emphasises an interconnectedness that is without threat, until
the poem's last line. Whales represent for Hughes "joy", "bliss",
"peace", "poise" and "the most terrible fall".

"An Otter" ends with a reference to the hounds as just another
image of a "natural" threat. The human responsibility behind this
threat is implicit. But the "fall" of the whale can only be attributable to
human hunters, so this poem ends with an accusation or warning. It
includes the human within nature's dynamics, although in a simple
way, uncomplicated by any sense of "water that nourishes and
drowns". This is both the poem's gain and its loss. The warning is
clear, but it seems to be simply stuck on to the end of the poem, and
not part of "the original Earth-drama" as some sort of death-process
should be, on the evidence of better poems, from "An Otter"
onwards.

When such celebrations exclude the tensions of Hughes's vision
of a creative – destructive universe, they run the risk of becoming
pastoral poems. But "October Salmon" in *River*[28] shows how far
Hughes, at his best, has come in celebrating this central dynamic in a
less urgent, less explanatory way than early poems such as "An Otter".
The poem brilliantly describes the physical state of the dying salmon,
whilst connecting this to changes in seasons, stars and the sea-river,
which gives and takes: "the river reclaiming his sea-metals". So nature

as flux is the constant image. But this is finally brought to a climax centred upon the salmon's "epic poise", a poise which means more in relation to the evidence here than the simple assertion of it in "Little Whale Song":

> The epic poise
> That holds him steady in his wounds, so loyal to his doom, so patient
> In the machinery of heaven.

Of course, the salmon does not choose his patience in his slow death. What Hughes is imagining is a contrast with human options of behaviour in a similar situation. It is, in fact, the dynamic tension of the destructive–creative universe that is being celebrated in the phrase "epic poise": the awareness of this slow death having been "inscribed in his egg", and the irony of the eventual "horrors" of his early home. "With a man it is otherwise", Hughes says explicitly in "Thrushes":

> his act worships itself – while for him,
> Though he bends to be blent in the prayer, how loud
> and above what
> Furious spaces of fire do the distracting devils
> Orgy and hosannah, under what wilderness
> Of black silent waters weep.[29]

The second feature of Hughes's particular combination of post-pastoral notions is that of human consciousness having been allowed to de-nature human nature. Self-consciousness about choice has produced, in "Thrushes", an act that "worships itself". The image is extended here to show a desire to be at one with the act, "blent in the prayer", that is always conscious of the act and therefore, in a sense, outside it. What are taken to be the devils distracting this mental process are, in fact, the suppressed capacities for fuller feeling. They "orgy and hosannah" and they weep in their distorted, repressed forms. This is Hughes's analysis of the underlying theme of Shakespeare's plays.[30] It is also redolent of Blake's "A Poison Tree" and "The Garden of Love".

So whilst Hughes wants to put human beings not only back in touch with their own animal selves, but with the cycles and tensions of a creative–destructive universe, he also recognises that consciousness causes a partial separation from that world. But the advantage of consciousness is conscience. That is, after all, what "Little Whale Song" is appealing to, and the poem, "The Black Rhino",[31] in the same

123

volume, was written to contribute to the preservation of this threatened species. These poems are the result of a logic which began with
"Thrushes" and developed through Crow's discoveries in the
sequence of poems in which outrage transforms compassion into the
beginnings of conscience: "That Moment", "Crow Tyrannosaurus"
and "Crow's Account of the Battle".[32]

Perhaps the best-known feature of Hughes's engagement with
the relationship between human nature and external nature is his
enacting the drama of this tension in poetic myths such as Crow. This
third feature of Hughes's post-pastoral achievement is represented in
Selected Poems 1957–1981 by at least seven mythic sequences, from
Wodwo through Crow and Cave Birds to "Prometheus on His Crag",
"Adam and the Sacred Nine" and "Seven Dungeon Songs". As
Heaney pointed out, the continuing student of anthropology was
well-chosen for the tribal role of Poet Laureate and public myth-
maker.

The function of Crow is to re-examine through this trickster a
range of assumptions taken for granted in our culture. But the hidden
narrative structure hinges upon Crow's search for the female figure
who is his creator. From my recordings of Hughes's public readings
during the 1970s I noted that Hughes generally put it like this: "During
his adventures he begins to wonder who his own creator is and he
encounters various female figures who are avatars of his creator, but
he never recognises her and always bungles the situation."[33] There is
actually one point in the sequence when Crow seems to come close
to defining her: "Crow's Undersong". The title might suggest two
things. Crow sings almost without realising what he is doing, "under
his breath" as it were, running through his mind what he knows of
her so far. The result is a riddle, a tentative "undersong". Secondly,
"Undersong" implies underground and the notion of underground
knowledge on Crow's part, of an underground presence not at home
on the "surface" of the city culture to which the poem refers. She is, in
fact, nature, glimpsed by Crow in all the paradoxes of her creative–
destructive reality: "She comes with the birth push" and "She stays/
Even after life even among the bones."

Decay is her continuity, just as much as procreation, and even if
"she cannot come all the way" into contemporary urban living, it is
her "distracting devils" which, as earlier in "Thrushes", are the sources
of those natural human potentials represented by "hope" and by
"crying". The poem ends:

She has come amorous it is all she has come for
If there had been no hope she would not have come
And there would have been no crying in the city
(There would have been no city)

The tentative emphasis of this poem has been continuously expressed against features of human culture such as instruments, clothes, wheels and houses. Counterbalancing this opposition to human life is an attractive sensuous delicacy and softness in the imagery which culminates in "She has come amorous." Procreation represents hope and the loss of hope results in crying. That crying is both a measure of our awareness of our loss in living in the city and of our potential for changing our alienated way of life. The latter is suggested by the positive act of her coming and the ironic reminder, in parenthesis, that the making of the city was originally an act of hope. Thus the final, tentative suggestion is that humans have both the capacity to still feel their urban alienation from nature and the hopefulness to act creatively to deal with it if they choose.

This subtle idea that nature's processes of decay and re-creation are internalised within human nature as capacities for "crying" and for "hope" is the fourth feature of Hughes's vision of nature. At least three critics feel that Hughes has created important insights into the way humans can perceive their connection with nature in the Epilogue poems from *Gaudete*.[34] Keith Sagar,[35] Len Scigaj[36] and Edward Larrissy[37] each admire the relationship between the speaker and the goddess to whom the poems are addressed. The Reverend Lumb, the speaker, has been a figure literally divided against himself throughout the narrative of *Gaudete* since he is a changeling made of wood. In a rather wooden interpretation of the gospel of Love he has been releasing repressed sexual impulses in a village that seems to be inhabited by stereotypes from "The Archers". When the real Lumb returns from the spirit world to replace the changeling who has been conducting this Dionysian ministry in his place, he brings with him a sequence of poems that loosely trace his engagement with the goddess. "The flaming darkness of the final poem is another occult image of transcendent unity in passionate ardor", writes Scigaj.[38] Passion and the equality of reciprocal unity are precisely the qualities missing from these poems, and from the final one in particular. Lumb glares in darkness and finds that it is aflame. He then realises that he has been acted upon by the goddess who has "come and gone again/With my skin."[39]

With one or two exceptions, the speaker's relationship with the goddess is one of adulation and distanced awe in these poems. Larrissy sees these poems rather differently: "A fundamentally lyric mode, of passionate, singing statement and address, controls clusters of images related to the more general idea of the Goddess, and others related to actual private experience."[40] His case for the latter in very few of the poems is convincing, but that glare is surely too uncomfortable to characterise one who is really at ease in a union with the goddess of nature, the female figure of "Crow's Undersong".

By contrast, the rediscovery of nature by the central figure of *Cave Birds* is symbolised as a marriage to a female figure who might well be that of "Crow's Undersong". Unity of internal and external nature is the central conception of Hughes's less tentative mythic sequence, *Cave Birds*. Like *Crow*, this book is flawed by its narrative structure having been hidden within the sequence itself. In a letter to Neil Roberts and myself Hughes explained that *Cave Birds* was at one point subtitled "The Death of Socrates and his Resurrection in Egypt – with some idea of suggesting that aspect of it which is a critique of sorts of the Socratic abstraction, and its consequences through Christianity to us."[41]

The cockerel protagonist in *Cave Birds* is put on trial for the neglect of his inner natural self. "The hero's cockerel innocence, it turns out, becomes his guilt", Hughes said in the unpublished narrative introduction to the radio broadcast of *Cave Birds* in 1975.[42] "His own self, finally, the innate nature of his flesh and blood, brings him to court."[43] After losing the complacently pastoral way in which he viewed the death-process in the opening poem of the sequence, the hero finally accepts the place of his own death within larger natural processes in "The Knight". He is then ready to be reintroduced to his natural self and regain a state of wholeness. This is achieved through the process described in "Bride and Groom Lie Hidden for Three Days".[44]

In this poem Hughes boldly uses images of machinery to convey a practical sense of the workings of the body in what is essentially an erotic poem moving towards a sexual climax. The delicate use of this imagery suggests the potential for a new symbolic self-awareness and reciprocal awareness through sexuality. The mechanical imagery prevents sentimentality whilst biologically endorsing the symbolism of a marriage of self and nature. Similarly the final image of "two gods of mud" acts in two ways by conveying a sense of ecstatic completeness, as though of a god, which is prevented from any suggestion of transcendence through the context of "mud".

This is the same physical symbolic discovery of wholeness that concludes the sequence called "Adam and the Sacred Nine", collected in *Moortown*.[45] After witnessing the completeness of being of nine sacred birds Adam makes a discovery of his own reciprocal oneness with the material world in a poem spoken by "The sole of a foot" which ends:

> I am no wing
> To tread emptiness.
> I was made
> For you.

The final poem in *Cave Birds*, "The Risen", indicates why the simplicity of the last poem of "Adam and the Sacred Nine" is ultimately not the whole story, and, indeed, why any single poem sequence cannot reach such a concluding completeness as "The Sole of a Foot" appears to do. The latter poem represents the realisation that Adam cannot be an animal or a bird: he must discover his own nature as a human being. But the last words of *Cave Birds* are a "Finale" of two lines:

> At the end of the ritual
>   up comes a goblin.

Self-discovery can never be complete. Not only that, but the dynamic interaction of inner natural self and consciousness continues to create complications.

The resurrection of the hero of *Cave Birds*, "in Egypt" according to Hughes's original sub-title, takes the form of a falcon. The falcon is the hieroglyph for Horus, who is in Hughes's words "beloved child and spouse of the Goddess".[46] What could be more complete? The last lines of "The Risen" are:

> But when will he land
> On a man's wrist.

This is not a question, but a statement. It is an ironic intrusion of a human tendency to want to control nature again. The image is from the human activity of falconry and it is a sudden shattering of the non-human terms of the mythic drama which suggests that, although the cockerel protagonist has achieved the wholeness of this falcon, readers may well have missed the allegorical point and may typically raise this question. To represent it as a statement has the same effect as putting it in inverted commas. So, "at the end of the ritual/up comes a goblin", in this case the old hubris of the desire to harness the wild energy of nature.

The hubris of control and exploitation represented by those last two lines of "The Risen" is exposed in the form of failed economic projects in Remains of Elmet. The "hope" of the economic enterprises of mills and farms is presented in some of those poems, but the dominant force of the collection is of failed attempts to control nature. The major achievement of this book is to convey a sense in which, even in the midst of decline and decay, there is a continuity between external and internal nature, not just in human individuals, but in human culture. Hence the poem title "Dead Farms, Dead Leaves". Perhaps the most effective image of this continuity is the title poem's vision of the Calder valley as a long glacial "gullet", digesting human activity which is itself feeding on successive generations.

This book is linguistically founded upon the fifth feature of Hughes's post-pastoral vision. If culture, individual human life, animal and bird life, and the workings of weather upon landscape are parts of an interactive whole, then it is possible to express this relationship through interchangeable images. The dead farms are the dead leaves of the culture of Calderdale. Walls, in the poem of that name, are "Spines that wore into a bowed/Enslavement".[47] Similarly natural processes can take on an image from human activity: "The hills went on gently/Shaking their sieve."[48] Such linguistic devices indicate a poet confidently at home in the natural world, accepting that the growth and decay of human activity is enacting long-term natural processes.

But perhaps a personal turning-point for Hughes came when he began to write poems in which he was no longer an external observer of this relationship, but a participant in it. A sixth dimension to the nature poetry of Ted Hughes emerged in 1979 with the publication of Moortown and the farming poems already referred to, which were republished separately ten years later as Moortown Diary. In these poems the poet himself takes practical responsibility for nature as a fully conscious, sensitive inhabitant of the natural world.

The anti-pastoral effect of public readings of the poem "February 17th" might detract awareness from that poem's drama of choices for the poet. The line-break of "I went/Two miles for the injection and a razor"[49] is not only a poetic effect; it represents an agonising decision which the poet actually had to make to save the life of one of his sheep. Thus the poem's final image of "the hacked-off head" staring up from the earth represents a lot more than an archetypal vision of death in life. The salutary dimension of this poetry for the academic critic is that the actions that generated these images were not made for poetic effect, but in a real trial actually undertaken by the poet. Readers will, of course, make their own readings of this text, but this is a good example of the oversimplification of Barthes's crude notion of "the death of the author".[50] Applied here it would screen the important element of the author's practical responsibility for nature in a text which is also symbolic, mythic, open to the reader's production of its meaning and ultimately the reader's verdict on both the text and the author.

This dimension of responsibility for nature is further extended by poems which describe the cost of this way of life to farm workers who are "the labourers at earth's furnace/Of the soil's glow and the wind's flash".[51] "A monument" is one of Moortown Diary's concluding sequence of elegies for Hughes's father-in-law and co-worker on the North Devon farm. In a note to this poem Hughes describes the apparent inner experience of the kind of tough job in terrible conditions which the poem evokes only in its external details: "The concentration with which he transformed himself into these tasks, and the rapt sort of delight, the inner freedom, they seemed to bring him – all without a word spoken – gave me a new meaning for the phrase 'meditation on matter'."[52] The poem "A Monument" describes Jack Orchard "in the knee-deep mud of the copse ditch" tightening a wire fence,

> Precise to the tenth of an inch,
> Under December downpour, mid-afternoon
> Dark as twilight, using your life up.[53]

This poem follows one entitled, "The Day He Died", so the reader understands the respect in the title of "A Monument" and the sudden poignancy of the poem's last phrase, "using your life up". In this poem Hughes has come a long way from the images of alienated people in "Thrushes". This poem is about action that does not "worship itself". Jack Orchard's actions reflect not only an animal acceptance of the conditions but a consciousness that, although unspoken, is "Precise to the tenth of an inch". If one wanted to go further, and see consciousness as conscience articulated in a wider responsibility for nature, the Preface to Moortown Diary is a radical attack upon "the EEC Agricultural

Policy War"[54] and the propaganda directed at the agribusiness of "new chemicals, new machinery, more chemicals, new methods, different chemicals, new gimmicks . . .".

In fact as early as 1978 Olwyn Hughes, the poet's sister and agent, informed me that Hughes had written letters to The Times anonymously "on fish stocks and on injecting cattle with steroids".[55] Hughes signed two letters about the threat to salmon in The Times[56] and Trout and Salmon.[57] Before the 1990 election Hughes responded to an invitation for writers to address the next Prime Minister by beginning:

> Dear Premier . . .
> Treat the Environmental cataclysm as a war on all its fronts. In other words, as an emergency, displacing every other concern that stands in its way.[58]

The Guardian of 16 April 1992 carried a photograph of Hughes together with the owner of a stretch of Devon river outside the courthouse in Plymouth after winning a battle against river pollution. So the poet's active responsibility towards nature extends beyond the farmer's accounts in Moortown Diary, the campaign poem "The Black Rhino" in Wolfwatching, and the two 1992 election poems published in The Times.[59]

The latter two poems provoked an outcry that actually undermined the purpose of the poems.[60] One of them, "Lobby Under the Carpet", attempting to convey the information that the chemical industry had caused "a 40% drop/in the sperm count of all Western Males",[61] failed as poetry due to the difficulty of finding an appropriate form. For Hughes this information was an important symptom of large-scale pollution: "What else falls when the sperm count falls?"[62] What we are observing here is the nature poet's attempt to be a green poet – to get his political activity into the poetry that might already be called that of the "Laureate of Nature". The extent of the practical conservation politics of the Poet Laureate has not been widely known, but in a letter referring to "Lobby Under the Carpet" to the present author Hughes reveals the extent of his sense of responsibility:

> The sperm-count detail was first aired in 1982 in a book by John Elkington called The Poisoned Womb (Penguin). The fall in average sperm-count was then 40% since the fifties. I sent a marked copy of the book to Maggie Thatcher in the mid-eighties. She passed it to her advisers and later very scrupulously sent it back. But it wasn't until

last year, 1992, that the detail became a public issue – by which time the count had fallen another 10%. That's 1% per year.

If the human race fails to survive all this it will be because it can't get interested in its own annihilation.[63]

In a recent radio interview Hughes has documented his greening as a poet.[64] Asked by Nigel Forde whether his interest in ecological and conservation issues had changed the way he looked at landscape, animals and poetry, Hughes replied:

It's changed my idea about the world, yes. I first became properly aware of it in the States in 1959. We used to go fishing on Cape Cod. And then, towards the end of 1959, there was an article, there, in a magazine called The Nation, which was a sort of radical little magazine and which used to publish things that couldn't get a hearing anywhere else. It was an account of the dumping of US atomic waste, off Boston, seven days a week, by a commercial dumper who had just simply contracted – with his ordinary dumping licence – to carry this stuff in barrels that would last about 15 years in sea water, out into 30 fathoms of water. Off Boston. This had been going on since 1945. It was then 1959 and the barrels were beginning to break up and the mackerel around Cape Cod were radioactive. They tried to get Kennedy involved and I think he did get involved eventually. But that was my revelation of what was happening.

And simultaneously, of course, Rachel Carson's book Silent Spring came out which suddenly revealed the whole of America as a poisoned land. By the time I came back to England I was aware of all this. And since then I just became very involved in it all. But it's a bad thing in that it spoils the world for you. I've become very involved with these rivers down here. To begin with I wasn't too worried and when I wasn't too aware of it and when these rivers were pretty full of fish they were just paradisal. They were just the most wonderful places. But now I look at these rivers and it's just like looking at a sort of dying relative. You can no longer see them as they were. . . .

Ted Hughes has provided for this book a footnote to Nigel Forde's interview which acts as a case-study of one contemporary poet's active, informed involvement with an aspect of nature over a lifetime. I make no apology for the detail of these quotations. This kind of documentation ought to be appearing now in books concerned with literature and the environment:

I was aware that silage killed fish ever since the 1940s – when I saw its effects on a farm in South Yorkshire. And I was aware of the chemical threat, after *Silent Spring*, and increasingly through the sixties, as we became more informed about its effect on bird life. But through the sixties these rivers seemed to be in good shape. When the salmon disease came – ulcerative dermal necrosis – in 1969, it seemed to have spread from rivers in Ireland, but we suspected the cumulative weakening effects on fish of the increasing chemical load of the rivers. Our main suspect was detergents – but the makers gave that a clean bill. The rivers got into more obvious trouble in the mid- to late seventies, with the farming revolution. By the early eighties we could see the catastrophe – but it was only in 1985, after a terrific battle over the river Torridge, which had been almost wiped out, that the River Authority finally accepted that it was indeed catas- trophe, and began to do something about it. Over this last few years we've been hopeful – and yet, in some essentials, things have got worse. Quite suddenly, for many stretches of rivers, trout have suddenly disappeared. Through and below Exeter, on the Exe, this last year or two, juvenile fish of all kinds are simply not there any more. At the same time, beginning with a court case in which a river fishery owner sued the South West Water Company for polluting his bit of river and won – using Common Law – we've become aware that the cocktail of chemicals are destroying the reproductive ability of the fish . . . . This is only one aspect of the problem. The other is: these fish are simply indicators of what is happening to us. Exeter, for instance, takes all its drinking water from the Exe.

This concern was for me triggered by my experience in the US, but that merely galvanised what I'd already known. From my earliest days I was hooked on fish – but I lived by a river, the West Yorks Calder, that had no life in it at all. Straight industrial effluent. And the Don, in South Yorks, which I expect you've glanced into, was worse. So my greening began you could say with everything that lay about me in my infancy. What focused my ideas maybe was just that devastation.[65]

In the radio interview Hughes frankly confronts his difficulty in writing green poetry: "I've written things about this, you know, I've tried to write sort of semi-protest pieces of verse about this sort of thing, but I don't think it works.[66] It may work as propaganda for a little bit for some people, for some readers, but I don't think it can ever be the real thing."

A notion of "the real thing" needs testing out in readings of some green poems in the next chapter, but it seems that poems with a narrow purpose demand an impossible simplification from a poet whose notion of nature is such a complex one. To summarise what has been deconstructed of Hughes's notion of nature so far, the farmer's practical action has been outlined as the sixth dimension of those integrated features of Hughes's writing which go beyond the anti-pastoral poems in constituting his particular post-pastoral vision. This later poetry accepts a direct responsibility for the welfare of nature. Hughes's vision of a dynamic creative–destructive universe confronts the alienating aspects of consciousness as well as the potentialities of conscience. This is characteristically explored in the poetic dramas of the mythic sequences. In a language of inter-changeable images in, for example, *Remains of Elmet*, connectedness between inner and outer processes has been explored in a cultural as well as an individual dimension.

Without detracting from any of the achievement indicated in the poems already discussed, it is now necessary to confront the prob-lems of the "paradisal" presented by *River*. This collection has been acclaimed by recent Hughes criticism as representing the real height of his achievement, and has stimulated some remarkable critical state-ments. One can read in Craig Robinson's book, *Ted Hughes As Shepherd Of Being*, that in one poem, "fish swim in a religious trance".[67] Len Scigaj, in his first book on Hughes, claimed that in *River* "Hughes follows the river to its source, where riverline meets horizon at a point that vanishes into the transphenomenal."[68] In his second book on Hughes, Scigaj goes even further by suggesting that in *River* "Hughes has constructed a cathedral of ecological vision to show readers how to enliven their imaginations and save our planet."[69] Such claims demand a careful scrutiny of the evidence in the poetry of *River*. Two poems admired by both Robinson and Scigaj are "Salmon Eggs" from *River* and the fishing poem "Earth-Numb" from *Moortown*. Each of these poems, however, presents a different, but equally important, direct contradiction of some of the features already outlined as characteristic of Hughes at his best.

"Salmon Eggs" carries the weight of being placed as the final poem of *River*. It begins well, with something of the mutual giving of "Bride and Groom Lie Hidden for Three Days":

The salmon were just down there –
Shuddering together, touching each other,
Emptying themselves for each other –
Now beneath flood-murmur
They curve away deathwards.[70]

There is a delicacy of perception established in "just", continued in "shuddering" and in "beneath flood-murmur". The sound of the third line quoted enhances the notion of repeated giving in the modulation of vowels from "emptying" to "each" to "other". The notion is similar to that suggested later in the same poem when the river is said to be "undergoing itself/In its wheel". But suddenly Hughes begins to introduce a series of religious images so that a natural process, already beautifully described, is heavily overlaid with religious significance. The salmon's "travail" to produce the eggs that are the subject of this poem becomes, in "raptures and rendings", a glib, formulaic enactment of the Christian notion of sacrifice suggested by "harrowing, crowned". One can see how the poet encourages, in this poem, those critics seeking evidence of transcendental significance in River. But the poem moves towards the river's undialectical statement, "Only birth matters". In his early poems, Hughes's anti-pastoral intentions sometimes produced misrepresentations in the other direction. "Relic", for example, suggested that in the sea, "Jaws/Eat and are finished and the jawbone comes to the beach"[71] without celebrating the life (such as that of "Little Whale Song") which is sustained by the death process. Since the "upbeat poems"[72] of Season Songs,[73] there has been a tendency to distort the creative–destructive dynamic in the more comfortable direction of "Only birth matters". This is the distortion that is characteristic of a pastoral and one has to admit that River contains many poems that are, in fact, as comfortably "coffee-table" as the photographs.

More serious, perhaps, is the problem presented by the fishing poems in River which David Moody has drawn attention to rather dramatically in discussion of the earlier fishing poem in Moortown, "Earth-Numb". In an article linking Craig Raine and Ted Hughes, entitled "Telling It Like It's Not",[74] Moody focuses on the death of the salmon at the end of "Earth-Numb" where it is described as:

Gagging on emptiness

As the eyes of incredulity
Fix their death-exposure of the celandine and the cloud.[75]

Moody writes: "My crude response to that is, 'You bastard!' The refinement of brute sensations into aesthetic effect is offensive if you have a feeling for live salmon and remember that this artist has just killed one, all the while carrying on about his sensations."[76]

The earlier structure of the poem has set up a sense of the

poet/fisherman feeling both threatened and exhilarated in a dangerous, terrifying practice amongst unknown, elemental forces. When the river grabs at him with "an electrocuting malice/Like a trap", he becomes a connector between river and sky, stiff with an electrical charge that is "something terrified and terrifying". Thus the final emergence of this "ghost" is a material image of poignant gain and loss. The last two lines are perhaps intended to produce pathos as the word "incredulity", *pace* Moody, is a projection into the sensations of the salmon. But can arguments about the fisherman respecting the salmon, paying his own dues with awe through his own terror – "killing with good karma" in the manner of an aboriginal hunter, be sustained in the cultural context in which Ted Hughes lives? L. Scigaj's suggestion that Hughes exercises a distinction between necessity and waste cannot be sustained in the case of fishing.[77] This is a leisure activity and could only possibly be an essential food source when he chooses to fish in the Alaskan wilderness.[78] Even then this need not be "essential" for a vegetarian. But Hughes is not a vegetarian poet. His notion of nature is one in which all natural things live off other natural things, in the plant[79] as well as the animal kingdom: "When I want to kill and eat a salmon I sink myself up to the fontanelle in evolution's mutual predation system within which every animal cell has been fashioned . . . When I'm not going to eat it I put it back."[80] Personally, I am convinced by the principle but not by the case. The fishing poems represent unnecessary pastoral exploitations of nature.

Of course, Hughes does not believe in equality between the human species and other species, although Scigaj has attempted to argue that he does.[81] The unease one might feel at Hughes's position as Poet Laureate, with which this chapter began, becomes relevant here. If, as a royalist, Hughes does not believe in social equality within the human species, it would be difficult to sustain an argument for equality between humans and other species.[82] But Hughes does not believe that whales can have responsibility for us, equal to ours for them. His interventions in conservation clearly indicate that, in the unequal capacity in which nature has placed us by developing our consciousness, we have to take some responsibility for the ecology of the planet. In a farming context Hughes has taken that responsibility directly, as he has for the rivers of Devon. Since 1957 Hughes has kept the question of our relationship with nature on the cultural agenda. Indeed, it might not be an exaggeration to say that his nature poetry, in its shifts from anti-pastoral to post-pastoral, has itself influenced the move towards environmentalism for a crucial generation of readers. The long-term importance of the influence of Ted Hughes through the education system on students and teachers might repay study in the future. His writing for children, radio and television talks, involvement in writing competitions, together with his essays, constitute a major cultural intervention for nature.[83] But what is most remarkable is the sustained commitment developed in his poetry to his exploration of our relationship with nature. In the ambitious projects of *Crow*, *Cave Birds*, *Remains of Elmet* and *Moortown* Hughes has pursued that question with more subtlety, power and insight than any other living writer.

One does have to admit that Hughes has failed to escape the cultural contradictions of his time, not least as an ecologically aware royalist, but also in his farming and fishing lifestyles. On the other hand he has used the Laureateship to challenge the establishment on behalf of nature. He is capable of occasional lapses into pastoral poetry, but also of writing a remarkably comprehensive body of post-pastoral poetry. He may not have available the deeply felt social and historical dimensions of the relationship with nature that the *Gaedhealtachd* gives the poetry of Sorley MacLean. He may not seek the personal and contemporary political sensitivity that the Irish context gives Seamus Heaney's use of nature imagery. But these partial contrasts, and reservations about some of the *River* poems, should not distort the main claim made here for the major work of Ted Hughes. The six features identified in this chapter indicate a complex vision of nature that has gone beyond that of other contemporary poets. Like MacLean and Heaney, Hughes has also, at his best, gone far beyond the necessary, but negative, anti-pastoral stance of Patrick Kavanagh. When many of the six features (that I have crudely separated for clarification) work together in a subtle play of tensions, in poems as different as "Crow's Undersong", "Bride and Groom Lie Hidden for Three Days", "February 17th", and "October Salmon", a contemporary post-pastoral poetry is giving us some of its richest food for thought. Art, says Hughes's American counterpart, Gary Snyder, should be "a matter of discovering the grain, a matter of uncovering the intricate and nonsymmetrical order, of the processes that bring about the natural world".[84] The continuing art of Ted Hughes is the most daring and comprehensive attempt at this that we have in poetry now.

Notes

1 "Hughes [in this poem] not only made a graceful gesture but reaffirmed an ancient tradition and re-established without sanctimoniousness, a sacerdotal function for the poet in the realm." *Belfast Review*, No. 10, March–May 1985, p. 6. "The Crow Man as Tribal Poet" was the headline of *The Times* leader, 22 Dec. 1984.

2 The *Observer*, 23 Dec. 1984, p. 7. Now in *Rain Charm For The Duchy and other Laureate Poems*, London: Faber & Faber, 1992, p. 1.

3 London: Faber & Faber, 1983.

4 London: Faber & Faber, 1982.

5 *The Hawk in the Rain*, London, Faber & Faber, 1957, p. 35.

6 ibid., p. 11.

7 Plate 14, W. H. Stevenson ed., *Blake: The Complete Poems*, London: Longman, 1971, p. 114.

8 ibid., p. 214.

9 London: Faber & Faber, 1978.

10 "The Tiger", Stevenson ed., *Blake: The Complete Poems*, p. 214.

11 "Perhaps the poem which has created the most misunderstanding, or which has been most misrepresented, but which is also recognised as one of his finest, is 'Hawk Roosting' . . . The way it has been read, or misread, depending on your point of view, has determined the way much of his later work has been read – or misread." D. Walder, *Ted Hughes*, Milton Keynes: Open University Press, 1987, p. 39.

12 *London Magazine* interview, January 1971, p. 8.

13 *Lupercal*, London: Faber & Faber, 1960, p. 26.

14 *Ted Hughes: A Critical Study*, London: Faber & Faber, 1981, p. 69.

15 *Crow*, London: Faber & Faber, 1970, p. 76.

16 ibid.

17 *Cave Birds*, p. 40.

18 *Remains of Elmet*, London, Faber & Faber, 1979, p. 14.

19 *Wolfwatching*, London: Faber & Faber, 1989, p. 1.

20 A recent study by L. M. Scigaj suggested that "nuclear" referred back to the sun in the previous stanza so that the problem can be avoided by reading thus: "The bird's eyes in 'A Sparrowhawk' . . . are 'wired direct' to the sun's core." *Ted Hughes*, Boston: Twayne, 1991, p. 152. The source of Hughes's over-straining language in this poem is perhaps to be found in a letter to Scigaj stating that in this poem Hughes wanted to suggest "Yeats' poetic self as Cuchulain reincarnated in a bird – a sort of Celtic Horus." ibid.

21 See, for example, "The Black Rhino", *Wolfwatching*, p. 26., "First Things First (An Election Duet performed in the Womb by foetal Twins)" in J. Porritt ed., *Save The Earth*, London: Dorling Kindersley, 1992, p. 192 and "Lobby from Under the Carpet", *The Times*, 9 Apr. 1992.

22 London: Faber & Faber, 1979, pp. 15–67.

23 *Moortown Diary*, London, Faber & Faber, 1989, p. 65.

24 ibid., p. 61.

25 *The Critical Forum: Ted Hughes and R. S. Thomas*, Norwich Tapes Ltd, 1978.

26 *Lupercal*, p. 46.

27 *Wolfwatching*, p. 47.
28 *River*, p. 110.
29 *Lupercal*, p. 42.
30 Argued first in his essay in *A Choice of Shakespeare's Verse*, London: Faber & Faber, 1971, revised edition, 1992 and more fully in *Shakespeare and the Goddess of Complete Being*, London: Faber & Faber, 1992.
31 *Wolfwatching*, p. 26.
32 *Crow*, pp. 18–22.
33 Gifford and Roberts, *Ted Hughes: A Critical Study*, p. 116.
34 London: Faber & Faber, 1977.
35 *The Art of Ted Hughes*, Cambridge University Press, 1975, second edition, 1978, p. 223.
36 *Ted Hughes*, p. 97.
37 *Reading Twentieth-Century Poetry: The Language of Gender and Objects*, Oxford: Blackwell, 1990, p. 135: "They are the first of his poems to address or speak of an Other on the implied basis of relationship, rather than describing or controlling or 'capturing' animals."
38 *Ted Hughes*, p. 100.
39 *Gaudete*, p. 200.
40 *Reading Twentieth-Century Poetry*, p. 136.
41 *Ted Hughes: A Critical Study*, London: Faber & Faber, 1981, p. 260.
42 BBC Radio 3, 23 Jun. 1975.
43 ibid.
44 *Cave Birds*, p. 56.
45 *Moortown*, p. 170.
46 *Ted Hughes: A Critical Study*, p. 260.
47 ibid., p. 33.
48 ibid., p. 56.
49 *Moortown Diary*, p. 30.
50 *Image-Music-Text*, London: Fontana, 1977, p. 143.
51 *Moortown Diary*, p. 34.
52 ibid., p. 67.
53 ibid., p. 55.
54 ibid., p. ix.
55 Unpublished interview, 1 Sept. 1978.
56 13 Aug. 1985.
57 July 1988.
58 *The Guardian*, 16 Aug. 90.
59 See note 21 above.
60 See D. J. Taylor's article "Keeping The Metre Running" in *The Guardian*, 20 Apr. 1992 and letter of 27 Apr. 1992.
61 "Lobby Under The Carpet", *The Times*, 9 Apr. 1992.
62 Letter to the present author, 17 Dec. 1993.
63 ibid.
64 "Bookshelf", BBC Radio 4, 20 Mar. 1992.
65 Letter to the present author, 17 Dec. 1993.
66 "I think the bits and pieces I had in my mind were odd verses I never published, or the piece in *Three Books* [London: Faber & Faber, 1993] titled

"1984 On 'The Tarka Trail' ", another titled "If" in the same book, and yes, the two *Times* pieces." Letter of 17 Dec. 1993.

67 London: Macmillan, 1989, p. 205.

68 *The Poetry of Ted Hughes*, University of Iowa Press, 1986, p. 290.

69 *Ted Hughes*, p. 144.

70 *River*, p. 120.

71 *Lupercal*, p. 44.

72 Hughes's description of them on the Norwich tape.

73 London: Faber & Faber, 1975.

74 *The Yearbook of English Studies*, p. 166–178.

75 *Moortown*, p. 96.

76 *The Yearbook of English Studies*, p. 176.

77 In Keith Sagar ed., *The Challenge of Ted Hughes*, London: Macmillan, 1994, p. 171.

78 See "Gulkana" in *River*, p. 78.

79 See "A Vegetarian" in *Wodwo*, p. 30.

80 Letter to the present author, 16 Jan. 1994.

81 After admitting that Hughes does not believe in "absolute equality", Scigaj then claims that Hughes does believe in "interspecies equality" before going on to praise the fishing poems in *River*, in *The Challenge of Ted Hughes*, p. 175.

82 I owe the essence of this sentence to Neil Roberts in an open discussion of Leonard M. Scigaj's paper at the conference which produced *The Challenge of Ted Hughes*, Manchester University, July 1990.

83 For the latest example of this see *Sacred Earth Dramas: An anthology of winning plays from the 1990 competition of the Sacred Earth Trust*, London: Faber & Faber, 1993.

84 "Nature Writing", *Resurgence*, No. 163, p. 29–30.

7
Many green voices

IF NOTIONS of nature are socially constructed this is as much true for criticism as creativity and for a "literary ecocriticism" as much as for the poetry it criticises. Criticism, like poetry is, as Heaney said of *The Great Hunger*, "of its own place and time". I have argued in Chapter 1 that in the exhilaration of freedom created by literary theory in the last decade, the ability to value freedom itself, or justice, or continuities in anything, including nature, has been rendered theoretically suspect. This book has been asking which notions of nature we should value in poetry, accepting the theoretical position that values are being used daily in relation to the environment and that therefore we had better have some analysis of those we are reading and some criteria for making distinctions between them, however provisional.

In our own time there has grown an increasing concern for the injury we are doing to the natural world in which we live. We now recognise that our construction of nature as unproblematic beauty has for too long been separate from our rapacious economic exploitation of nature (including sections of human nature). Nowhere is this separation of aesthetics from economics better illustrated in practice than in the quarrying that takes place within our National Parks. Of course, we use motorways to experience nature in National Parks where the hills are being destroyed in order to provide motorways. But paradoxes such as this also exist on a global scale as the "first world" exploits the natural resources of the "third world" that sustain life on the planet itself. The social construction of nature as "ecology" has prompted a better informed concern for our effects upon the planet that is our home. It is widely agreed that it is currently our best construction of nature since it makes us accept our part in a dynamic ecosystem. Literary criticism should also be informed by science and apply that learning with what appears to be the best rigour of clarification available at the time. To call this "literary ecocriticism", as Jonathan Bate does,[1] risks inviting another fashionable conformity. All criticism that discusses literature and the environment should learn from and clarify the implications of ecology. When Bate suggests that Clare's "language that is ever green" must be reclaimed in our reading of Wordsworth,[2] there is an implication that this language is both unproblematically recognisable and in need of reclamation from disuse. This chapter will demonstrate further that a great variety of green languages are alive and well. It will also extend the question that has been pursued through the previous chapters: "Which green language?"

What, then, have emerged as the criteria for valuing one "green language" rather than another? What notions of nature in poetry have been endorsed, despite the flaws and the reservations, in the foregoing chapters? Three key words have been used repeatedly in valuing much of the poetry of these writers: "connection", "commitment" and "responsibility". These words have been defined in relation to specific poems. Usually all three qualities have come together in the poetry that has been most valued. Often this has been achieved by a recognition that each of these qualities expresses something that is problematic. Patrick Kavanagh's expression of frustration, for example, turns out to be the characteristic contemporary experience: some sense of disconnection is felt whilst knowing that unity with external nature is possible. When an engaged commitment is made to either work, or place, or inner energies in relationships, a responsibility for nature can, in turn, make a recognition of connectedness. Hughes's poem "Bride and Groom Lie Hidden for Three Days" has been claimed to be a fine example of this. What this poem also illustrates is that the notion of connectedness that has been valued here is always an interactive one. Human beings are in a continuously active relationship with a dynamic natural world. Inner natural forces in the writer or the persona of the poem are seen as themselves a part of the external natural cycles and the continuous dynamics of a creative–destructive universe. Poetry which suggests static notions of nature and of our relationship with it tends towards pastoral. Thus what might have been claimed to be the green language of George Mackay Brown, as his own use of the phrase "the green fable"[3] implies, has been shown to be recreating the lie that simple unchanging cycles govern rural life.

So if one can be explicit in general terms about the notion of nature that underpins the best nature poetry examined so far, to what extent can this be found in the many other contemporary voices that might be described as in some ways using Clare's "language that is ever green"? What other poets are really writing further versions of pastoral and what other poets, in their best work, reach beyond the closed circuit of pastoral/anti-pastoral poetry?

Peter Redgrove has made it his life's work to explore the possibilities of a "green language". Redgrove's particularly idiosyncratic poetry attempts to articulate often unconscious connections between inner and outer nature. Some poets have used images of external nature to mirror tensions in their own nature. Sylvia Plath is the obvious example, but others, such as the Welsh poet Christine Evans, also deploy the notion of nature as mirror. For a quietly growing group of rock-climbing poets their hands-on engagement with nature provides a practical meeting-place for inner and outer nature. Poetry about mountains then raises the wider question of what notions of nature underlie the poetry of place. Culture is located in a poetry of place for Heaney and MacLean in particular, but what notions of nature have been introduced into British poetry by the self-displaced poets from the Caribbean and from Asia? What might the "green languages" of Grace Nichols, John Agard and Debjani Chatterjee, for example, bring to the current debate? Finally, Ted Hughes has raised the question of how successful didactic or campaigning green poetry can be at its best. What, for example, is the meaning of the *Whale Nation*[4] phenomenon which has linked words and images on page, stage and TV screen? These questions indicate the scope of the present chapter.

Writing in 1987, Terry Eagleton observed that Peter Redgrove "was for long England's leading ecological poet *avant la lettre*, and has now had the pleasure of seeing the letter catch up with him".[5] Neil Roberts, in a recent study of Redgrove's work, puts the following gloss on Eagleton's statement: "His poems have not been made into high-profile green statements like Heathcote Williams's *Whale Nation* or Ted Hughes's 'Black Rhino' but he, more than anyone writing in England, is entitled to be named the poet of Gaia, whom he calls the Black Goddess."[6]

Such claims might suggest that Redgrove's poetry deserved a major chapter in this book. The gap between these claims, Redgrove's intentions and the actual achievements of the poetry therefore requires clarification. In Chapter 1 I referred to Redgrove's pursuit of invisible forces in the natural world through an examination of images of the Black Goddess in his book of that name. What Roberts is claiming is that Redgrove adopts a particularly interconnected approach to the making of a poem that reflects the very notion of Gaia,[7] and himself as a part of the organism of Gaia:

> What I particularly wish to emphasise is that this is not merely a "thematic" element. The body of the language, the method of composition, the metaphorical and syntactical structure, testify to a subject that is not an onlooker, externally in command of the world and experience, but more akin to Julia Kristeva's "sujet en procès" (in process/on trial). The narrative dynamic of dream, or "active imagination", which structures many of the poems, shifts and dissolves the subject in ways that dramatise the play between the ego, the Jungian "self" and nature.[8]

This helps to explain the characteristic features of Redgrove's later poetry, such as "The Big Sleep", the final poem in *Poems 1954–1987*.[9] This poem links the rhythms of the sea with, firstly, the pull of bees towards honey, then the magnetic forces of the earth, the pull of the moon, the effects of weather on dreams, and, finally, patterns of procreation. The lack of conventional syntactical links creates a sense of all these forces shifting together simultaneously, but within a pattern that is contained by references to a giant clock. The poem begins:

> Sea, great sleepy
> Syrup easing round the point, toiling
> In two dials, like cogs
>
> Of an immense sea-clock,
> One roping in, the other out.
> Salt honey, restless in its comb,
>
> Ever-living, moving, salt sleep,
> Sandy like the grains at eyes' corners
> Of waking, or sleepiness, or ever-sleeping.[10]

What opens as a series of descriptive images of the sea shifts in the third stanza to suggest a presence "at the eyes' corners" of three different states. And what might be assumed to be human or organic states in "waking, or sleepiness" clearly shift into a rather different dimension in the third state of "ever-sleeping". Are these states to be perceived as different or the same? What does it mean for "ever-

143

living, moving, salt sleep" to be a presence "at the eyes' corners" of all three states? One suspects that such questions are too conventionally "rational" for the mode of Redgrove's poems, which Roberts characterises as "the 'logic', or more accurately the narrative grammar, of dream".[11]

In a letter to Neil Roberts, Redgrove described three "modes" in his poetry:

> I begin to distinguish three modes of poetry in my own work, and am looking at this in others'. I call the schema, not entirely facetiously, "The Poet's Favorite [sic] Day".
>
> The three modes are "The Lover"; "The Dreamer"; "The World". The pattern is that the poet makes love, and that is one kind of poem; he falls asleep and dreams after making love, and that is another kind of poem; he wakes after this sleep and sees the world with rinsed senses, or cleans'd perceptions, and that makes the third kind of poem. (16 Apr. 1983)[12]

Roberts suggests that "the three modes are more characteristically present in a single poem (note that it is only the third kind that the poet actually 'makes', out of a vision provided by the other two)".[13] Actually the pattern seems to be in reverse in "The Big Sleep" which begins with visionary images and proceeds through dreams before concluding with the erotic touching of waters from which "a bone begins to grow". If one allows that the rather "literal" textual questions raised earlier are inappropriate to the poetic mode of holistic "cleans'd perception",[14] the question of the identity of the female figure referred to in the poem is too strong to be ignored. She has been identified in the poem as "the big one" whose dreaming or storming affects the inhabitants of Falmouth. So the female figure appears to be the Goddess, Gaia, the internally interactive, self-regulating organism that is the planet Earth. But what has been controlling everything in the first half of the poem has been a giant clock, which has become "the big one". So the notion of Gaia underlying this poem is a remarkably fatalistic, one-way interaction which is totally controlling. Redgrove appears to be content, even amused with this notion of nature.[15] If, in *The Great Hunger*, Patrick Kavanagh is a poet of pessimistic fatalism, in "The Big Sleep" Peter Redgrove is a poet of optimistic fatalism.

The problem with "The Big Sleep", which represents the problem with Redgrove's *oeuvre*, is that, having suggested connections which are in themselves obviously potent and important, he cannot be made accountable for having said anything *about* them, for his work apparently requires the suspension of the very mode that might evaluate his explorations: rational discussion of what his poetry implies about its subject.

In what terms, for example, can one sympathetically suggest that the image of a clock was always going to imply a deterministic Gaia by the end of the poem? How can one challenge "the logic of dream"? In his prose studies Redgrove seeks to help readers accommodate themselves to external natural patterns and rhythms. This assumes a degree of human choice.[16] But the ending of "The Big Sleep" presents human procreation as simply one of "her accustomed patterns".

Ultimately the poem has nowhere to go because it is only making links, not exploring them. Under the cover of humour, in the visual image of women pregnant with "a big drop . . . in their bellies", a shift is made from small-scale genetics to large-scale evolution in order to get back to the opening of the poem. But this circular pattern is to be understood as "dreaming" and originates from a figure who is now mythologised as "the Dreamer", on the internal evidence as much for the poet as for the women in the poem. What appears to be, by the last line of the poem, a circle of links, has in fact been a straight line from a "source": "the Dreamer". The notion of nature at work here is ultimately a very limited un-interactive one.

By now it will be clear that, in my view, with a few exceptions in the early work,[17] Redgrove's poetry does not live up to the expectations raised by his prose. Indeed, "The Big Sleep" illustrates the way in which the shifting structure of "the logic of dream" can result in a poem which actually achieves the opposite of what is being claimed for Redgrove as "the poet of Gaia". It must be said that Redgrove is at least attempting, with a carnivalesque spirit, to explore an aspect of nature that is necessarily the most difficult to articulate in poetry. His may be a case for defining the limits of criticism.

In a poem which uses a number of remarkably similar images and ideas (moon, sleep, nightmare and procreation), Gillian Clarke weaves in "The Hare" a more subtle sense of relationship between inner and outer nature. Ultimately it is one that also provides a clarification of the differences and similarities between people, in contrast to the Falmouth automata of "The Big Sleep".

Gillian Clarke swims with seals[18] and is powered by wind![19] She is a maker of original images for the elements and of musical poems that celebrate the Welshness, in voice and place, of her experience of those elements. "Neighbours",[20] a poem about the fall-out from Chernobyl having linked Welsh communities with other European communities through shared concerns, indicates that she is not narrowly parochial. A European dimension informs her strong cultural location, as it does Sorley MacLean's.

"The Hare" is the most powerful poem in her latest collection, Letting in the Rumour.[21] It is a poem in which a connection with the rhythms of the moon brings her closer to her fellow-poet, Frances Horovitz, who died of cancer in 1983 and to whose memory the poem is dedicated. "The Hare" describes how the two women went out of a house late at night to investigate a cry they first thought to be a baby's, but realised that it was a hare caught by a fox or a trap. The darkness in which they had, in the previous stanza, felt calmly at ease, has been turned into something "terrible".

The experience of the natural world through darkness is important to Redgrove's emphasis on our physical and emotional reconnection with the dynamics of nature. His intention is to expand our conception of nature, especially in our directly sensuous and "extrasensuous perception"[22] of it. His early poem "Without Eyes"[23] characterises his belief that knowledge can be gained through the heightened senses of working in darkness. In Gillian Clarke's poem darkness provides a less comfortable, more ambiguous experience of the natural world than that of "The Big Sleep".

Darkness in "The Hare" contains both peace and suffering. This is important not only because it brings the women together in their guilty wakefulness, but because it anticipates the suffering of Frances Horowitz, whose memory, the writer says at the end of the poem, "can calm me still". This duality is held, in the final images of the poem, to offer, as it were, icons of understanding for that death and that calm:

> At your great distance you can calm me still.
> Your dream, my sleeplessness, the cattle
> asleep under a full moon,
> and out there
> the dumb and stiffening body of the hare.

The image of the full moon refers back to a personal link between the two women established earlier in the poem:

Then, that joke we shared, our phases of the moon.
"Sisterly lunacy" I said. You liked
the phrase. It became ours.

This in turn is associated with the references to mothering in the
poem that come to a poignant climax in the lines:

Even in dying you
menstruated as a woman in health
considering to have a child or no.

Thus the poem reverberates beyond the moving personal relationship – the closeness of two women who are actually "Different/as
earth and air" – to recognise that the dualities of calmness and
suffering, and of mothering and dying, are woven not only within
female experience but in the whole of nature. Gillian Clarke's achievement is to have implicitly constructed this notion of nature through
the accumulating associations of her images. It is thus a poetic discovery rather than an illustration of a theory as "The Big Sleep" appears
to be.

Gillian Clarke draws upon images of nature to give meaning to the
events, processes and tensions in her life. In many ways this is the
most common use of nature in contemporary poetry and one might
have examined this in the work of say, Anne Stevenson[24] or Michael
Longley.[25] Fraser Harrison was quoted in Chapter 1 as offering a lucid
explanation for the importance of nature symbolism in helping us
"keep up our courage in the face of our mortality and vulnerability to
suffering".[26] Perhaps the best example of this poetic process has been
the work of Seamus Heaney, whose understanding of politics, love
and his role as a writer are worked out through a major body of nature
poetry. Many other poets in our time use nature in order to "decentre"
their own natural inner tensions. The work of another Welsh poet,
Christine Evans, provides a problematic example of this.

Christine Evans repeatedly enters into darkness with her son to
search for Halley's Comet in the long poem which gives the title to her
third collection, *Cometary Phases.*[27] This leads to the discovery of a
number of links between herself and nature, but ultimately what she
learns from nature is that, as a mother, she must let her son go: "Once
core, I grow towards husk."[28] In this poem she makes seven nocturnal
reflections, from November to April, on both the comet and her
twelve-year-old son, whose fascination with it she shares. Really that

fascination is for the darkness that is teeming with life and with death, on a time-scale that is quite different from the domestic time-scale of the sequence. It is to be understood in two ways in this poem: that of explicit knowledge represented by quantum physics, space exploration, "Tomorrow's World", which has also given us air pollution and dumpsites that "glow and tick";[29] and intuitive knowledge that is sensitised by being, in Redgrove's term, "without eyes". It is the combination of the perspectives derived from the former and the values derived from the latter that enables the writer to end the poem with the achievement of "some old clutching having been let go".[30]

This might appear, from such a summary, to be a characteristic contemporary "green poem" in the domestic sense of a mother sharing with her son a scientific curiosity whilst also being aware of the long-term dangers of pollution and radiation. The problem is that this particular "green language" is merely token in the poem. The battle between scientific and intuitive perspectives in the sequence has been described by Linden Peach as "the tension between 'centred' and 'decentred' perspectives on time".[31] The weakness of the sequence lies in the stasis of that tension. There is an intellectual failure to do more than juxtapose scientific and intuitive knowledge derived from these two perspectives. Attempts to bring them into a unified vision result in the trite simplicity of:

> we are all – Caligula
> the singing whale, ingenious quick
> bacterium or bristlecone
> petals on the same bright flower
> dying and sprouting
> in the same warm working dark.[32]

To simply say that we are living in the same working world as whales or bacterium is to take our understanding no further, but to grasp for what is called a few lines later, "a kind of consolation".

Sylvia Plath, on the other hand, rejects all easy consolations. When she appears to find them they actually entail great risks, such as confrontation with her own death. With characteristic daring and wit she "centres" or projects her inner tensions on external nature, using nature as a mirror to look deeper into herself. The poem "I Am Vertical", for example, echoes, in her different voice, the frustration of *The Great Hunger* that is dominated by alienation, yet knows that in death there will be an ultimate and ironic unification with nature. The poem's title is also its first line:

I Am Vertical

But I would rather be horizontal.
I am not a tree with my root in the soil
Sucking up minerals and motherly love.[33]

It is characteristic of Plath to alliterate from "minerals" to
"motherly love", claiming that only a tree receives the latter
"naturally", as it were. The other "verticals" in nature are better off than
she is. This poem refuses Fraser Harrison's suggestion that living with
a tree must necessarily help us "keep up our courage in the face of our
mortality".[34] The "I" in this poem cannot love nature because her
consciousness alienates her from it. Her conclusion is that death will
be her most "natural" state and will connect her at last to trees and
flowers: "I shall be useful when I lie down finally." The practical and
playful "touch" of the trees' roots is expressed in a similar tone to one
of the lines about Maguire's death in The Great Hunger: "He'll know the
names of the roots that climb down to tickle his feet."[35] For all the
explicit earnestness of Christine Evans's poem, there is nothing that
matches this ironic sense of final organic connection with the external
natural world. That is because those roots are moving, reaching representatives of interactive processes, rather than simply being, in Evans's
words, "petals on the same bright flower".

The power of "I Am Vertical" lies in its bold exaggeration of the
central problem of the human species' relationship with nature,
which has recurred throughout this study: human consciousness,
which perhaps defines our species, seems, at the same time, to
separate us from the rest of nature. It is a problem to which poets have
found at least a working resolution if, like Wordsworth, they have
recognised that the human brain is itself a product of nature as has
been shown in Chapter 5. Sylvia Plath's resolution of the problem is to
choose death in this poem. That choice is already implicit in the poet's
initial preference for the "horizontal". All references to nature that
follow in the poem are used to mirror that inner state. In other poems
Plath makes different choices.

Although she is not usually thought of as speaking "a language that
is ever green", Sylvia Plath's inner states are continually projected on
to socially constructed images of nature. Bats, blood and stars, for
example, are recurrent images which carry socialised associations that
are played upon in the dramatic explorations of her poems. In the
later poem "Nick and the Candlestick",[36] Plath the mother chooses

149

her son to represent a future potential that can outflank the negative natural forces evoked in the poem by images such as "black bat airs" that "wrap" Plath herself. The horror associated with the "blooming" of blood is outflanked here by the strength of kinship and the new start the child offers. The force of motherly love in this poem is both celebrated and let go. The poem ends:

> You are the one
> Solid spaces lean on, envious.
> You are the baby in the barn.

The "one/Solid spaces lean on" is in obvious contrast to the final image of "I Am Vertical", although the implications for Plath herself, still suffering the "pain" in this poem, have not necessarily changed.

Because Plath uses nature imagery to externalise her inner life and because she dramatically examines the social construction of meaning in that imagery, there is implicit in her poetry a remarkable diversity of notions of nature. In the poem "Child", written thirteen days before her death, she is capable of a desperate sentimentality in images such as "Little/Stalk without wrinkle".[37] It is perhaps worth noting that in the manuscript[38] drafts Plath was struggling to set this image of innocence against a final image of a sky devoid of, not of a single star, as Hughes inserted in the published version, but of a whole universe. Hughes's final line, "Ceiling without a star" is not one of the alternatives she considered. After crossing out "moon and planets" she has actually left uncorrected the words "with no constellations". It is a small change, but one which has so far gone unobserved and which adds to the current concern about the history of the editing of Plath.[39] To be without constellations is to be without other living universes rather than just a single star.

The better known case of the editing of Ariel[40] provides a last example of the diversity of Plath's use of nature images to be considered here. Her own plan was to end the collection with the bee sequence, and with the poem "Wintering" in particular.[41] This would have concluded a sequence (and a collection) of daring self-examination with the tentative natural potential for regeneration in the following lines:

> Winter is for women –
> The woman, still at her knitting,
> At the cradle of Spanish walnut,
> Her body a bulb in the cold and too dumb to think.

Will the hive survive, will the gladiolas
Succeed in banking their fires
To enter another year?
What will they taste of, the Christmas roses?
The bees are flying. They taste the spring.[42]

Here, of course, Sylvia Plath does "take courage" from her particular construction of bulbs and bees. Sadly her inner nature (and the interrelated social tensions[43]) could not ultimately be healed by the explorations of self through images of external nature. The mirrored implications of her construction of nature in "I Am Vertical" finally overwhelmed that at the end of "Wintering".

A positive attitude towards nature is essential to the survival of a number of poets who physically explore their own inner nature by direct contact with elemental forces. Rock-climbing poetry is a sub-genre that has so far escaped critical attention. This group of poets publish their climbing poems alongside other kinds of poetry: David Craig,[44] Alison Fell,[45] Graham Mort[46] and Libby Houston,[47] for example. This is a form of nature poetry that has a long tradition going back to Wordsworth and "the first piece of climbing literature in English"[48] which describes an engagement with nature that must have been made by children ever since the human species lived under steep rocks. Then, collecting the eggs of cliff-nesting birds will have been for food, rather than for money as it was for the young Wordsworth:[49]

> Oh! When I have hung
Above the raven's nest, by knots of grass
And half-inch fissures in the slippery rock
But ill sustain'd, and almost, as it seem'd,
Suspended by the blast which blew amain,
Shouldering the naked crag. . . . [50]

David Craig has suggested that "at such points Wordsworth was taking poetry over a watershed into new mental country".[51] The direct experience of needing to literally read nature in those "half-inch fissures in the slippery rock" is a mental and also an emotional discipline which Wordsworth's poetry is celebrating here for the first time. Nature poetry has no exact precedents by which to construct the meaning of this physical way of learning from nature.

On the larger scale of "reading" mountains, later Romantic poets were to take on the challenge of "Thinking like a Mountain".[52] Their

work and that of climbing poetry up to 1960 is probably best represented in Wilfred Noyce's *The Climber's Fireside Book*.[53] But in the last two
decades, the more macho culture of climbing publishing has been
highly suspicious of climbing poetry. The reasons for this I have
explored elsewhere.[54] Nevertheless, despite the equal suspicion of
non-climbing poetry reviewers,[55] a small number of books con-
taining climbing poems have recently been published.[56] At the 1991
International Festival of Mountaineering Literature, seventeen British
climbing poets were invited to read.[57] Among them was a young poet
whose climbing poems might be taken to represent an interesting
point of development in this form of nature poetry.

Kym Martindale's poetry is the opposite of macho, not because it
describes women climbing, but because the acceptance of inner fears
leads, through tuning in to the rock, to a sensitivity towards the whole
of nature. In "The Climber and the Moth", the dialectic of climber and
rock is echoed in the formal juxtaposition of the story of the climber
against the death of a moth:

> She starts up the green tainted rock,
> Soothes her fears with the cool mechanics
> Of placing protection
> And feeling slick, hauls into another climb.
>
> > The moth lies dead and perfect,
> > pinned out in the mud,
> > a delicate death
> > between the massive ruts
> > of bootprints.[58]

That last line just hints at humans trampling over the natural
world, unaccommodated and uncaring. Some of them are probably
climbers, their bootprints having given them away as they
approached the crag. Meanwhile, this climber finds that she is having
difficulty tuning in to nature: "Again and again she sinks back/To read
the rock." What this actually means is described with an alert sense of
integration with the forces of nature: "thrusting" her hands into a
rock-form she pulls and

> Suddenly the move is clear;
> She eases into dips and shallows,
> In the footsteps of wind and rain,
> And finally holds the top.

Leaping and scrambling the descent,
Hands burning, tender from the scrape of rock,
She only just avoids,
With pleasure in her quick delicacy,
Crushing a dead, white moth.

The form has held the story of the moth separate on the page from that of the climber, but when they coincide in the poem's last line, the moth is used to indicate just how the climber's physical alertness to nature has also become a moral one. She avoids the moth, offering respect for it even though it is dead, with conscious "pleasure in her quick delicacy". A subtle suggestion of caring beyond the self carries this poem away from any suspicion of embarrassing hedonistic self-indulgence that might be feared by editors of the climbing press. This delicate poem, from a then unpublished poet, was actually written on a creative writing course which explored in writing the experience of rock-climbing.[59] It is a small indication of the value that the recent cultural development of residential writing courses could have for the future of nature poetry. But this poem was the beginning, not the peak of Kym Martindale's poetic development. A poem written a year later brought a feminist perspective to bear on the social construction of the climbing experience. This poem was written for a writing competition, indicating that another increasingly popular cultural development can have a significance for the production of not only new poetry, but in this case at least, nature poetry that does new things.

The 1991 competition launched by *High* magazine invited a retelling of a climbing event under the appalling title "High was there".[60] Martindale's poem is written in the voice of an old African woman who remembers watching in her youth the making of a film called *Seo* featuring climbing by the French woman, Catherine Destivelle. The most impressive parts of this film show unroped climbing above a village in Mali. The poem "Caterina of the Rocks"[61] makes a myth for an oral culture out of the significance of the event for this watching woman. It begins by planting the following idea in the process of denying it:

It is no myth: listen child, to me,
I saw the white woman climb.
Slow dancer on the rocks,
On this monster cliff ending in the sky.

The speaker sees this climber as a creature in her element:

> And she inched like a snake on its prey,
> Into the folds and seams and up.

But the significance of this amazing achievement, for the woman watching, is an empowering one. The poem quietly suggests that a woman in tune with nature can achieve an inner power that may be denied her in a patriarchal society. The poem ends with the village's celebration feast for the French woman:

> Then we feasted and sang.
> The men put on their costumes and danced,
> But their hearts were small and their feet were dead.
> She shrank their hearts.
> But we swayed and called
> Tall into the nights and days.
> Yes, child, she came, the white woman who climbed to climb,
> Who needed no-one but herself.
>
> Down the years of toiling,
> Of bearing boys who want to be men,
> When my back and heart ache,
> I dream that day again,
> Eyes closed,
> My hand still on the warm rough stone.

The ambiguity of the last line is itself a subtle celebration of the link between the speaker, the climber and the rock. The speaker has become the climber, taken something of her strength, in reliving the experience. At the same time she has become "stilled" in herself as a result of understanding the experience of connecting with "warm rough stone". Outer and inner nature have been linked to create something that is parallel to the knowing "calm" at the end of Gillian Clarke's "The Hare". The notion of nature constructed in these two poems by Kym Martindale is more engaged and life-enhancing than those of Christine Evans or Sylvia Plath in the sense that she achieves a more healing combination of connection and responsibility. Ironically this is achieved through a commitment to facing the experience of possible physical disconnection from external nature!

If the "green voices" of rock-climbing poets spring from a tactile experience that tests their ability to "read" nature, both in themselves and in the steepest places, the poetry which focuses particularly on place should be able to "read" and reflect the individual qualities and tensions of that place. Each of the previous chapters has produced interesting examples of the mediated "green voices" of place. The cultural constructions of nature in place have always been reflected in nature poetry, as the earlier quotations from Pope, Goldsmith, Crabbe and Clare have shown. But in recent years there have been two developments which deserve special attention. One is an extension of the Romantic fascination for mountains and the other is the critical and creative case made for "a poem that is like a place" by Jeremy Hooker.[62]

The cultural identity invested in the nature of a place, and the desire for visitors to make meaning out of nature in that place, has recently produced a number of anthologies that are each collections of regional nature poetry.[63] Among these, *The Lake District*,[64] *Poems of the Scottish Hills*[65] and *The Poetry of Snowdonia*[66] indicate that mountains have a particular importance in contemporary British poetry.[67] The large anthology of mountain poetry, *Speak to the Hills*,[68] contains over 600 poems by more than 300 writers, most of them living, and many of them publishing elsewhere. Clearly since the "bourgeois invention" of the Lake District, as Auden put it, mountains have continued to attract poets in particular. To explore the reasons for this would be to begin another book which would have rich material to reflect upon. Certainly part of the popular meaning of mountains is as escape and much of the poetry in *Speak To The Hills* and *Poems of the Scottish Hills* is indeed in the escapist pastoral mode.

One of the most popular contemporary Scottish poets who is well known throughout the rest of Britain, and writes about the mountains of the north-west of Scotland, is Norman MacCaig. For his eightieth birthday Chatto & Windus published his *Collected Poems*[69] and there appeared the inevitable *Critical Essays*[70] from Scottish academics in generous mood. Jack Rillie's review essay[71] of the latter is a good example of the way in which what elsewhere might be regarded as weaknesses in the poetry become the indicators of MacCaig's achievement. "A preference for nouns over adjectives, or metaphors",[72] which Rillie accepts as a feature of MacCaig's poetry, is admired because "he may rend metaphor and demand the world in its selfhood – glacier, water, bread, wood ... reference unjeopardised".[73] In fact, despite a few poems of whimsical uncertainty about his relationship to the natural world,[74] his poetry celebrates the unproblematic relationship of an escapist to "glacier, water, bread, wood". In MacCaig's poetry these doubts and celebrations are the two sides of the same pastoralist coin: his poetry fails to transcend the reality of his working in Edinburgh and his holidaying at his cottage in Assynt. The definitive example of MacCaig's form of escapism is "The Pass of the Roaring" where "The tall cliffs unstun my mind./Thank God for a place where no history passes."[75] Whilst "unstun" is an unusually effective verb, it is undone by the following line which reveals it to be part of an escapist process. The perverse idea that there is no history in what is likely, in this poem, to be Sutherland can only come from an escapist weekender.[76] This suspicion is confirmed in the final stanza:

> There's always a returning. A cottage glows
> By a dim sea and there I'll slump by the fireside –
> And another grace will gather, from human
> Intercommunications, a grace
> Not to be distinguished from the one that broods
> In fingerling waters and gulfs of space.

The effect of "tall cliffs" in "unstunning" the mind has merely resulted in this ahistorical "slump" into the "grace" of the north-west Highlands.

One has to admit that pastorals such as this tend to dominate the anthologies of mountain poetry. Those contemporary poems which come close to finding the sharp sense of meaning in mountains that is achieved by Sorley MacLean's "The Cuillin" are poems of active engagement such as Kym Martindale's. It seems to be the case that currently, as far as mountains are concerned, poems about climbing them are more successful than landscape poems about them. One might expect more, perhaps, from Jeremy Hooker who has, over the last decade, been both critically[77] and creatively elaborating a poetry of place.

Born near Southampton and having spent many years in mid-Wales, Hooker's poetry has focused entirely on these two rural areas. In his collection *Master of The Leaping Figures*[78] he appends an explanation of his concept of "a poem that is like a place":

> Entering a place that is new to us, or seeing a familiar place anew, we move from part to part, simultaneously perceiving individual persons and things and discovering their relationships, so that, with time, place reveals itself as particular identities belonging to a network, which continually extends with our perception, and beyond it. And by this process we find ourselves, not as observers

only, but as inhabitants, citizens, neighbours, and locate ourselves in a space dense with meanings.[79]

One example of this approach is the poem sequence "Itchen Water", in which Hooker "followed the chalk stream from source to sea, learning more of its quick continuous changes, and deep historical passages". The poems themselves in this collection are disappointing. They tend to be simply descriptive or to bring in historical information which is not thought through in the development of the poem. Indeed, the poet hardly seems to be present in any kind of thinking, feeling sense. The reason is revealed in the poem "At Ovington" where the poet is looking at the river and at hawking swifts in the company of a sculptor. The poem ends:

> I would let all go again,
> saying – it is perfect without us,
> but we meet here, we share
> words and your hand shaping
> the flow, the brute
> and graceful wings.
> And our feet beat solidly on the bridge.[80]

The poet actually prefers to be an observer of what is "perfect without us". But poet and sculptor must make "shapes", even if in the poet's case they do not quite make meaning, as in the last line of this poem. The implications of those solid enough foot-beats in that place are unfortunately left entirely open.

In his first book, *Soliloquies of a Chalk Giant*,[81] Hooker had explored an interesting network of meanings perceived in both the human-made image of the Cerne Abbas giant and the natural context in which it lies. Here Hooker was dealing not so much with culturally specific meanings invested in place as with his own informed perceptions of possible meanings. The poem "A Chalk Pebble" takes an image of what is "perfect without us" as a starting point for exploration:

> This is perfect:
> A chalk pebble,
> Smooth and round,
> Like an egg.[82]

This is in fact the giant's view of a pebble as a giant's egg, a hubris that is mocked by his chalk hand crumbling as it makes contact with the hard pebble. So when the giant perceives the advancing saurian as having a "familiar" head that is "small and mean", a serious hint about future life-forms is made with a lightness of touch. The end of the poem finally brings together the organic and the inorganic elements of nature in the poem, reminding the reader that here the organic makes the inorganic. Thus any possible hubris of human achievement in the making of the giant is undercut with quiet simplicity:

> The dead sponge mingles
> With alchemic water
> For the slow formation
> Of a perfect stone.

The image of the chalk giant gives these poems from Hooker's 1972 collection a symbolic structure for his exploration of the meanings of natural forces located in the chalk downs of Dorset. The result is an authentic poem of place that expresses an integrated notion of humans and landscape, the organic and the inorganic, processes of making and unmaking.

Symbolic cultural meanings for nature can be attached to single items which come to represent place. Consider, for example, the following list: rose, thistle, shamrock, leek, yam, palm tree, elephant. More than places, the rose, thistle, shamrock and leek have come to represent the national cultures of England, Scotland, Ireland and Wales. But British poetry now has to accept the new cultural constructions behind references, in some poetry now published here, to yams and palm trees and elephants. Caribbean and Asian nature is now part of British nature poetry. New "green voices" are singing in the Forest of Arden. Some of them have been here for almost all of the period covered by this book.

James Berry, who has been in Britain since 1948, is able to celebrate a different culture by simply naming the "fruits of nature" from the Caribbean to be found in a London market. His poem "The Coming of Yams and Mangoes and Mountain Honey" begins:

> Handfuls hold hidden sunset
> stuffing up bags
> and filling up the London baskets.
> Caribbean hills have moved and come.
>
> Sun's alphabet drops out of branches.
> Coconuts are big brown Os,
> pimentoberries little ones.[83]

The delight in the word-play of alliteration, rhyme and metaphor expresses the poet's delight in identifying with these "fruits" of a Caribbean sun. But it is also a statement about the images of nature in London having changed, which has added, of course, to the language as well. The poem ends:

Caribbean hills have moved
and come to London
with whole words of the elements.
Just take them and give them
to children, to parents and the old folks.

James Berry can write in a variety of voices, but one of the most distinctive individual voices in British poetry at present is the ironic wit of the Guyana-born poet John Agard. He makes a salutary comment on cultural constructions of nature in his poem "Palm Tree King":

Because I come from the West Indies
certain people in England seem to think
I is a expert on palm trees

So not wanting to sever dis link
with me native roots (know what ah mean?)
or to disappoint dese culture vulture
I does smile cool as seabreeze

and say to dem
which specimen
you interested in[84]

The wit of this poem sharpens as the poet answers more and more difficult questions:

If 6 straw hat
and half a dozen bikini
multiply by the same number of coconut tree
equal one postcard
how many square miles of straw hat
you need to make a tourist industry?

In a different context this is quite as sharp a comment on a clash of cultural constructions of nature as the anti-pastoral section XIII of The Great Hunger. It is also a voice that is self-evidently Caribbean in a self-consciously playful way: "I does smile cool as a seabreeze."

The different voice of Grace Nichols, who left Guyana with John Agard in 1977, explores with a gentle wit the disconnectedness of a

West Indian in Britain in her collection *The Fat Black Woman's Poems*.[85]
The collection opens with a typical celebration that draws its strength
from a sensuous unity with Caribbean nature:

Beauty
is a fat black woman
riding the waves
drifting in happy oblivion
while the sea turns back
to hug her shape[86]

The simplicity of this is acknowledged in "happy oblivion" and is
a deliberate challenge to the reader that is echoed by the form. It is an
apparent pastoral that is self-declared: why shouldn't this "fat black
woman" relax, at one with the sea that doesn't just accept her beauty,
but "hugs" it? The irony that undercuts that "happy oblivion" is the
knowledge that lies behind the reality of being both fat and black in
Britain today.[87] In fact the humour of the sequence from which the
book takes its title is derived from the way "fat" acts as a complementary social stigma in an all-white society to being "black" in a racist
mixed-race society. Implicitly a white "fat" woman is assumed to be in
a parallel social position to that of a "black" woman in contemporary
Britain. Thus the opening poem is saying not only "black is beautiful",
but also "fat is beautiful". But the poet and the reader know that the
social reality for the "fat black woman" will not allow a "happy
oblivion" to last for long.

Less ironic is the childhood memory of "Those Women" which is
about work, but also about women being so at ease at work in "their
own element" that the child viewer in the poem senses a laughing
sexuality in those "contriving" women:

How I remember those women
sweeping in the childish rivers
of my eyes

and the fish slipping
like eels
through their laughing thighs[88]

By contrast, images of nature from the Caribbean are used by
Grace Nichols as political metaphors in her book-length sequence *i is a
long memoried woman*.[89] The poem "This Kingdom", which begins, "This

Kingdom Will Not Reign/Forever", starts to paint a pastoral picture
before suddenly warning

> Swamps can send plagues –
> dysentery, fevers
>
> plantations can perish
>
> lands turn barren
>
> And the white man
> no longer at ease
> with the faint drum/
> beat
>
> no longer indifferent
> to the sweating sun/
> heat
>
> can leave exhausted
> or
> turn his thoughts
> to death[90]

The rhythm of this and its expression in the punctuation ("drum/
beat"; "sun/heat") is closer to Black American than previous British
poetry. The experience of nature from which the political metaphors
are drawn is also obviously more Caribbean than British. Yet this is a
poem from a sequence first published by a small press in London,
then collected in the Virago *Fat Black Woman's Poems*, from a poet who is
reported as saying that it was only when she came to Britain that she
became a "serious" poet.[91]

So these powerful poems by Grace Nichols must now be
regarded as part of a new extension of British nature poetry, as must
the poems dominated by nature imagery by James Berry, John Agard
and A. L. Hendriks, for example, to be found a decade ago in
anthologies such as *News for Babylon: The Chatto Book of Westindian-British
Poetry*. This Caribbean-influenced poetry is a new "green voice",
speaking in its varied rhythms. It is politicised, witty and exploring
what it means to live with the constructions of nature located in two
places. In some senses this has been true for all the non-English poets
discussed here. They each have to work with, for example, a Scottish–
English, or a Welsh–English awareness of their references to nature.
For poets originally from Ulster but living in the Republic, like Heaney
and Montague, there is a three-way dimension of awareness. The old
traditions and their more recent continuations which have been the

subject of this book have been complemented by the addition of yams to cultural constructions such as thistle. Indeed, within the thistle itself there is probably an Italian flower waiting to bloom out of Glasgow. But what of the elephant?

British Asian poetry has been slower to make an impact, although its richness of mythological associations with nature and long traditions of poetic forms will make an obvious enlargement when it gathers momentum. Debjani Chatterjee is an Indian poet who has recently been published by a British press.[92] When I interviewed her about the possibilities of Asian contributions to British nature poetry she said:

> British publishers, on the whole, have not really shown interest in poetry by writers who come from Asia, so Asian notions of nature have not yet had a chance to make an impact on British poetry. A famous exception was the publication of the Oxford student Dom Moraes in 1957.[93] He produced three collections[94] here before going back to India. Just now things are beginning to change.[95] But British readers will not only miss much through translation but will be unaware that, for example, the rainy season is the season of poetry throughout the sub-continent. It is the season that poets love to write about because it is the best and the worst of seasons. The monsoons have actually produced a genre of lyric poetry that is frequently expressed as song.[96]

When this tradition finds its way into British nature poetry the meaning of "rain", as discussed in Chapter 1, will again be expanded and enriched. "But most of all, perhaps, what British readers will need help with are the mythological meanings and symbolism associated with animals, birds, and in some poetic forms, such as ghazal, the traditional significance of desert, orchard and rose."[97] In fact, with the exception of the poem "Flamingoes", every reference to an animal or bird in I Was That Woman is culturally specific. Two poems about elephants from I Was That Woman illustrate two culturally constructed meanings for the writer that this animal represents.

The child in the poem "The Elephant" is actually more interested in monkeys. The opening line of the poem states her dislike of elephants in a wicked play upon an English cliché that "is also intended as a visual joke":[98] "Elephants were not her cup of tea."[99] When her father says in the poem, " 'But this is an Indian elephant' ", she goes "to greet her majestic compatriot":

> She avoided those massive tree trunk legs
> and looked straight up at the eyes.
> A storehouse of sorrow was locked in its brain.
> Tentative, she reached out a hand and patted
> the incredible trunk stretched out to her.

Reaching out to each other are two "compatriots" in a "wet, cold, foreign land".[100] For the child it is enough that this is an Indian elephant. The significance for the reader derives from the fact that the elephant is representative of India. For the reader this is nature as symbol rather than association. But in India there is more to the elephant than this. The elephant in Hindu folklore is associated with Ganapati, the elephant-headed god of wisdom who is also the god of literature.[101] Debjani Chatterjee's poem about him is a profound exploration of just what that wisdom might be. The poem addresses Ganapati's mother, the goddess of the Himalaya who married the god Shiva:

> Parvati, because you loved us, you bade us love the world a little.
> Radiant goddess of the mountains, you married the outcast god who
> haunted cemeteries.
> We saw that we should embrace the children of two races:
> they are the strong links of connection and bear your blessing,
> they are rainbows spanning gulfs of silence, swamps of intolerance.
> You wanted to stretch our notions of humanity.[102]

Mountains and cemeteries represent the "two races", those of the upper world and the underworld, that should be embraced through their children. This comes to symbolise a social lesson that should "span . . . intolerance". In this poem, embracing the forces of life and of death in nature should lead to a moral expansion so that the very notion of "humanity" is extended. By the end of the poem this comes to imply an inclusion of all organic nature in the concept of "humanity", bizarre as that might seem to a homocentric view of the world. The crucial breakdown of "our notions of humanity" comes at the centre of the poem. The elephant's "creature compassion" is so expansive that it clearly transcends our taken-for-granted divisions:

> We accepted that the brain within the massive skull
> was more than animal, human or divine – all wisdom.
> He personified a bond that we knew was powerful.

This is prosaic as poetry, especially considering the potentially powerful images that might evoke that bond. What produces this rather cerebral poetry is the desire to communicate the unusual notion of bonding personified by the elephant. That bond is not only between the elephant and us, the animal and the human, but unites animal, human and divine in one vision that is "all wisdom". In fact the story of Ganapati (whose mother is the "you" referred to in the following quotation) should "stretch our notions of humanity" to include plants as well:

> Ganapati, because he loved us, he bade us love the world a little.
> Radiant god, he married the bashful banana tree with its veil of fertile
> leaves.
> You celebrated this union and gave your blessing.
> All the world loves a bride – we joined in and draped
> our friend's elegant wife in a red bordered sari, we blew conch
> shells.
> We stretched our notions of humanity.

Three comments from the author are helpful here. Firstly, an explanation that the notion of "loving the world a little" derives from the Hindu belief "that the world is *maya*, an illusion, only temporary. We are creatures in creation and should delight in that, but we shouldn't let it bind us too much."[103] Secondly, the idea of "stretching" relates to the sequence of "bondings" in the poem. "With each combination that we recognise we're enriched more than the simple sum of the two halves, so our humanity is stretched." Thirdly, the tone of the poem ("all the world loves a bride") is deliberately playful because "it is important to be no longer in awe of the god; it is important to be able to laugh at him. You need that familiarity to be able to love him and to observe the lessons of his life."

The lessons of Ganapati's life as told in this poem integrate what can be recognised as "green" notions, of embracing all aspects of the natural world, plant and animal, life-forces and death-forces, together with humanitarian notions of tolerance even for behaviour which might appear bizarre. It may take a contribution to British nature poetry from an Asian perspective to show Europeans that we do not necessarily need to "move from red to green" as Jonathan Bate suggests we should.[104] The choice is a false one and there are other poems that endorse Debjani Chatterjee's implication that a concern for humanity should be part of a green concern.

In fact there are didactic green poems written by David Craig and by Tony Harrison which show how wrong Bate's modish notion is.

They are among the radical green voices that have risen to a peak in our time. This would include very different poems by Heathcote Williams, Hilary Llewellyn-Williams, Philip Gross, and Adrian Mitchell, to name a representative few whose work has not been discussed so far. The cultural context of this rise in green consciousness was outlined in Chapter 1. There is a sense in which green poetry is a version of the anti-pastoral poetry that was considered in Chapter 2. These poems are based upon the premise that a pastoral construction of nature is inadequate to our current environmental crisis. Certainly some poems written by the writers considered in earlier chapters would demand to be included in any discussion of green poetry. Sorley MacLean's "Screapadal"[105] and Ted Hughes's "The Black Rhino"[106] are obvious examples. But the link the ecofeminists make between the exploitation of the earth and of fellow human beings, especially women, was already present, in an early Marxist form, in The Country and the City.

The spur to the writing of The Country and the City was Raymond Williams's objection to the respect paid by Cambridge English studies in the 1960s to the country-house novels and to pastoral poetry: "The values of the rural capitalist order which first imposed the notion of mastery [of nature] are now being presented as the height of civilization."[107] He complained in The Country and the City, with what he later admitted to be an "autobiographical" anger,[108] about "an unreflecting celebration of mastery – man's mastery of nature – as if the exploitation of natural resources could be separated off from the accompanying exploitation of man".[109] In the last essay Williams published on this subject he concluded: "The most helpful social and political movement of our time is the very different and now emergent 'green socialism', within which ecology and economics can become, as they should be, a single science and source of values, leading on to a new politics of equitable livelihood."[110] This is the theoretical answer to Bate's commendation of a political movement "from red to green". An examination of the current state of poetry written in the "language that is ever green" indicates not only that what passes for "green" reveals divergent attitudes towards "ecology and economics", towards nature and human beings, but that a green poetry that does not engage with both is in danger of returning to the pastoral in new "green" forms.

Perhaps the most didactic green poem to have been published in the period covered by this study is David Craig's "Against Looting". It

expresses the political concerns of the green movement with a directness that is none the less powerfully poetic. It begins:

> Leave the mahogany where it is!
> Leave the mahogany trees in Borneo
> Where the orangs embrace them gently.
>
> Leave the geodes where they are!
> Great egg-wombs, toothed with crystal,
> Leave them in the Brazilian darkness.
>
> Leave the edelweiss where it is!
> Its foliage woven of frost,
> Leave it to root on the bergs of the Dolomites.
>
> Leave the ambergris where it is!
> Leave it, oily and fragrant,
> In the gut of the sperm whale.[111]

The power of this derives from the tension released after each
imperative by the gentle tone of delicate, sensuous observation. Here
is descriptive nature poetry put to a didactic purpose: the survival of
each part of nature that is being described. It is, of course, the human
species that is threatening the survival of all twelve organic and
inorganic parts of nature mentioned in the poem. Mention of the
sperm whale touches upon what has become a symbol of the green
movement's campaigns. But in this poem Craig is careful to distance
himself from the tendency, implicit in "the move from red to green",
to let concern for external nature override concern for suffering
within the human species. Again, the answer to Jonathan Bate is to be
found in the concern for all forms of exploitation in the final stanza of
"Against Looting":

> Leave them in memory of the slaves
> Stowed like carcases in the holds,
> In memory of the elephants chained and swaying
> In concrete hangers, in memory of the gorilla
> Counting the links of his chain
> Over and over and over, and leave them
> For the sake of the children
> That they may never laugh at a prisoner
> Or try to buy a life with a coin.

That last line concisely sums up the fact that the problem of humans
exploiting both each other and the rest of nature originates in the
same way of thinking. As Raymond Williams suggests, and as Debjani

Chatterjee's poem "Ganapati"[112] illustrates, our notions of nature reflect our notion of "humanity".

David Craig's cry for the protection of the sperm whale, within a shared concern for humans too, invites comparison with Heathcote Williams's *Whale Nation*. An interesting aspect of the social construction of meaning invested in whales is that they represent, for some people, a morally higher form of life than human beings and that they are therefore more worthy of our concern than our fellow humans. This is the implication at the end of the long, lavishly illustrated poem which has proved to be so highly popular, *Whale Nation*.

The debate about whether this is really poetry[113] seems to me to be easily resolved. Much of the time, as poetry, it is prosaic, but at other times the resources of poetry express its content. Look, for example, at the expression of the build-up of speed and then the smooth passing of whales in the following:

Naked,
With skin like oiled silk,
Smooth as glass
They move at fifty miles an hour.
Attaining faultless streamlining
By subtly changing the shape of their bodies:
Altering ridges of cartilage, and indentations of flesh
To correspond to constantly differing patterns of water;
To accommodate minute oscillations with vibrant inflexions of
muscle and skin,
So that layers of liquid glide over each other,
In an easy, laminar flow.
No drag, no turbulence.
A velvet energy.[114]

Simile and metaphor, at the beginning and end of this passage, relieve a somewhat wooden middle section. This is poor poetry, but it is poetry. It is also a superb example of what a book of green poetry can be, with its well-researched pictures and its anthology of source material. At this time it is crucial that the old boundaries of "the two cultures"[115] are dissolved, just as Raymond Williams argued that boundaries between ecology and economics should be loosened. If nature poetry is to be able to engage with the future of the planet, then scientific, cultural, economic and political information should be its source material. As I argued in presenting Ted Hughes's documentation of river pollution, nature poetry now needs to be informed in its description of the natural world if it is to have any effect on attitudes towards nature.

Whale Nation ends with a contrast detrimental to the human species:

> In the water, whales have become the dominant species,
> Though they do not broodily guard their patch with
> bristling security.
>
> In the water, whales have become the dominant species,
> Without trading innocence for the pretension of possessions.
>
> In the water, whales have become the dominant species,
> Though they acknowledge minds other than their own.
>
> In the water, whales have become the dominant species,
> Without allowing their population to reach plague proportions.
>
> In the water, the whale is the dominant species;
> An extra-terrestrial, who has already landed . . .
>
> A marine intelligentsia, with a knowledge of the deep.
>
> From space, the planet is blue.
> From space, the planet is the territory
> Not of humans, but of the whale.[116]

This appears not only to very deftly challenge a homocentric view of the planet, but to imply that the human species is less worth "saving" than the whale. The danger of this notion of nature is that it can lead to the position of some animal rights activists who value human life less highly than that of exploited or endangered animals.[117]

Whale Nation, although weak as poetry, is an important poem for both the whale and for nature poetry. It demonstrates that a densely informed nature poetry is not only possible, but can be popular. However, the companion poem, *Falling for a Dolphin*,[118] is actually better poetry and is based upon a direct relationship with a dolphin in Dingle Bay. This poem is more reflective, searching for meaning in historical and cultural visions of the dolphin:

> Is there a ghost of an ancestral treaty
> For mutual survival,
> As you shared
> And share
> This earth's fragile hospitality?
> And what explains the sense of some ancient, hidden nature
> Overlapping somewhere along the line with man's . . .
> A nature venerated in antiquity,
> When this shape-shifting sea-sprite

Was Poseidon's messenger, a Gaian pilot . . .
A demi-god.

All much less quirky, less sentimental
When you are inches away
Looking into its lake-like eye.[119]

More than *Whale Nation*, *Falling for a Dolphin* explores the interrelationship between its subject and humans, including the mythic meaning of the creature. But it does not do this at the expense of drawing upon scientific knowledge. Of course, the whole notion of taking a holiday to swim with a dolphin, as is now being commercially advertised not just for Dingle Bay but for locations world-wide,[120] raises questions about whether we are exploiting the dolphin – whether we are projecting on to dolphins a "friendliness"[121] we cannot find in our own species and whether the dolphin provides a focus for a pastoral escapism. Journalist Judith Williamson wrote in 1991:

> I am sure that advertisers are already calling this the Year Of The Dolphin: when in doubt, bung one in, seems to be their motto at present. "Son, you have swum with the dolphins. . . ." says the right-on father in the building society ad, an index of his awareness . . . The dolphin now carries the floating burden of all the values we think are good but cannot easily find in our society. After all, trust, affection and playfulness were not qualities that "Eighties culture" had much time for. . . . We are increasingly preoccupied with nature exactly when we seem to find our own nature almost unbearable.[122]

If this is true – and it is an interesting theory – it is not true of *Falling for a Dolphin*. Heathcote Williams does not isolate his experience with the dolphin in a sealed, escapist preciosity. He includes in the poem the cynical comments of the local fishermen about both dolphin-watchers and "the fuckin' dolphin".[123] He has not escaped from his reality or from himself. By "looking into its lake-like eye" he is learning about himself as well as about the dolphin. In meeting the dolphin he confronts his fear and the sea's cold. The poem he brings back from this encounter expresses an enlargement of knowledge about internal and external nature for our species.

In complete contrast to this poetry of green directness, there is an escapist green poetry that appears to raise questions, makes the right references to ecological concerns, but evaporates into rhetoric when it comes to consider the final responsibilities. The second collection of Hilary Llewellyn-Williams, *Book of Shadows*,[124] takes its title from the sequence which concludes the book. It is based upon the notion of nature elaborated by the Renaissance philosopher Giordano Bruno. The Italian monk, who visited England between 1583 and 1586 and became a friend of Sir Philip Sidney, was a magician and poet whose philosophy, as Llewellyn-Williams describes in her Notes, had much in common with what Oelschlaeger conjectures as "a Paleolithic idea of wilderness":[125] that all nature is alive and is sacred; that matter and spirit are indivisible; that all life-forms are interrelated; that the universe is infinite; that the poet is able to use ritual to shape natural events.[126] Bruno's notion that all parts of the material universe are in continual motion and are continually renewed from within has been of particular interest to Llewellyn-Williams. But she is concerned in "Book of Shadows" with our contemporary disconnection from nature: "I am not writing about history, but about what concerns us all: the world we live in, our environment – physical, spiritual and emotional."[127]

This all sounds a rich field of exploration. But the poems merely touch upon the ideas before throwing up their hands in despair. The poem "Alchemy", for example, enters into the world of darkness and the "alchemy" of sleep. If sleep leaves us slightly transformed, the poem suggests, it is the larger "darkness" of unseen processes that is continually changing us in a manner that links us to the rest of the material universe:

> Star particles link us with trees
> dolphins and stones, travel through us
>
> creating the universe. Base matter
> becomes gold: in the Cauldron
> of Annwn, in the crucible of mind
> we're all magicians.[128]

The fundamental notion of nature at work in this poem is the same as that in "The Big Sleep": nature making in us "new patterns while we sleep"; the processes that link organic and inorganic nature; and the power of the imagination to find an articulation of all this. So what can our imagination as "magicians" produce to build upon these "links"?

> As darkness
> rises, and we grope wildly, perhaps
> out of chaos the magic will come right.

That "perhaps" is surely an abdication of responsibility, leaving our future to a rather Hardyesque "hoping it might be so".[129] Really we should be using this reconnectedness to be more disciplined than "groping wildly" if we are to stem the "rising darkness" of environmental problems which our disconnectedness has produced. An earlier poem in the sequence, "Turning North", ends in a quite different spirit, perhaps reflecting the current frustrated form of alienation:

> We won't wait for justice:
> we'll take it, we'll wield it, a thrown
>
> hunting-spear, a sword. Remember, the lords are few
> and frightened. There's danger: this could be
> the last waving light before dark – what can we lose?[130]

But blind anger at "our masters, our lords" simply will not do. This poem has been written as though the green movement had done nothing to draw attention to individual responsibility for pollution, to say nothing of corporate responsibility for poisoning the sea and bulldozing forests. This is no longer a feudal society and confusion is no longer an excuse. Blind lashing-out with the sword is crude stuff – less cunning than the selective application of the monkey wrench.[131]

Against this bankrupt green rhetoric needs to be put the Brechtian fable by Philip Gross, "What This Hand Did", first published in the green issue of *Poetry Review*.[132] It begins:

> This is the one. This is the hand
> that scraped a castle in the sand.
>
> When the tide turned present to past
> this hand tried to hold it fast.
>
> When drops trickled through its grip
> this hand let the moment slip.

The hand turns to its "mate", to prayer, to the sword, to the laws, and then to an image of what journalist Judith Williams called " 'eighties culture' ".[133]

> When the laws began to break
> this hand grabbed what it could take.
>
> When the whole world's banks went bust
> this hand scratched the moon for dust.
>
> When the seasons came undone
> this hand tried to forget the sun.

> When the sun began to rise
> this hand tried to shield its eyes.
>
> This hand. This one.
> What has it done? What has it done?

The singular subject of this poem allows it to stand for both individual and shared responsibility for what has been done. The poem exposes a notion of nature that is also, of course, a social and economic attitude: "When the hour was getting late/this hand reached out for its mate." The self-centred greed of the hand tries everything too late, out of desperation rather than commitment.

If this poem acts as a comment on the present, implying a need for a reversal of this attitude towards nature, Adrian Mitchell offers a warning for the future in his poem "On the Beach at Cambridge". After the nuclear holocaust a bureaucrat from the Ministry of the Environment emerges from a bunker in Cambridge to record what he sees. The poem ends with the realisation that the ashes all around have come not only from the buildings and books of Cambridge which "Spread their wings/And became white flames":

> But in one moment all the children in Cambridge
> Spread their wings
> And became white flames
> And then black ash.
>
> And all the children of America, I suppose.
> And all the children of Russia, I suppose.
>
> And I am standing on the beach at Cambridge
> And I am watching the broad black ocean tide
> Bearing on its shoulders its burden of black ashes.
>
> And I am listening to the last words of the sea
> As it beats its head against the dying land.[134]

Apocalyptic "green voices" such as this are most effective when they are founded in fact. As the sea-level rises after the melting of the ice-caps, not only would Cambridge become a beach, but it may only be a temporary one as the ocean continues to rise and the land "dies" under the water.

War threatens nature to the core since large scale long-term damage can be inflicted on the environment even if the damage to the human species is relatively small-scale and short-term. The most recent reminder of this has been the Gulf War. Tony Harrison's "Initial

Illumination",[135] was first published in The *Guardian* during the Gulf war on 5 March 1991 and thus represents what might be called "topical green poetry". This indicates the potential penetration into the wider culture[136] of poetry that can explore concern about both war and its environmental consequences.

The poet is in a train passing cormorants off Lindisfarne which recall those cormorants drawn around the " 'I' " of the words "*In principio*" in a Saxon illuminated Bible made by the monks on Lindisfarne. The poem suggests that the Gulf War is not being fought for principle and certainly not for "the word of God much bandied by George Bush". The opening lines catch a vivid glimpse of what might be the beginning of an English pastoral:

> Farne cormorants with catches in their beaks
> shower fishscale confetti on the shining sea.

What dominates the end of the poem is the image published in the newspapers of a cormorant in the Gulf Sea struggling in oil:

> Is it open-armed at all that victory V,
> that insular initial intertwined
> with slack-necked cormorants from black lacquered sea,
> with trumpets bulled and bellicose and blowing
> for what men claim as victories in their wars,
> with the fire-hailing cock and all those crowing
> who don't yet smell the dunghill at their claws?

That photograph of the oiled cormorant came to represent the terrible damage and suffering of both people and the environment caused by the war. The inversion of natural patterns of behaviour in war is shown by the almost Shakespearian image[137] of the cock in Baghdad crowing in the dawn-bright light of a bombing raid. But the poem itself weaves images of cormorants with those of "raiders gung-ho for booty and berserk" and "the burial of the blackened in Baghdad". The final line echoes the starting point of *Cave Birds* with its image of human beings as arrogant cockerels whose complacence prevents them from realising that they have made a stinking dunghill out of the environment and the lives that are grasped so firmly in "their claws".

Cave Birds still stands as one of the major achievements of post-pastoral contemporary nature poetry, but poems like "Initial Illumination", "What This Hand Did", "On the Beach at Cambridge" and "Against Looting" indicate the power of a new kind of campaigning green poetry that accepts Hughes's notion of nature as including human nature. All these poems confound the premise implied in *Whale Nation* and in Bate's "from red to green" that concerns about the exploitation of nature should be separate from concerns about human exploitation. "If we alienate the living process of which we are a part", Raymond Williams wrote, "we end, though unequally, by alienating ourselves."[138]

When Ted Hughes admitted that his own green poems somehow never quite seemed to be "the real thing" he was touching upon an old question about political poetry: can directness be as successful as indirectness in poetry that seeks to engage with political issues? Hughes has reflected further on "the real thing" in green poetry:

> Poetry loses its power, as a medium, maybe, when it takes sides in any conflict – loses its power, I mean, to persuade any of the opposite side . . . . Poetry has to be on all sides at once – or it has to take form at a level beneath that on which taking sides begins. . . . In the Environmental Wars it is very easy to become righteously embattled against the individuals who seem responsible for the damage. The real problem as I see it, is the difficulty of avoiding that easy but exhilarating battle with them, and of finding *effective ways* of making them painfully aware of the human folly in which we are all implicated. Maybe some kind of poem could do it. (Maybe some kinds of poem have helped.)[139]

Surely the green poet ought to be able to make imaginative use of the resources of poetry to engage with forms of thought directly. Sometimes this will necessitate taking sides in a poetical mode. But poetry does not persuade, it provokes; it does not state, it suggests; it does not set out a position, it explores its implications. Green poetry is likely to fail as poetry when it is either simple propaganda or vague right-on rhetoric. What I have tried to show here is that powerful green poetry is possible in a variety of modes of engagement: Brechtian fable ("What This Hand Did"), topical reflection ("Initial Illumination"), futuristic projection ("On the Beach at Cambridge"), or even direct didacticism ("Against Looting").

I do not want to argue that green poetry is the only kind of poetry appropriate to our current environmental crisis. What this book has been arguing is that post-pastoral nature poetry in all its forms is developing our understanding of the paradoxes of our relationship with nature. What the survey of this chapter has shown is not only that nature poetry has a vitality beyond the work of MacLean, Heaney and Hughes discussed in earlier chapters, but also that the diversity of notions of nature within the traditions of nature poetry in Scotland, Ireland, Wales and England are being extended by poetry being written now. The pastoral trap remains seductive, particularly, it seems, for poets concerned with landscape such as MacCaig and Hooker. The anti-pastoral remains a necessary corrective at times, and has been extended by the satire of John Agard and the green poetry of David Craig. But the best of the post-pastoral voices discussed in this chapter complement those of MacLean, Heaney and Hughes by searching for forms of connection, commitment and responsibility that will help us confront a long-standing and now urgent question of our time: how to live with a notion of nature that will improve our relationship with the rest of the planet and with ourselves.

In the last chapter six features of the work of Ted Hughes provided the most comprehensive indication of what a post-pastoral notion of nature might be in our time. A dynamic sense of what Gary Snyder calls "the gift-exchange quality of our give-and-take" could supersede the self-consciousness that has alienated us from our inner selves and from our global environment in much of the poetry of the twentieth century. Myth-making can enact the drama of our ecological relationships and confirm our inner capacities for ebb and flow as links with larger processes in the natural world. Both the personal and the cultural dimensions of growth and decay could be understood in relation to the breathing of Gaia. Ultimately consciousness, which appeared to set us apart, could be seen from a biocentric view to be the human species' opportunity to take responsibility for its ecological relationships and its survival.

The impact of post-pastoral poetry on our social consensus has perhaps only just begun. Poetry that acknowledges and informs our responsibility for each other and the planet upon which we depend is arguably the most important poetry being written today. This poetry will not, in itself, save us or the planet, but it is one of the ways in which our culture revisits what it takes for granted and revisions the possibilities. An enquiry that began by recognising that "nature poetry" had become a pejorative term has not only shown that it is alive, if ignored in some fashion-forming quarters, but that it is essential to our survival. Ironically, Blake Morrison, one of the editors of *The Penguin Book of Contemporary British Verse* quoted at the beginning of this book as evidence that nature poetry is having a bad time, writes of

175

Hughes in 1994 that "the nature poet has never been so important".[140]

Adrian Noble's 1993 RSC production of *King Lear* at Stratford created a striking image of our times. Through the first half of the play there hung over the stage a gauzed moon which imperceptibly transformed into a globe. Lear's curse against nature caused this globe to crack and grains of sand to spill from it on to the stage. By the time the audience returned from the interval a considerable pile of sand had accumulated on the stage. Time is running out for "unaccomodated man". The nature poet has never been more important because we need images that will help us heal that crack in "Nature's moulds" from which "all germens spill at once".[141] It is a quarter of a century since Ted Hughes wrote that "the subtly apotheosized misogyny of Reformed Christianity" has resulted in the self-exile of our species from "Mother Nature – from both inner and outer nature".[142] He knew that a healing power would come only from works that explored "one all-inclusive system": "in them the full presence of the inner world combines with and is reconciled to the full presence of the outer world".[143] Whether those potentially healing images are Sorley MacLean's woods of Raasay, Gillian Clarke's hare, Debjani Chatterjee's elephant god, Ted Hughes's gods of mud or Seamus Heaney's Bog Queen, we shall only know if they really *can* heal by closely examining them as imaginative notions of nature.

Our social construction of nature is a continuing process, informed by both scientists and poets. It is now more urgent than ever that notions of nature in literature are scrutinised and debated. This study has proposed a theoretical framework and tentative criteria for further debate, defined by discussion of poems by twenty-five poets. Our continuing explorations of the nature of nature in our time will be conducted through the imaginative activities of both criticism and creativity. In support of this holistic spirit of drawing upon all our faculties, I would like to conclude (and continue) this enquiry in the voice of poetry.

"The Stone Spiral" (for Gill)

It squats in stone
Buddha-like, biding its time,
Accepting its own nature,
Its ribbed shell now
A spiral of white arches
Settled into the flat planes
Of sea-sediment stone.

An ammonite in Freiburg
Decorates a window ledge
Borrowed time for a smart flat.
The trees of the Black Forest
Fold inwards under each year's
Crop of industrial rainfall.

A glass case in Finale Ligure
Cages a flotsam collection
Of the tiny sea creatures.
The turquoise pool of the Mediterranean
Clouds a little more with the swirls
Of each year's sewage and oil.

Even here in Provence
Where aromas rise on the thermals
Under the white heat of Mont St Victoire
Herbs have been harvesting
Radiation from the rain storms
Spiralling out of Russia.

And as we turn the circle
Of our rock-climbing journey towards
Home and names of sites for locking
Time-bombs of waste in rain-tight rock
I wonder by what form – bunker or core,
A menhir or a Henry Moore – our species
Will be known to its inheritors.[144]

Notes

1 *Romantic Ecology*: Wordsworth and the Environmental Tradition, London: Routledge, 1991, p. 11.
2 ibid., p. 19.
3 *The Wreck of the Archangel*, London: John Murray, 1989, p. 104.
4 London: Jonathan Cape, 1988.
5 "Rituals of the Mind", *The Literary Review*, Aug. 1987, p. 24.
6 *The Lover, the Dreamer and the World: a Study of Peter Redgrove's Poetry*, Sheffield Academic Press, 1994, p. 16.
7 See Chapter 1 for James Lovelock's definition of his Gaia theory.
8 *The Lover, the Dreamer and the World*, p. 16.
9 Harmondsworth: Penguin, 1989.
10 *Poems 1954–1987*, p. 227.
11 *The Lover, the Dreamer and the World*, p. 128.
12 ibid., p. 11.
13 ibid.

14 Note the hint at Blakean perception, the reference for which I have quoted in discussing "Egghead" by Ted Hughes in Chapter 6.

15 At a reading recently I asked Redgrove if I was right in my impression that in his poems people discover their connection with external nature, but do not make choices. He replied, "If we find that we are lived by forces, our choices are reduced." He acknowledged that some choices are currently crucial: "We must stop pumping out ozone-depleting gases." But he accepted that in his poetry nature is controlling us in ways that we are hardly aware of: "We have cut ourselves off from some knowledge in nature" (Waterstone's Bookshop, Sheffield, 11 Apr. 1992).

16 In answer to another question at the above reading, Redgrove suggested that people could learn to control and influence their dreams for their own good health.

17 See T. Gifford and N. Roberts, "Hughes and two contemporaries: Peter Redgrove and Seamus Heaney" in K. Sagar ed., *The Achievement of Ted Hughes*, Manchester University Press, 1983.

18 "Swimming with Seals", Fraser Steel ed., *The Poetry Book Society Anthology*, No. 1, New Series, London: Hutchinson, 1990, p. 99.

19 "The national grid has left me out./For power I catch wind": "At One Thousand Feet", *Letting in the Rumour*, Manchester: Carcanet, 1989, p. 7.

20 ibid., p. 8.

21 ibid.

22 *The Black Goddess and the Sixth Sense*, London, Bloomsbury, 1987, p. 110.

23 *Poems 1954–1987*, p. 16.

24 Her fine poem "Himalayan Balsam" (*Selected Poems*, Oxford University Press, 1987, pp. 112–13), is given an interesting reading by Alan Robinson in *Instabilities in Contemporary British Poetry*, London: Macmillan, 1988, pp. 182–84.

25 See "The Hebrides" in *Poems 1963–1983*, London: Secker & Warburg, 1991, for an early example, or more recently "Northern Lights" in *Gorse Fires*, London: Secker & Warburg, 1991, p. 32.

26 *The Living Landscape*, London: Pluto Press, 1986, p. 32.

27 Bridgend: Seren Books, 1989.

28 ibid., p. 105.

29 ibid., p. 99.

30 ibid., p. 106.

31 "A Decentred Self?: the long poems of Christine Evans", *Poetry Wales*, Vol. 27, No. 1, p. 37.

32 *Cometary Phases*, p. 100.

33 *Sylvia Plath: Collected Poems*, London: Faber & Faber, 1981, p. 162.

34 *The Living Landscape*, p. 32.

35 Kavanagh, *Collected Poems*, London: Martin Brian & O'Keefe, 1972, p. 54.

36 ibid., p. 240.

37 ibid., p. 265.

38 Published as a single poem in a limited edition of 325 copies, *Child*, Exeter: The Rougemont Press, 1971.

39 See J. Rose, *The Haunting of Sylvia Plath*, London: Virago, 1991.

40 Of the 41 poems in the folder Plath left titled *Ariel*, Hughes omitted 14 "of the more personally aggressive poems" (*Collected Poems*, p. 15) and added 13

poems, 10 of them written later than those in the original folder. This was first drawn attention to by M. Perloff in "The Two Ariels: The (Re)making Of The Sylvia Plath Canon", *The American Poetry Review*, Nov.–Dec. 1984.

41 *Collected Poems*, p. 295.

42 ibid., p. 219.

43 She finished the bee sequence on the day she wrote to her mother that she would seek a divorce. (Anne Stevenson, *Bitter Fame: A Life of Sylvia Plath*, London: Viking, 1989, p. 264.)

44 See, for example, "Into Rock" in *Against Looting*, Clapham: Giant Steps, 1987, p. 48.

45 See "Photograph of the Alps seen from New South Wales" in *The Crystal Owl*, London: Methuen, 1988, p. 84.

46 See "Climbing at Heptonstall Quarry" in *Sky Burial*, Coventry: Dangaroo Press, 1989, p. 56.

47 See "On Location" in *At The Mercy*, London: Allison & Busby, 1981, p. 39.

48 David Craig, *Native Stones*, London: Secker & Warburg, 1987, p. 128.

49 A dead raven or an egg would gain four pence from the church warden, who hung them on the church railings or from nails on the church door. The following event presumably took place "ere I had seen/Nine summers" (*The Prelude*, 1805, Book I, lines 310–11), if the "plunderer"'s activities that follow this phrase are to be read as a list. The earliest recorded evidence of Wordsworth's rock-climbing has been fixed at the year 1783 by Stephen Gill (*William Wordsworth: A Life*, Oxford University Press, 1989, p. 21). In fact the thirteen-year-old Bill Wordsworth did not climb to the raven's nest at Yewdale Crags, Coniston on the day he refers to because the first boy on the top-rope became cragfast and had to be rescued. (T. W. Thompson, *Wordsworth's Hawkshead*, Oxford University Press, 1970, p. 211ff.)

50 *The Prelude*, 1805, Book I, lines 341–6.

51 *Native Stones*, p. 134.

52 This powerful concept is actually the title of an essay by the American ecologist Aldo Leopold, collected in his *Sand County Almanac*, Oxford University Press, 1949. It is quoted in Max Oelschlaeger, *The Idea of Wilderness*, New Haven: Yale University Press, 1991, p. 232. See Byron, *Childe Harold's Pilgrimage*, canto iv, stanza 156, J. J. McGann ed., *Lord Byron: The Complete Poetical Works*, Oxford University Press, 1980, Vol II, p. 176; Shelley, "Mont Blanc", T. Hutchinson ed., *The Complete Poetical Works of Percy Bysshe Shelley*, Oxford University Press, 1912, p. 528; John Keats, "Read me a lesson, Muse, and speak it loud", *Poetical Works*, Oxford University Press, 1956, p. 390.

53 London: Heinemann, 1964. This anthology includes the work of poets such as Geoffrey Winthrop Young (p. 123), Menlove Edwards (p. 180), William Bell (p. 193), Noyce himself (p. 221) and the best of the pre-1960 climbing poets, Michael Roberts (p. 198). Roberts's two collections are worthy of further study: *Poems*, London: Jonathan Cape, 1936 and *Orion Marches*, London: Faber & Faber, 1939.

54 T. Gifford, "Poetry and the Climbing Press", *High*, No. 20, July 1984, p. 35 and revised version, *The Climbing Art* (USA), fall 1990, p. 12.

55 "I had my doubts as to what I, as a non-climber, would get out of this book." (Review of T. Gifford, *Outcrops*, Todmorden: Littlewood, 1991 in *Inkshed*, autumn 1991 by Bernard Young.) "It isn't often that poems one has no experience of can chill, delight, move." (Review of *Outcrops* by F. Sedgwick, *NATE News*, Sheffield: NATE, spring 1992, p. 39.)

56 In addition to those four books mentioned in notes 51–4 above: E. Drummond, *A Dream of White Horses*, London: Diadem, 1987 (see "To Climb Or Not To Climb", p. 11); A. Greig, *The Order of the Day*, Newcastle upon Tyne: Bloodaxe, 1990 (see "The Winter Climbing", p. 15); T. Gifford, *The Stone Spiral*, Clapham: Giant Steps, 1987 (see "The Stone", p. 37); T. Gifford, *Outcrops*, (see "Activities in Zone 2–4000", p. 52).

57 This is an annual event at Bretton Hall College, Leeds University, organised by the present author.

58 *High*, No. 100, March 1991, p. 112.

59 "Writing on Rock", The Arvon Foundation, Lumb Bank, July 1990, tutors: T. Gifford and G. Mort.

60 *High*, No. 103, June 1991, p. 3.

61 In T. Gifford and R. Smith eds, *The Orogenic Zones: the First Five Years of The International Mountaineering Literature Festival*, Leeds: Bretton Hall College, 1994.

62 *Master of the Leaping Figures*, Petersfield: Enitharmon Press, 1987, p. 76.

63 For example, T. Curtis ed., *The Poetry of Pembrokeshire*, Bridgend: Seren, 1989 and D. M. Thomas ed., *Granite Kingdom: Poems of Cornwall*, Penryn: Tor Mark Press, 1970.

64 Norman Nicholson ed., Harmondsworth: Penguin, 1978.

65 H. Brown ed., Aberdeen University Press, 1982.

66 T. Curtis ed., Bridgend: Seren Books, 1989.

67 Not only for readers but for writers as well – witness the provision of two courses offering "Writing in Mountains" at the Taliesin Trust's residential centre, Tŷ Newydd, Criccieth, July 1991 and September 1992, tutors: T. Gifford and L. Houston.

68 H. Brown and M. Berry eds., Aberdeen University Press, 1985.

69 London: Chatto & Windus, 1990.

70 J. Hendry and R. Ross eds., Edinburgh University Press, 1990.

71 *Chapman*, No. 66. p. 51.

72 ibid., p. 48.

73 ibid., p. 51.

74 See, for example, "In a Mist", *Collected Poems*, p. 262, or "1,800 feet up", p. 326.

75 *Collected Poems*, p. 278.

76 It is likely that any pass in Sutherland will have seen the sad consequences of the Clearances as a diaspora took place over two generations from the late eighteenth into most of the nineteenth century. Two examples from Sutherland: "Two thousand people had been banished from the strath [Kildonan] by 1820" (David Craig, *On The Crofters' Trail*, London: Jonathan Cape, 1990, p. 144). At Ousdale "106 families amounting to 700 people were cleared over two generations" (ibid., p. 148).

An unconvincing attempt to describe MacCaig as "The History Man" is made in an essay of that title by R. Ross in Hendry and Ross, *Norman MacCaig: Critical Essays*, pp. 7–21. "A conscious detachment" (p. 21) is the best comment that Ross can offer on MacCaig's few references to history in a lifetime's poetry.

77 *The Poetry of Place*, Manchester: Carcanet, 1982.
78 Petersfield: Enitharmon, 1987.
79 ibid., p. 76.
80 ibid., p. 46.
81 Petersfield: Enitharmon, 1974.
82 *A View from the Source: selected poems*, Manchester: Carcanet, 1982, p. 38.
83 J. Berry, *Chain of Days*, Oxford University Press, 1985, p. 93.
84 *News for Babylon*, London: Chatto & Windus, 1984, p. 173.
85 London: Virago, 1984.
86 ibid., p. 7.
87 "Shopping in London winter/is a real drag for the fat black woman", p. 11, confirms that the sequence is located in Britain.
88 ibid., p. 39.
89 London: Karnak House, 1983.
90 ibid., p. 71.
91 "Free Verse", interview with Suzie Mackenzie, *The Guardian*, 16 Oct. 1991.
92 *I Was That Woman*, Frome: Hippopotamus Press, 1989.
93 *A Beginning*, London: Parton Press, 1957.
94 *A Beginning*, plus *Poems*, London: Eyre & Spottiswoode, 1960 and *John Nobody*, London: Eyre & Spottiswoode, 1965. See also *Collected Poems 1957–1987*, Bombay: Penguin India, 1989.
95 Debjani Chatterjee drew attention to the following: S. Bhatt, *Brunizem*, Manchester: Carcanet, 1989 and *Monkey Shadow*, Manchester: Carcanet, 1991; M. Khalvati, *Persian Minatures*, Huddersfield: Smith/Doorstop, 1990; G. S. Sharat Chandra, *Once or Twice*, Frome: Hippopotamus Press, 1974; Rushkana Ahmed ed., *We Sinful Women*, London: Women's Press, 1991; D. Chatterjee and R. Islam eds, *Barbed Lines*, Sheffield: Bengali Women's Support Group and Yorkshire Arts Circus, 1990; E. de Souza, *Ways of Belonging: selected poems*, Edinburgh: Polygon, 1990; T. Latif, *Skimming The Soul*, Todmorden: Littlewood Arc, 1991; Mahmood Jamal, ed., *The Penguin Book of Modern Urdu Poetry*, Harmondsworth: Penguin, 1986; D. Chatterjee *et al.*, *The Sun Rises in the North*, Huddersfield: Smith/Doorstop, 1991.
96 Interview with the present author, 3 Jan. 1992.
97 ibid.
98 ibid.
99 *I Was That Woman*, p. 19.
100 "Actually this was in Japan": interview, 3 Jan. 1992.
101 *I Was That Woman*, Notes p. 57.
102 ibid., p. 51. The full stop after "intolerance" is a correction on the advice of the author from the comma in the published text.
103 My interview of 3 Jan. 1992 is the source of this and the two quotations which follow.
104 *Romantic Ecology*, p. 8.
105 *From Wood to Ridge*, Manchester: Carcanet, 1989, p. 305.
106 *Wolfwatching*, London: Faber & Faber, 1989, p. 26.
107 *Politics and Letters*, London: New Left Review, 1979, p. 312.
108 ibid.
109 *The Country and the City*, London, Chatto & Windus, 1973, Paladin edn 1975,

p. 50.

110 "Between Country and City", in R. Mabey *et al.* eds., *Second Nature*, London: Jonathan Cape, 1984, p. 219; reprinted in Simon Pugh ed., *Reading Landscape: country-city-capital*, Manchester University Press, 1990, p. 18.

111 *Against Looting*, p. 7.

112 *I Was That Woman*, p. 51.

113 "This is no ordinary piece of writing. There are at least three things it makes you want to do: wonder at whales, defend humans, and ponder the difference between poetry and prose." Matt Holland's review suggests that sections "read like the *National Geographic* . . . and others that read like . . ., well, like poetry". *Poetry Review*, Vol. 78, No. 4, winter 1988/9, p. 55.

114 *Whale Nation*, p. 14.

115 C. P. Snow, *The Two Cultures*, Cambridge University Press, 1959.

116 *Whale Nation*, p. 100.

117 An article in the *Sunday Times Magazine* claimed that in *Whale Nation* Williams is "testifying to the . . . moral superiority of whales and dolphins". John Ryle, "Heathcote and the Whale", 17 Jul. 1988, p. 64.

118 London: Jonathan Cape, 1988.

119 ibid., p. 34.

120 The 1992 brochure of a Carlisle company called "Discover the World" offers a holiday swimming with dolphins in the Bahamas.

121 The particular dolphin in this poem is known as "Friendly Fungie": see Judith Williamson, "The year of the dolphin", the *Guardian*, 23 May 1991.

122 ibid.

123 *Falling for a Dolphin*, p. 45.

124 Bridgend: Seren Books, 1990.

125 *The Idea of Wilderness*, New Haven: Yale University Press, 1991, p. 12.

126 Llewellyn-Williams, *Book of Shadows*, p. 95.

127 ibid., p. 46.

128 ibid., p. 77.

129 The final line of "The Oxen", *Poems of Thomas Hardy: a New Selection*, ed. T. R. M. Creighton, London: Macmillan, 1974, p. 91.

130 *Book of Shadows*, p. 69.

131 "Monkeywrenching is an extremely moral way of resisting the industrialisation of natural places . . . It's one tool. Sometimes you lobby; sometimes you write letters; sometimes you file lawsuits. And sometimes you monkeywrench." Dave Foreman, founder of Earth First!, quoted by Roderick Nash, *The Rights of Nature*, University of Wisconsin Press, 1989, p. 191. The term derives from Edward Abbey's brilliant novel *The Monkey Wrench Gang*, London: R. Clark, 1991.

132 Vol. 80, No. 2, summer 1990, p. 7.

133 "The Year of the Dolphin", the *Guardian*, 23 May 1991.

134 *On The Beach At Cambridge*, London: Allison & Busby, 1984, p. 96.

135 *A Cold Coming: Gulf War Poems*, Newcastle upon Tyne: Bloodaxe, 1991, p. 4.

136 Harrison insisted that this poem was published in the news pages rather in the arts pages. (Reading at Bretton Hall College, 24 Nov. 1993.) The *Guardian* commissioned six poems from David Milsted for its weekly "Environment" pages starting on 22 Nov. 1991. Unfortunately this "Gallery of Greens" was a series of stereotypical portraits written in doggerel.

137 *Hamlet*, I.i.60: "The bird of dawning singeth all night long."

138 "Ideas of Nature", in *Problems In Materialism and Culture*, London: Verso, 1980, p. 84.

139 Letter to the present author, 17 Dec. 1993.

140 "Myth in the Making", the *Independent on Sunday*, 6 Nov. 1994, p. 29.

141 *King Lear*, III.ii.8.

142 *Winter Pollen: Occasional Prose*, ed. W. Scammell, London: Faber & Faber, 1994, p. 129.

143 ibid., p. 150.

144 T. Gifford, *The Stone Spiral*, p. 7.

Bibliography

Abbey, Edward, *The Monkey Wrench Gang*, London: R. Clark, 1991.

Ahmed, Rushkana, ed., *We Sinful Women*, London: Women's Press, 1991.

Anderson, W., *Green Man: The Archetype of our Oneness with the Earth*, London: HarperCollins, 1990.

Andrews, Elmer, *The Poetry of Seamus Heaney*, London: Macmillan, 1988.

Auden, W. H., *Collected Poems*, London: Faber & Faber, 1976.

Barrell, John and Bull, John, eds, *The Penguin Book of English Pastoral Verse*, London: Allen Lane, 1974, and Harmondsworth: Penguin, 1982.

Barthes, R., *Image-Music-Text*, London: Fontana, 1977.

Bate, Jonathan, *Romantic Ecology: Wordsworth and the Environmental Tradition*, London: Routledge, 1991.

Belsey, Catherine and Moore, Jane eds, *The Feminist Reader*, London: Macmillan, 1989.

Berger, Peter L. and Luckmann, Thomas, *The Social Construction of Reality*, Harmondsworth: Penguin, 1987.

Berman, Marshall, *All That Is Solid Melts Into Air: the Experience of Modernity*, New York: Simon and Schuster, 1982.

Berry, J., *Chain of Days*, Oxford University Press, 1985.

Bhatt, S., *Brunizem*, Manchester: Carcanet, 1989.

——*Monkey Shadow*, Manchester: Carcanet, 1991.

Blunden, Edmund, *Nature in English Literature*, London: Hogarth Press, 1929.

Bold, Alan, *George Mackay Brown*, Edinburgh: Oliver & Boyd, 1978.

Bramwell, Anna, *Ecology in the Twentieth Century: A History*, London: Yale University Press, 1989.

Brown, George Mackay, *Fisherman with Ploughs*, London: Chatto & Windus, 1971.

——*The Wreck of the Archangel*, London: John Murray, 1989.

Brown, H., ed., *Poems of the Scottish Hills*, Aberdeen University Press, 1982.

Brown, H. and Berry, M. eds, *Speak To The Hills*, Aberdeen University Press, 1985.

Chatterjee, Debjani, *I Was That Woman*, Frome: Hippopotamus Press, 1989.

Chatterjee, Debjani, and Islam, R., eds, *Barbed Lines*, Sheffield: Bengali Women's Support Group and Yorkshire Arts Circus, 1990.

Chatterjee, Debjani, *et al.*, *The Sun Rises in the North*, Huddersfield: Smith/Doorstop, 1991.

185

Clarke, Gillian, *Letting in the Rumour*, Manchester: Carcanet, 1989.

Corcoran, Neil, *Seamus Heaney*, London: Faber & Faber, 1986.

Craig, David, *Against Looting*, Clapham: Giant Steps, 1987.

——*Native Stones*, London: Secker & Warburg, 1987.

——*On the Crofters' Trail*, London: Jonathan Cape, 1990.

Creighton, T. R. M., ed., *Poems of Thomas Hardy: a New Selection*, London: Macmillan, 1974.

Curtis T., ed., *The Poetry of Pembrokeshire*, Bridgend: Seren Books, 1989.

——*The Poetry of Snowdonia*, Bridgend: Seren Books, 1989.

Daly, Mary, *Gyn/ecology: The Metaphysics of Radical Feminism*, Boston: Beacon Press, 1978.

Davis, H., ed., *Pope: Poetical Works*, Oxford University Press, 1966.

Deane, Seamus, *Celtic Revivals*, London: Faber & Faber, 1985.

Diamond, Irene and Orenstein, Gloria Feman, eds, *Reweaving the World: The Emergence of Ecofeminism*, San Francisco: Sierra Club Books, 1990.

Dobson, A., ed., *The Poetical Works of Oliver Goldsmith*, London: Bell, 1895.

Drummond, E., *A Dream of White Horses*, London: Diadem, 1987.

Dunn, S. and Scholefield, A., eds, *Beneath the Wide, Wide Heaven*, London: Virago, 1991.

Dyson,A. E., *Three Contemporary Poets: Thom Gunn, Ted Hughes, R. S. Thomas*, London: Macmillan, 1990.

Emerson, Ralph Waldo, *Selected Works*, Oxford University Press, 1990.

Empson, William, *Some Versions of Pastoral*, London: Chatto & Windus, 1935.

Evans, Christine, *Cometary Phases*, Bridgend: Seren Books, 1989.

Fell, Alison, *The Crystal Owl*, London: Methuen, 1988.

Gifford, T., *The Stone Spiral*, Clapham: Giant Steps, 1987.

——*Outcrops*, Todmorden: Littlewood, 1991.

Gifford, T., ed., *John Muir: The Eight Wilderness-Discovery Books*, London: Diadem, 1992.

Gifford T. and Roberts, N., *Ted Hughes: A Critical Study*, London: Faber & Faber, 1981.

Gifford, T. and Smith, R., eds, *The Mountaineering Literature Festival*, see p. 180, Leeds: Bretton Hall, 1994.

Gill, Stephen, *William Wordsworth: A Life*, Oxford University Press, 1989.

Gill, Stephen, ed., *William Wordsworth: Poems and Selected Prose*, Oxford University Press, 1984.

Gillies, W., ed., *Ris a' Bhruthaich: The Criticism and Prose Writings of Sorley MacLean*, Stornoway: Acair, 1985.

Gregory G., ed., *Elizabethan Critical Essays*, Oxford University Press, 1904.

Greig, A., *The Order of the Day*, Newcastle upon Tyne: Bloodaxe, 1990.

Grieve, M. and Aitken, W. R., *The Complete Poems of Hugh MacDiarmid*, Vol. I, Harmondsworth: Penguin, 1985.

Griffin, A. Harry, *A Lakeland Mountain Diary*, Swindon: Crowood, 1990.

Haffenden, John, ed., *Viewpoints*, London: Faber & Faber, 1981.

Hardy, Thomas, *Tess of the d'Urbervilles*, London: Macmillan, 1967.

Harrison, Fraser, *The Living Landscape*, London: Pluto Press, 1986.

Harrison, Tony, *A Cold Coming: Gulf War Poems*, Newcastle upon Tyne: Bloodaxe, 1991.

Heaney, Seamus, *Death of a Naturalist*, London: Faber & Faber, 1966.

——*Door Into The Dark*, London: Faber & Faber, 1969.

——*North*, London: Faber & Faber, 1975.

——*Wintering Out*, London: Faber & Faber, 1972.

——*Field Work*, London: Faber & Faber, 1979.

——*Preoccupations*, London: Faber & Faber, 1980.

——*Station Island*, London: Faber & Faber, 1984.

——*The Haw Lantern*, London: Faber & Faber, 1987.

——*The Government of the Tongue*, London: Faber & Faber, 1988.

——*Seeing Things*, London: Faber & Faber, 1991.

Hendry, J. and Ross, R., *Norman MacCaig: Critical Essays*, Edinburgh University Press, 1990.

Hooker, Jeremy, *Soliloquies of a Chalk Giant*, Petersfield: Enitharmon Press, 1974.

——*A View from the Source: selected poems*, Manchester: Carcanet, 1982.

——*The Poetry of Place*, Manchester: Carcanet, 1982.

——*Master of the Leaping Figures*, Petersfield: Enitharmon Press, 1987.

Houston, Libby, *At The Mercy*, London: Allison & Busby, 1981.

Hughes, Ted, *The Hawk in the Rain*, London: Faber & Faber, 1957.

——*Lupercal*, London: Faber & Faber, 1960.

——*Crow*, London: Faber & Faber, 1970.

——*A Choice of Shakespeare's Verse*, London: Faber & Faber, 1971, revised edition 1992.

——*Wodwo*, London: Faber & Faber, 1971.

——*Season Songs*, London: Faber & Faber, 1975.

——*Gaudete*, London: Faber & Faber, 1977.

——*Cave Birds*, London: Faber & Faber, 1978.

——*Moortown*, London: Faber & Faber, 1979.

——*Remains of Elmet*, London: Faber & Faber, 1979.

——*Selected Poems 1957–1981*, London: Faber & Faber, 1982.

——*River*, London: Faber & Faber, 1983.

——*Moortown Diary*, London: Faber & Faber, 1989.

——*Wolfwatching*, London: Faber & Faber, 1989.

——*Shakespeare and the Goddess of Complete Being*, London: Faber & Faber, 1992.

——*Rain Charm For The Duchy and other Laureate Poems*, London: Faber & Faber, 1992.

——*Three Books*, London: Faber & Faber, 1993.

——*Winter Pollen: Occasional Prose*, ed. W. Scammell, London: Faber & Faber, 1994.

Hulse, M., Kennedy, D., and Morley, D., eds, *The New Poetry*, Newcastle upon Tyne: Bloodaxe, 1993.

Hutchinson, T., ed., *The Complete Poetical Works of Percy Bysshe Shelley*, Oxford University Press, 1912.

Jackson, H. J., ed., *Samuel Taylor Coleridge: Selected Poems and Prose*, Oxford University Press, 1985.

Jamal, Mahmood, ed., *The Penguin Book of Modern Urdu Poetry*, Harmondsworth: Penguin, 1986.

Jones, P. and Schmidt, M., eds, *British Poetry since 1970: a Critical Survey*, Manchester: Carcanet, 1980.

Kavanagh, Patrick, *Self-Portrait*, Dublin: Dolmen Press, 1964.

——*Collected Poems*, London: Martin Brian & O'Keefe, 1972.

Kaplin, K., *Tongues in Trees*, Bideford: Green Books, 1989.

Keats, John, *Poetical Works*, Oxford University Press, 1956.

Khalvati, *Persian Miniatures*, Huddersfield: Smith/Doorstop, 1990.

King, A. and Clifford, S., eds, *Trees Be Company*, Bristol Classical Press, 1989.

Larrissy, Edward, *Reading Twentieth-Century Poetry: The Language of Gender and Objects*, Oxford: Blackwell, 1990.

Latif, T., *Skimming The Soul*, Todmorden: Littlewood Arc, 1991.

Leavis, F. R., *New Bearings in English Poetry*, London: Chatto & Windus, 1932, Peregrine edition, 1973.

Leopold, Aldo, *Sand County Almanac*, Oxford University Press, 1949.

Liu, Alan, *Wordsworth: the Sense of History*, California: Stanford University Press, 1989.

Llewellyn-Williams, Hilary, *Book of Shadows*, Bridgend: Seren Books, 1990.

Longley, Edna, *Poetry in the Wars*, Newcastle upon Tyne: Bloodaxe, 1986.

Longley, Edna, ed., *Edward Thomas: Poems and Last Poems*, London: MacDonald & Evans, 1973.

Longley, Michael, *Poems 1963–1983*, London: Secker & Warburg, 1991.

——*Gorse Fires*, London: Secker & Warburg, 1991.

Loughrey, Bryan, ed., *The Pastoral Mode*, London: Macmillan, 1984.

Lovelock, James, *Gaia: a New Look at Life on Earth*, Oxford University Press, 1987.

Lucas, J., ed., *A Selection from George Crabbe*, London: Longman, 1967.

Lucas, John, *England and Englishness*, London: Hogarth Press, 1990.

Lynen, John F., *The Pastoral of Robert Frost*, New Haven: Yale University Press, 1960.

Mabey, R., *et al.*, eds, *Second Nature*, London: Jonathan Cape, 1984.

MacAulay, D., ed., *Modern Scottish Gaelic Poems*, Edinburgh: Canongate, 1976.

MacCaig, Norman, *Collected Poems*, London: Chatto & Windus, 1990.

McGann, J. J., ed., *Lord Byron: The Complete Poetical Works*, Oxford University Press, 1980, Vol. II.

McKibben, Bill, *The End of Nature*, Harmondsworth: Penguin, 1990.

MacLean, Sorley, *Spring Tide and Neap Tide: Selected Poems 1932–72*, Edinburgh: Canongate, 1977.

——*Poems 1932–82*, Philadelphia: Iona Foundation, 1987.

——*From Wood to Ridge*, Manchester: Carcanet, 1989.

Marinelli, Peter V., *Pastoral*, London: Methuen, 1971.

Marsh, Edward, ed., *Georgian Poetry 1911–1912*, London: The Poetry Bookshop, 1912, 8th edition 1913.

Marshall, Peter, *Nature's Web: An Exploration of Ecological Thinking*, London: Simon & Schuster, 1992.

Miller, R. and Luther, S., *Eday and Hoy: A Development Survey*, Department of Geography, University of Glasgow, 1968.

Mitchell, Adrian, *On The Beach At Cambridge*, London: Allison & Busby, 1984.

Montague, John, *The Rough Field*, Dublin: The Dolmen Press, 1972, revised edition, Newcastle upon Tyne: Bloodaxe, 1989.

Moraes, Dom, *A Beginning*, London: Parton Press, 1957.

——*Poems*, London: Eyre & Spottiswoode, 1960.

——*John Nobody*, London: Eyre & Spottiswoode, 1965.

——*Collected Poems 1957–1987*, Bombay: Penguin India, 1989.

Morrison, Blake, *Seamus Heaney*, London: Methuen, 1982.

Morrison, Blake, and Motion, Andrew, eds, *The Penguin Book of Contemporary British Poety*, Harmondsworth: Penguin, 1982.

Mort, Graham, *Sky Burial*, Coventry: Dangaroo Press, 1989.

Motion, Andrew, *The Poetry of Edward Thomas*, London: Routledge, 1980.

Muir, Edwin, *The Estate of Poetry*, London: Hogarth Press, 1962.

——*Selected Poems*, London: Faber & Faber, 1965.

Nash, Roderick, *Wilderness and the American Mind*, New Haven: Yale University Press, 1967, 3rd edition 1982.

——*The Rights of Nature*, University of Wisconsin Press, 1989.

Nemo, John, *Patrick Kavanagh*, London: George Prior, 1979.

Newby, Howard, *Country Life: a Social History of Rural England*, London: Weidenfeld & Nicolson, 1987, Cardinal edition, 1988.

Nichols, Grace, *i is a long memoried woman*, London: Karnak House, 1983.

——*The Fat Black Woman's Poems*, London: Virago, 1984.

Nicholson, Norman, *Sea to the West*, London: Faber & Faber, 1981.

——*Selected Poems 1940–1982*, London: Faber & Faber, 1982.

Nicholson, Norman, ed., *The Lake District*, Harmondsworth: Penguin, 1978.

Noyce, Wilfred, ed., *The Climber's Fireside Book*, London: Heinemann, 1964.

O'Brien, Darcy, *Patrick Kavanagh*, London: Bucknell University Press, 1975.

Oelschlaeger, Max, *The Idea of Wilderness*, New Haven: Yale University Press, 1991.

Parker, Michael, *Seamus Heaney: The Making of the Poet*, London: Macmillan, 1993.

Plant, Judith, ed., *Healing the Wounds: The Promise of Ecofeminism*, Philadelphia: New Society Publishers, 1989.

Plath, Sylvia, *Child*, Exeter: Rougemont Press, 1971. (Limited edition.)

——*Collected Poems*, London: Faber & Faber, 1981.

Porritt, J., ed., *Save The Earth*, London: Dorling Kindersley, 1992.

Pugh, Simon, *Garden-nature-language*, Manchester University Press, 1988.

Pugh, Simon, ed., *Reading Landscape: Country-city-capital*, Manchester University Press, 1990.

Quinn, Antoinette, *Patrick Kavanagh: Born-Again Romantic*, Dublin: Gill & Macmillan, 1993.

Rae, S., ed., *The Orange Dove of Fiji: Poems for the World Wide Fund for Nature*, London: Hutchinson, 1989.

Raine, Craig, *A Martian Sends a Postcard Home*, Oxford University Press, 1979.

Rawson, C., ed., *The Yearbook of English Studies*, Modern Humanities Research Association, 1987.

Redgrove, Peter, *The Black Goddess and the Sixth Sense*, London: Bloomsbury, 1987.

——*Poems 1954–1987*, Harmondsworth: Penguin, 1989.

Ricks, Christopher, *The Force of Poetry*, Oxford University Press, 1984.

Roberts, Michael, *Poems*, London: Jonathan Cape, 1936.

——*Orion Marches*, London: Faber & Faber, 1939.

Roberts, Neil, *The Lover, the Dreamer and the World: a Study of Peter Redgrove's Poetry*, Sheffield Academic Press, 1994.

Robinson, Alan, *Instabilities in Contemporary British Poetry*, London: Macmillan, 1988.

Robinson, Craig, *Ted Hughes as Shepherd of Being*, London: Macmillan, 1989.

Robinson, E. and Summerfield, G., eds, *Selected Poems and Prose of John Clare*, Oxford University Press, 1967.

Rosaldo, Michelle Zimbalist and Lamphere, Louise eds, *Women, Culture and Society*, Stanford University Press, 1974.

Rose, Arnold M., ed., *Human Behaviour and Social Processes: an Interactionist Approach*, London: Routledge, 1982.

Rose, J., *The Haunting of Sylvia Plath*, London: Virago, 1991.

Ross, R. H., *The Georgian Revolt*, London: Faber & Faber, 1967.

Ross, R. J. and Hendry, J., eds, *Sorley MacLean: Critical Essays*, Edinburgh: Scottish Academic Press, 1986.

Roszak, Theodore, *The Voice of the Earth: An Exploration of Ecopsychology*, London: Bantam Books, 1993.

Sagar, Keith, *The Art of Ted Hughes*, Cambridge University Press, 1975, second edition 1978.

Sagar, Keith, ed., *The Achievement of Ted Hughes*, Manchester University Press, 1983.

——*The Challenge of Ted Hughes*, London: Macmillan, 1994.

Sales, Roger, *English Literature in History 1780–1830: Pastoral and Politics*, London: Hutchinson, 1983.

Scammell, William, ed., *This Green Earth: A Celebration of Nature Poetry*, Maryport: Ellenbank Press, 1992.

Scigaj, L. M., *The Poetry of Ted Hughes*, University of Iowa Press, 1986.

——*Ted Hughes*, Boston: Twayne, 1991.

Sharat Chandra, G. S., ed., *Once or Twice*, Frome: Hippopotamus Press, 1974.

Showalter, Elaine, ed., *The New Feminist Criticism*, London: Virago, 1986.

Smith, Iain Crichton, *Biobuill is Sanasan-reice*, Glasgow: Gairm Publications, 1965.

Smith, Stan, *The Inviolable Voice*, Dublin: Gill & Macmillan and Humanities Press, 1982.

——*Edward Thomas*, London: Faber & Faber, 1986.

Snow, C. P., *The Two Cultures*, Cambridge University Press, 1959.

Snyder, G., *The Practice of the Wild*, San Francisco: North Point Press, 1990.

——*No Nature*, New York: Pantheon Books, 1992.

Sola Pinto, V. de and Roberts, W., eds, *The Complete Poems of D. H. Lawrence*, London: Heinemann, 1972.

Souza, E. de, *Ways of Belonging: selected poems*, Edinburgh: Polygon, 1990.

Steel, Fraser, ed., *The Poetry Book Society Anthology*, No. 1, New Series, London: Hutchinson, 1990.

Stevenson, Anne, *Selected Poems*, Oxford University Press, 1987.

——*Bitter Fame: A Life of Sylvia Plath*, London: Viking, 1989.

Stevenson, W. H., ed., *Blake: The Complete Poems*, London: Longman, 1971.

Terrill, R., *R. H. Tawney and His Times*, Cambridge, Mass.: Harvard University Press, 1973.

Thomas D. M., ed., *The Granite Kingdom: Poems of Cornwall*, Penryn: Tor Mark Press, 1970.

Thomas, Keith, *Man and the Natural World*, London: Allen Lane, 1983.

Thomas, R. G., ed., *The Collected Poems of Edward Thomas*, Oxford: Clarendon Press, 1978.

——*Pietà*, London: Rupert Hart-Davis, 1966.

——*H'M*, London: Macmillan, 1972.

——*Selected Poems 1946–1968*, St Albans: Granada, 1973.

——*What Is a Welshman?*, Llandybie: Christopher Davies, 1974.

——*Laboratories of the Spirit*, London: Macmillan, 1975.

——*Frequencies*, London: Macmillan, 1978.

——*Later Poems 1972–1982*, London: Macmillan, 1983.

——*Counterpoint*, Newcastle upon Tyne: Bloodaxe, 1990.

Thomas, R. S., *Bluyddyn yn Llyn*, Gwasg Gwynedd, 1991.

Thomson, Derick, *An Introduction to Gaelic Poetry*, London: Gollancz, 1977.

Thomson, William, P. L., ed., *Orkney Heritage*, Kirkwall: Orkney Heritage Society, 1981.

Thoreau, Henry David, *Walden and Civil Disobedience*, Harmondsworth: Penguin, 1983.

Walder, D., *Ted Hughes*, Milton Keynes: Open University Press, 1987.

Wiener, M. J., *English Culture and the Decline of the Industrial Spirit 1850–1980*, Cambridge University Press, 1981.

Wilde, Oscar, *De Profundis and Other Writings*, Harmondsworth: Penguin, 1984.

Williams, Heathcote, *Falling for a Dolphin*, London: Jonathan Cape, 1988.

——*Whale Nation*, London: Jonathan Cape, 1988.

Williams, J., *Twentieth-Century British Poetry: A Critical Introduction*, London: Edward Arnold, 1987.

Williams, Raymond, *The Country and the City*, London: Chatto & Windus, 1973, Paladin edition, 1975.

——*Keywords*, Glasgow: Fontana, 1976.

——*Politics and Letters*, London: New Left Review, 1979.

——*Problems In Materialism and Culture*, London: Verso, 1980.

Windrath, H., ed., *No Earthly Reason?: Poetry on Green Issues*, Manchester: Crocus, 1989.

Yeats, W. B., *Collected Poems*, London: Macmillan, 1950, Papermac edition, 1982.

Young, Hugo, *One of Us*, London: Macmillan, 1989, revised edition, 1990.

Index

Page references in **bold** indicate the main reference